YOUR PERSONAL HOROSCOPE 2026

LARS MELLIS

YOUR PERSONAL HOROSCOPE 2026

**Month-by-month
forecast for every sign**

Thorsons

Thorsons
An imprint of HarperCollins*Publishers*
1 London Bridge Street
London SE1 9GF

www.harpercollins.co.uk

HarperCollins*Publishers*
Macken House, 39/40 Mayor Street Upper
Dublin 1, D01 C9W8, Ireland

First published by Thorsons 2025

1 3 5 7 9 10 8 6 4 2

info@stardatamedia.com

Star ★ Data asserts the moral right to be
identified as the author of this work

A catalogue record of this book is
available from the British Library

Star Signs & Horoscopes

ISBN 978-0-00-874716-9

Printed and bound in India by
Replika Press Pvt Ltd

The author is grateful to the people of STAR ★ DATA, who truly fathered this book and without whom it could not have been written.

Contents

Introduction

Welcome to the fascinating and intricate world of astrology!

For thousands of years the movements of the planets and other heavenly bodies have intrigued the best minds of every generation. Life holds no greater challenge or joy than this: knowledge of ourselves and the universe we live in. Astrology is one of the keys to this knowledge.

Your Personal Horoscope 2026 gives you the fruits of astrological wisdom. In addition to general guidance on your character and the basic trends of your life, it shows you how to take advantage of planetary influences so you can make the most of the year ahead.

The section on each sign includes a Personality Profile, a look at general trends for 2026 and in-depth month-by-month forecasts. The Glossary (*page 5*) explains some of the astrological terms you may be unfamiliar with.

One of the many helpful features of this book is the 'Best' and 'Most Stressful' days listed at the beginning of each monthly forecast. Read these sections to learn which days in each month will be good overall, good for money and good for love. Mark them on your calendar – these will be your best days. Similarly, make a note of the days that will be most stressful for you. It is best to avoid booking important meetings or taking major decisions on these days, as well as on those days when important planets in your horoscope are retrograde (moving backwards through the zodiac).

The Major Trends section for your sign lists those days when your vitality is strong or weak, or when relationships with your co-workers or loved ones may need a bit more effort on your part. If you are going through a difficult time, take a look at the colour, metal, gem and scent listed in the 'At a Glance' section of your Personality Profile. Wearing a piece of jewellery that contains your metal and/or gem will strengthen your vitality, just as wearing clothes or decorating your room or office in the colour ruled by your sign, drinking teas made from the herbs ruled by your sign or wearing the scents associated with your sign will sustain you.

Another important virtue of this book is that it will help you to know not only yourself but those around you: your friends, co-workers, partners and/or children. Reading the Personality Profile and forecasts for their signs will provide you with an insight into their behaviour that you won't get anywhere else. You will know when to be more tolerant of them and when they are liable to be difficult or irritable.

I consider you – the reader – my personal client. By studying your Solar Horoscope I gain an awareness of what is going on in your life – what you are feeling and striving for and the challenges you face. I then do my best to address these concerns. Consider this book the next best thing to having your own personal astrologer!

It is my sincere hope that *Your Personal Horoscope 2026* will enhance the quality of your life, make things easier, illuminate the way forward, banish obscurities and make you more aware of your personal connection to the universe. Understood properly and used wisely, astrology is a great guide to knowing yourself, the people around you and the events in your life – but remember that what you do with these insights – the final result – is up to you.

A Note on the 'New Zodiac'

Recently an article was published that postulated two things: the discovery of a new constellation – Ophiuchus – making a thirteenth constellation in the heavens and thus a thirteenth sign, and the statement that because the Earth has shifted relative to the constellations in the past few thousand years, all the signs have shifted backwards by one sign. This has caused much consternation, and I have received a stream of letters, emails and phone calls from people saying things like: 'I don't want to be a Taurus, I'm happy being a Gemini', 'What's my real sign?' or 'Now that I finally understand myself, I'm not who I think I am!'

All of this is 'much ado about nothing'. The article has some partial truth to it. Yes, in two thousand years the planets have shifted relative to the constellations in the heavens. This is old news. We know this and Hindu astrologers take this into account when casting charts. This shift doesn't affect Western astrologers in North America and Europe. We use what is called a 'tropical' zodiac. This zodiac has nothing to do with the constellations in the heavens. They have the same names, but that's about it. The tropical zodiac is based on the Earth's revolution around the Sun. Imagine the circle that this orbit makes, then divide this circle by twelve and you have our zodiac. The Spring Equinox is always 0 degrees (Aries), and the Autumn Equinox is always 0 degrees Libra (180 degrees from Aries). At one time a few thousand years ago, these tropical signs coincided with the actual constellations; they were pretty much interchangeable, and it didn't matter what zodiac you used. But in the course of thousands of years the planets have shifted relative to these constellations. Here in the West it doesn't affect our practice one iota. You are still the sign you always were.

In North America and Europe there is a clear distinction between an astrological sign and a constellation in the heavens. This issue is more of a problem for Hindu astrologers. Their zodiac is based on the actual constellations – this is called the 'sidereal' zodiac. And Hindu astrologers have been accounting for this shift all the time. They keep close tabs on it. In two thousand years there is a shift of 23 degrees, and they subtract this from the Western calculations. So in their system many a Gemini would be a Taurus and this is true for all the signs. This is nothing new – it is all known and accounted for, so there is no bombshell here.

The so-called thirteenth constellation, Ophiuchus, is also not a problem for the Western astrologer. As we mentioned, our zodiac has nothing to do with the constellations. It could be more of a problem for the Hindus, but my feeling is that it's not a problem for them either. What these astronomers are calling a new constellation was probably considered a part of one of the existing constellations. I don't know this as a fact, but I presume it is so intuitively. I'm sure we will soon be getting articles by Hindu astrologers explaining this.

Glossary of Astrological Terms

Ascendant

We experience day and night because the Earth rotates on its axis once every 24 hours. It is because of this rotation that the Sun, Moon and planets seem to rise and set. The zodiac is a fixed belt (imaginary, but very real in spiritual terms) around the Earth. As the Earth rotates, the different signs of the zodiac seem to the observer to rise on the horizon. During a 24-hour period every sign of the zodiac will pass this horizon point at some time or another. The sign that is at the horizon point at any given time is called the Ascendant, or rising sign. The Ascendant is the sign denoting a person's self-image, body and self-concept – the personal ego, as opposed to the spiritual ego indicated by a person's Sun sign.

Aspects

Aspects are the angular relationships between planets, the way in which one planet stimulates or influences another. If a planet makes a harmonious aspect (connection) to another, it tends to stimulate that planet in a positive and helpful way. If, however, it makes a stressful aspect to another planet, this disrupts that planet's normal influence.

Astrological Qualities

There are three astrological qualities: *cardinal*, *fixed* and *mutable*. Each of the 12 signs of the zodiac falls into one of these three categories.

Cardinal Signs
Aries, Cancer, Libra and Capricorn
The cardinal quality is the active, initiating principle. Those born under these four signs are good at starting new projects.

Fixed Signs
Taurus, Leo, Scorpio and Aquarius
Fixed qualities include stability, persistence, endurance and perfectionism. People born under these four signs are good at seeing things through.

Mutable Signs
Gemini, Virgo, Sagittarius and Pisces
Mutable qualities are adaptability, changeability and balance. Those born under these four signs are creative, if not always practical.

Direct Motion

When the planets move forward through the zodiac – as they normally do – they are said to be going 'direct'.

Grand Square

A Grand Square differs from a normal Square (usually two planets separated by 90 degrees) in that four or more planets are involved. When you look at the pattern in a chart you will see a whole and complete square. This, though stressful, usually denotes a new manifestation in the life. There is much work and balancing involved in the manifestation.

Grand Trine

A Grand Trine differs from a normal Trine (where two planets are 120 degrees apart) in that three or more planets are involved. When you look at this pattern in a chart, it takes the form of a complete triangle – a Grand Trine. Usually (but not always) it occurs in one of the four elements: Fire, Earth, Air or Water. Thus the particular element in which it occurs will be highlighted. A Grand Trine in Water is not the same as a Grand Trine in Air or Fire, etc. This is a very fortunate and happy aspect, and quite rare.

Houses

There are 12 signs of the zodiac and 12 houses of experience. The 12 signs are personality types and ways in which a given planet expresses itself; the 12 houses show 'where' in your life this expression takes place. Each house has a different area of interest. A house can become potent and important – a house of power – in different ways: if it contains the Sun, the Moon or the 'ruler' of your chart; if it contains more than one planet; or if the ruler of that house is receiving unusual stimulation from other planets.

1st House
Personal Image and Sensual Delights

2nd House
Money/Finance

3rd House
Communication and Intellectual Interests

4th House
Home and Family

5th House
Children, Fun, Games, Creativity, Pleasure and Love Affairs

6th House
Health and Work

7th House
Love, Marriage and Social Activities

8th House
Transformation and Regeneration, Fears and Anxieties

9th House
Foreign Travel, Higher Education and Spiritual Philosophy

10th House
Career and Legacy

11th House
Friends, Group Activities and Fondest Wishes

12th House
Spirituality and Mental Health and Wellness

Karma

Karma is the law of cause and effect which governs all phenomena. We are all where we find ourselves because of karma – because of actions we have performed in the past. The universe is such a balanced instrument that any act immediately sets corrective forces into motion – karma.

Long-term Planets

The planets that take a long time to move through a sign show the long-term trends in a given area of life. They are important for forecasting the prolonged view of things. Because these planets stay in one sign for so long, there are periods in the year when the faster-moving (short-term) planets will join them, further activating and enhancing the importance of a given house.

Jupiter
stays in a sign for about 1 year

Saturn
2½ years

Uranus
7 years

Neptune
14 years

Pluto
15 to 30 years

Lunar

Relating to the Moon. See also 'Phases of the Moon', below.

Natal

Literally means 'birth'. In astrology this term is used to distinguish between planetary positions that occurred at the time of a person's birth (natal) and those that are current (transiting). For example, Natal Sun refers to where the Sun was when you were born;

transiting Sun refers to where the Sun's position is currently at any given moment – which usually doesn't coincide with your birth, or Natal, Sun.

North and South Nodes

Points in the zodiac where the Moon's orbit intersects with the Earth's orbit (also known as the ecliptic). The signs the nodes occupy typically indicate which signs the eclipses will be in for that year. The north node is associated with increase and the south node with shedding.

Out of Bounds

The planets move through the zodiac at various angles relative to the celestial equator (if you were to draw an imaginary extension of the Earth's equator out into the universe, you would have an illustration of this celestial equator). The Sun – being the most dominant and powerful influence in the Solar system – is the measure astrologers use as a standard. The Sun never goes more than approximately 23 degrees north or south of the celestial equator. At the Winter Solstice the Sun reaches its maximum southern angle of orbit (declination); at the Summer Solstice it reaches its maximum northern angle. Any time a planet exceeds this Solar boundary – and occasionally planets do – it is said to be 'out of bounds'. This means that the planet exceeds or trespasses into strange territory – beyond the limits allowed by the Sun, the ruler of the Solar system. The planet in this condition becomes more emphasized and exceeds its authority, becoming an important influence in the forecast.

Phases of the Moon

After the full Moon, the Moon seems to shrink in size (as perceived from the Earth), gradually growing smaller until it is virtually invisible to the naked eye – at the time of the next new Moon. This is called the waning Moon phase, or the waning Moon.

After the new Moon, the Moon gradually gets bigger in size (as perceived from the Earth) until it reaches its maximum size at the time of the full Moon. This period is called the waxing Moon phase, or waxing Moon.

Planetary Rulers

Planets have dominion over specific signs which inform interpretation of the natal chart and astrological transits. Planets in a particular sign are influenced by that sign's planetary ruler. Houses of a natal chart are also influenced by the planetary ruler of the sign on the house's cusp. Traditional planetary rulers only include the first seven planetary bodies (the Sun to Saturn), while modern planetary rulers include all ten. The planetary rulers are as follows:

Aries
Mars

Taurus
Venus

Gemini
Mercury

Cancer
The Moon

Leo
The Sun

Virgo
Mercury

Libra
Venus

Scorpio
Mars (traditional); Pluto (modern)

Sagittarius
Jupiter

Capricorn
Saturn

Aquarius
Saturn (traditional); Uranus (modern)

Pisces
Jupiter (traditional); Neptune (modern)

Power Word

Similar to a 'Totem' (see definition below), but for each monthly horoscope. A power word is a single word that encapsulates the essence of the monthly horoscope.

Retrogrades

The planets move around the Sun at different speeds. Mercury and Venus move much faster than the Earth, while Mars, Jupiter, Saturn, Uranus, Neptune and Pluto move more slowly. Thus there are times when, relative to the Earth, the planets appear to be going backwards. In reality they are always going forward, but relative to our vantage point on Earth they seem to go backwards through the zodiac for a period of time. This is called 'retrograde' motion and tends to weaken the normal influence of a given planet.

Short-term Planets

The fast-moving planets move so quickly through a sign that their effects are generally of a short-term nature. They reflect the immediate, day-to-day trends in a horoscope.

Moon
stays in a sign for only 2½ days

Mercury
20 to 30 days

Sun
30 days

Venus
approximately 1 month

Mars
approximately 2 months

Totem

A literary device for this book; your totem for the year serves as an archetype to hold onto, providing an understanding of the thesis of the year for each sign.

T-square

A T-square differs from a Grand Square (see above) in that it is not a complete square. If you look at the pattern in a chart it appears as 'half a complete square', resembling the T-square tools used by architects and designers. If you cut a complete square in half, diagonally, you have a T-square. Many astrologers consider this more stressful than a Grand Square, as it creates tension that is difficult to resolve. T-squares bring learning experiences.

Transits

This term refers to the movements or motions of the planets at any given time. Astrologers use the word 'transit' to make the distinction between a birth, or Natal, planet (see 'Natal', above) and the planet's current movement in the heavens. For example, if at your birth Saturn was in the sign of Cancer in your 8th house, but is now moving through your 3rd house, it is said to be 'transiting' your 3rd house. Transits are one of the main tools with which astrologers forecast trends.

YOUR PERSONAL HOROSCOPE
2026

Aries

$\vee$

THE RAM

Birthdays from
March 21 to
April 20

Personality Profile

ARIES AT A GLANCE

Element – Fire

Ruling Planet – Mars
   Career Planet – Saturn
   Love Planet – Venus
   Money Planet – Venus
   Planet of Fun, Entertainment, Creativity and Pleasure – Sun
   Planet of Health and Work – Mercury
   Planet of Home and Family Life – Moon
   Planet of Spirituality and Mental Health – Jupiter
   Planet of Travel, Education, Religion and Philosophy – Jupiter

Totem – the Hierophant

Colours – carmine, red, scarlet

Colours that promote love, romance and social harmony – green,
  jade green

Colour that promotes earning power – green

Gem – diamond

Metals – iron, steel

Scent – honeysuckle

Quality – cardinal (= activity)

Quality most needed for balance – caution

Strongest virtues – abundant physical energy, courage, honesty, independence, self-reliance

Deepest need – action

Characteristics to avoid – haste, impetuousness, over-aggression, rashness

Signs of greatest overall compatibility – Leo, Sagittarius

Signs of greatest overall incompatibility – Cancer, Libra, Capricorn

Sign most helpful to career – Capricorn

Sign most helpful for emotional support – Cancer

Sign most helpful financially – Taurus

Sign best for marriage and/or partnerships – Libra

Sign most helpful for creative projects – Leo

Best Sign to have fun with – Leo

Signs most helpful in spiritual matters – Sagittarius, Pisces

Best day of the week – Tuesday

Understanding an Aries

Aries is the activist *par excellence* of the zodiac. The Aries need for action is almost an addiction, and those who do not really understand the Aries personality would probably use this hard word to describe it. In reality 'action' is the essence of the Aries psychology – the more direct, blunt and to-the-point the action, the better. When you think about it, this is the ideal psychological makeup for the warrior, the pioneer, the athlete or the manager.

Aries likes to get things done, and in their passion and zeal often lose sight of the consequences for themselves and others. Yes, they often try to be diplomatic and tactful, but it is hard for them. When they do so they feel that they are being dishonest and phoney. It is hard for them even to understand the mindset of the diplomat, the consensus builder, the front office executive. These people are involved in endless meetings, discussions, talks and negotiations – all of which seem a great waste of time when there is so much work to be done, so many real achievements to be gained. An Aries can understand, once it is explained, that talk and negotiations – the social graces – lead ultimately to better, more effective actions. The interesting thing is that an Aries is rarely malicious or spiteful – even when waging war. Aries people fight without hate for their opponents. To them it is all good-natured fun, a grand adventure, a game.

When confronted with a problem many people will say, 'Well, let's think about it, let's analyse the situation.' But not an Aries. An Aries will think, 'Something must be done. Let's get on with it.' Of course, neither response is the total answer. Sometimes action is called for, sometimes cool thought. But an Aries tends to err on the side of action.

Action and thought are radically different principles. Physical activity is the use of brute force. Thinking and deliberating require one not to use force – to be still. It is not good for the athlete to be deliberating the next move; this will only slow down his or her reaction time. The athlete must act instinctively and instantly. This is how Aries people tend to behave in life. They are quick, instinctive decision-makers and their decisions tend to be translated into action almost immediately. When their intuition is sharp and well tuned, their actions are powerful and successful. When their intuition is off, their actions can be disastrous.

Do not think this will scare an Aries. Just as a good warrior knows that in the course of combat he or she might acquire a few wounds, so too does an Aries realize – somewhere deep down – that in the course of being true to yourself you might get embroiled in a disaster or two. It is all part of the game. An Aries feels strong enough to weather any storm.

There are many Aries people who are intellectual. They make powerful and creative thinkers. But even in this realm they tend to be pioneers – outspoken and blunt. These types of Aries tend to elevate (or sublimate) their desire for physical combat in favour of intellectual, mental combat. And they are indeed powerful.

In general, Aries people have a faith in themselves that others could learn from. This basic, rock-solid faith carries them through the most tumultuous situations of life. Their courage and self-confidence make them natural leaders. Their leadership is more by way of example than by actually controlling others.

Finance

Aries people often excel as builders or estate agents. Money in and of itself is not as important as are other things – action, adventure, sport, etc. They are motivated by the need to support and be well-thought-of by their partners. Money as a way of attaining pleasure is another important motivation. Aries function best in their own businesses or as managers of their own departments within a large business or corporation. The fewer orders they have to take from higher up, the better. They also function better out in the field rather than behind a desk.

Aries people are hard workers with a lot of endurance; they can earn large sums of money due to the strength of their sheer physical energy.

Venus is their money planet, which means that Aries need to develop more of the social graces in order to realize their full earning potential. Just getting the job done – which is what an Aries excels at – is not enough to create financial success. The co-operation of others needs to be attained. Customers, clients and co-workers need to be made to feel comfortable; many people need to be treated properly in order for success to happen. When Aries people develop these abilities – or hire someone to do this for them – their financial potential is unlimited.

Career and Public Image

One would think that a pioneering type would want to break with the social and political conventions of society. But this is not so with the Aries-born. They are pioneers within conventional limits, in the sense that they like to start their own businesses within an established industry.

Capricorn is on the 10th house of career cusp of Aries's solar horoscope. Saturn is the planet that rules their life's work and professional aspirations. This tells us some interesting things about the Aries character. First off, it shows that, in order for Aries people to reach their full career potential, they need to develop some qualities that are a bit alien to their basic nature: they need to become better administrators and organizers; they need to be able to handle details better and to take a long-range view of their projects and their careers in general. No one can beat an Aries when it comes to achieving short-range objectives, but a career is long term, built over time. You cannot take a 'quickie' approach to it.

Some Aries people find it difficult to stick with a project until the end. Since they get bored quickly and are in constant pursuit of new adventures, they prefer to pass an old project or task on to somebody else in order to start something new. Those Aries who learn how to put off the search for something new until the old is completed will achieve great success in their careers and professional lives.

In general, Aries people like society to judge them on their own merits, on their real and actual achievements. A reputation acquired by 'hype' feels false to them.

Love and Relationships

In marriage and partnerships Aries like those who are more passive, gentle, tactful and diplomatic – people who have the social grace and skills they sometimes lack. Our partners always represent a hidden part of ourselves – a self that we cannot express personally.

An Aries tends to go after what he or she likes aggressively. The tendency is to jump into relationships and marriages. This is especially true if Venus is in Aries as well as the Sun. If an Aries likes you, he or she will have a hard time taking no for an answer; many attempts will be made to sweep you off your feet.

Though Aries can be exasperating in relationships – especially if they are not understood by their partners – they are never consciously or wilfully cruel or malicious. It is just that they are so independent and sure of themselves that they find it almost impossible to see somebody else's viewpoint or position. This is why an Aries needs as a partner someone with lots of social graces.

On the plus side, an Aries is honest, someone you can lean on, someone with whom you will always know where you stand. What he or she lacks in diplomacy is made up for in integrity.

Home and Domestic Life

An Aries is of course the ruler at home – the Boss. The male will tend to delegate domestic matters to the female. The female Aries will want to rule the roost. Both tend to be handy round the house. Both like large families and both believe in the sanctity and importance of the family. An Aries is a good family person, although he or she does not especially like being at home a lot, preferring instead to be roaming about.

Considering that they are by nature so combative and wilful, Aries people can be surprisingly soft, gentle and even vulnerable with their children and partners. The sign of Cancer, ruled by the Moon, is on the cusp of their solar 4th house of home and family. When the Moon is well aspected – under favourable influences – in the birth chart, an Aries will be tender towards the family and will want a family life that is nurturing and supportive. Aries likes to come home after a hard day on the battlefield of life to the understanding arms of their partner and the unconditional love and support of their family. An Aries feels that there is enough 'war' out in the world – and he or she enjoys participating in that. But when Aries comes home, comfort and nurturing are what's needed.

Horoscope for 2026

When the Universe gives you stage directions, do you listen, Aries? This year your totem is the Hierophant, one of 'the major arcana' tarot cards. When the Hierophant presents itself in a tarot spread, there is a call for spiritual evolution. Saturn, the planet of discipline and hard lessons, spent a brief period in your sign during 2025. This changes this year as Saturn will spend 10½ months of the year in your sign (from February 13 to December 31). Saturn won't leave Aries until April, 2028. Saturn isn't the only heavy hitter entering your sign. Neptune, the planet of spirituality, dreams and illusion, also had a short stay in Aries during 2025 and is extending its journey through Aries in 2026. Indeed, Neptune will now stay in Aries for 13 years, from January 26 through to 2039. Consider this to be the start of a new cycle of spiritual evolution.

Saturn entering Aries signifies a notable milestone in taking responsibility for your progress in pursuit of long-term goals. One area of life significantly under review this year is the company you keep and how it impacts your progress towards these goals. This includes groups of friends, professional organizations and any other greater community you immerse yourself in. Pluto, the planet of transformation, stays in your career sector all year. In addition to that, the first eclipse of the year also lights up this area of life. Eclipses are evolutionary transits which stimulate growth through scrutiny and shake-ups.

Like the company you keep, one-on-one partnership is another important topic for Aries in 2026. Venus, the planet of union and intimacy, will be retrograde in your relationship sector during the autumn. Relationships are especially under review during the second half of the year because the solar eclipse in Leo on August 12 will light up the romance sector of your chart. It's a big year for evaluating the seriousness of existing partnerships, or for re-evaluating your desire for a relationship if you're single. Mars, the planet of drive and ambition, will heat up your romance sector this fall as well.

The Hierophant is a weighty card to choose in a tarot spread, because along with the spiritual path it calls you to journey on is also a process of shedding aspects of your identity or beliefs which no longer serve you. This is a theme all year with Saturn and Neptune being co-present in your sign. In order to make room for the new, you need to do away with the old. This is a year to say yes to going deeper – going deeper within yourself to really understand your convictions and who or what you're fighting for. Aries has strong associations with being the pioneer. This is a year you're called to explore heightened expressions of discipline and routine to usher in holistic abundance.

For a quarterly view of your year ahead, the first quarter of 2026 centres around physical wellness and routines, in addition to evaluating your existing spiritual value system. The second quarter of the year features some scrutiny around budgeting your finances. The third quarter of the year brings attention to creative self-expression and romance. And the final quarter of the year centres more intently on partnership, routines and physical wellness.

Health (1st/6th/12th houses)

(Please note that this is an astrological perspective on health and not a medical one. Any health-related symptoms should be evaluated by a qualified healthcare professional.)

Understanding astrological trends with health can be divided up into physical and mental wellness for the year. Mars, your planetary ruler and physical health planet, is very busy this year buzzing through nine of the twelve zodiac signs. Unlike in 2025, Mars will not be retrograde this year, providing you with some forward momentum in creating routines that centre around physical health. Spring is an important season for physical health. In March, the lunar eclipse in Virgo lights up this sector of your chart, scrutinizing patterns of behaviour around diet and exercise. This is an invitation to take long-standing physical health matters seriously. Moreover, if you haven't had a physical exam from a doctor in a while, this transit could also be an invitation to do so. The spring also features Mars, occupying your sign from April 10 to May 19. Among many significations, Mars rules inflammation and heat. Beware of consuming foods which cause inflammation or similar reactions during this period.

Your mental health planet, Jupiter, spends the first half of 2026 (January 1 to June 30) in your home and family sector – linking this sector to your overarching mental wellness. Carving out a sanctuary space in your home where you can retreat and rejuvenate is strongly recommended, if possible. This space should be an area in the home where you can be alone and where others can only enter by invitation. (For clients living in smaller spaces or spaces where this isn't possible, I've recommended the bathtub as their special place to calm down and centre.) This sanctuary space should also ideally be a conducive area for wellness practices such as meditation, mindfulness or journalling. Your mental health planet enters fiery Leo on June 30 and stays in the sign for the remainder of the year. This shift will draw the focus from the home to either creative self-expression or children. Processing emotion through song, dance, making art or a multitude of other creative endeavours is recommended with your mental health planet in Leo.

Here are the specific areas of the body to focus on this year:

- Face and head: the face and head are perennial areas of focus for you, Aries, as your sign rules these parts of the body in medical astrology. With Saturn and Neptune co-present in your 1st house for the majority of the year, placing greater emphasis on facial and cranial wellness is recommended. Methods of support for this part of the body include diet and specialized massage.
- Digestive system: the digestive system is the second area of focus given the activity occurring in your physical wellness sector this year. The spring is an especially heightened time of

focus on supporting this part of the body, given the lunar eclipse occurring in this sector of your chart and your physical health planet occupying your sign for a majority of the season.

- Ankles and feet: the north node continues to occupy the sign of Pisces, which rules the feet, until July 27 when it enters Aquarius, which rules the ankles. The north node will also be occupying the sectors of your chart related to these parts of the body as well. Proper maintenance through stretching and reflexology is recommended.

Love and Social Life (5th/7th/11th houses)

Social life is more of an area of focus for you this year than relationships. Your social life planet, Saturn, enters your sign in mid-February and stays in Aries for the rest of the year. A major theme within this area of life is taking stock of the reciprocity of your existing social groups and relationships. Is your proverbial cup being filled by others as much as you're filling theirs? This is an ever-present question in 2026 for Aries and applies to circles of friends and professional organizations. Speaking of professional organizations, the astrology of 2026 suggests getting more involved in professional circles, and even assuming positions of power or authority within these networks. The first three months of 2026 are especially pertinent to social life as there are multiple astrological influences affecting this area of life. Mars, your planetary ruler, enters your social life sector on January 24 and stays there until March 3. Mars rules drive, ambition, assertion and conflict. Mars in your social life sector will empower you to have more agency in deciding whether the networks you associate with actually uplift and fuel you. Take stock of how you feel after spending time with these circles of friends. The first quarter of 2026 also features a solar eclipse in Aquarius, in your friendship sector. This transit supports exploring and immersing yourself in new groups or networks.

Your relationship planet, Venus, remains relatively neutral until the end of 2026, when it will be retrograde from October 3 to November 13. Venus's retrogrades are times to re-evaluating your values related to relationships, in addition to functioning as audits of existing relationships. A Venus retrograde is *not* a time to fear! This is a time to slow down and actually consider how you're feeling in an existing partnership. Do you need to advocate for any of your needs which aren't being met? For couples in relationships, such a period can actually draw them closer, if they collaborate in this recalibration. For those who are single, a Venus retrograde will be a period of time to rethink your approach to pursuing a relationship – or if you even want to pursue one in the first place. Taking yourself on dates is a good way to get in touch with the way you seek to be treated by others. Venus's retrograde in Libra from October 25 to November 13 is an especially potent time for this.

Jupiter, the planet of growth and expansion, leaves Cancer and enters Leo on June 30, where it'll stay for the rest of the year. This is important because Jupiter will begin its transit in your romance sector on this day. Moreover, Jupiter gets busy forming aspects with Uranus, Neptune and Pluto during July, making it an especially hot summer for you, Aries.

Career and Finances (10th/2nd/8th houses)

Saturn, the planet of discipline and hard work, is your career planet. Saturn enters your sign in February and will stay there for the next two years. This year your totem, the Hierophant, reminds you of the importance of seeking out mentorship or guides to advance or promote yourself in your career. With Saturn occupying your sign, this year is very much, 'If at first I don't succeed, try, try again.' Incremental progress is better than no progress at all, so make sure you celebrate the little victories this year. Your career planet meets up with Neptune, the planet of dreams, on February 20, encouraging you to audit your existing career aspirations and your existing action plan to achieve these goals. The first question to answer, Aries, is: 'Do I even have a thorough action plan to achieve my career goals?' Start there and work step by step this year. As mentioned above, Saturn rules hard work, so strap on your boots and get to it!

Venus is your finance planet and is relatively neutral until the end of the year. Essentially, what you put in you'll get out. Intentionally carving out and adhering to a budget earlier in the year is recommended to mitigate any turbulence when your finance planet turns retrograde in October. Venus's retrogrades are times where frugality is especially recommended. Retrograde periods are periods where a planet is moving slower than normal, resulting in delays or stalling in the areas of life it rules. Venus's retrograde in Scorpio and Libra also pertains to partnership or collaborations which generate income. Use the retrograde period to audit the efficacy of any existing partnerships or to suss out new partnerships for financial endeavours. However, it is not recommended to start a new financial project until after the retrograde period is over (after November 14).

Home and Domestic Life (4th house)

This year starts off with abundant Jupiter in your home sector. If a move or upgrade to the home did not materialize in 2025, the first half of 2026 is ripe with possibility. Jupiter in Cancer centres around cultivating abundance in the home. Consulting a feng shui expert to maximize the energy and flow of your living space is absolutely recommended. As mentioned in the health section of this Horoscope, Jupiter is your mental health planet, so with it transiting your home sector it is important to carve out a 'sanctuary space' in your home. For more information, please review the health section again. Jupiter is also your spirituality planet. Jupiter in your home sector also indicates the importance of having an altar or some form of physical reflection of your spiritual value system. Having an altar aligns with the overarching theme of cultivating abundance in the home this year. If you feel called to do so, Jupiter in Cancer strongly supports honouring your ancestors with this altar as well. Photos, mementos, family relics can all be included in the altar.

Your home planet is the Moon, so it's important to track monthly New and Full Moons to better understand the ebb and flow of energy in your living space. February, March and August are three noteworthy months for this area of life as eclipses occur in all three of them. Take extra care of the physical infrastructure of your home during these months.

Self-improvement (3rd/5th/9th houses)

If you've been craving to become a student again, 2026 is a great year to do so. Uranus, the planet of innovation and individuality, enters Gemini and stays in the sign for six and a half years. Uranus in Gemini strongly supports educating yourself again. Jupiter is your planet of higher education and enters Leo at the end of June. The latter half of 2026 will feature Jupiter and Uranus harmoniously aligning over the summer and staying in complementary signs for the remainder of the year. Uranus transiting Gemini also supports further developing an understanding of new and innovative technology. Familiarizing yourself better with advances in AI, machine learning, self-driving cars and any other new form of technology which piques your interest is strongly recommended.

Creative self-expression is another facet of life supported for Aries in 2026. Jupiter, the planet of growth and expansion, enters your creativity sector over the summer. Jupiter in Leo supports forms of creativity which appease your inner child. Picking up or making more time for singing, dancing, painting or any other creative activity you used to love to partake in will pay long-lasting dividends in giving you the motivation to level up in this Hierophant year.

Month-by-month Forecasts

January

Best Days Overall: 1–4
Most Stressful Days Overall: 24–27
Best Days for Love: 3–6
Best Days for Money: 9–12
Best Days for Career: 16–19
Power Word: Gentle

Happy new year, Aries! The month and year start off with a water Full Moon in Cancer on the 3rd. This lunation encourages you to start the year by taking care of your inner child and making it happy. Relationships with parents, and also the parent–child relationship which exists within you, are likely to be an emotional focus for the first week of the year. January 6 features the Sun meeting up with Venus. For Aries, this is a career-oriented transit which is perfect for beginning the quest to tackle the big goals you seek to achieve this year. This is an ideal day to schedule specific deliverables or actions to start you off on this year's adventures. However, it's important you do not bite off more than you can chew as the energy leading into and out of the weekend of the 10th is busy and chaotic. Please prioritize your peace during this weekend!

The New Moon in Capricorn on the 18th is also a career-oriented lunation. It'd be wise to schedule some of those deliverables I mentioned earlier for the week following this lunation to capitalize on this fertile career energy. Aquarius's season kicks off on January 19, which is your annual spotlight on your social life and the groups you immerse yourself in. Treat the start of this season as an invitation to reach out to a few of your closest friends and express gratitude for all the ways they support you. After Aquarius's season kicks off, Mercury enters Aquarius and both Mercury and the Sun meet up with each other *and* Pluto on the 22nd and 23rd respectively. Pluto rules all not-so-fun things to talk about, like shame, vulnerability, power dynamics, etc. As a result, the start of Aquarius season may be a little heavy, so be gentle with yourself, sweet Ram.

January wraps up with your planetary ruler, Mars, also entering Aquarius, on the 23rd. Mars rules drive, ambition and assertion, among many other significations. Mars in Aquarius is an especially social transit for Aries, so just make sure you balance your social life with much-needed recharge time as well. Mars will also meet up with Pluto on the 27th, which may trigger shake-ups in friend groups or organizations you're a part of. If you feel on edge, just remember to give yourself space to process how you're feeling and to articulate that appropriately, instead of reacting in the moment – if possible. Lastly, Neptune enters your sign where it will stay until 2039. You'll be feeling a call towards incorporating spirituality more intentionally into your daily life this year.

February

Best Days Overall: 20–24
Most Stressful Days Overall: 15–16; 27–28
Best Days for Love: 1–3; 21–22
Best Days for Money: 10–14
Best Days for Career: 2–5; 20
Power Word: Responsibility

Happy February, Aries! This month's cosmic weather starts off on the 1st with a bright Full Moon in Leo. This is a creative and romantic lunation for you so plan on snuggling up with a special someone or carving out some time for play. Mercury and Venus will both square off with Uranus between the 5th and the 8th, so expect the unexpected. Mercury moves into Pisces on the 6th and Venus does the same on 10th. These shifts promote nesting, resting and self-compassion. Pisces is the mutable water sign of the zodiac, so anticipate a spike in emotions over the next few weeks.

One of the most anticipated astrological events of 2026 occurs on February 13 with Saturn entering your sign! Saturn is the planet which rules responsibility, discipline and restriction. Starting this month and for the rest of the year, you're being tasked to mature and take ownership of your decisions. As mentioned in the yearly overview above, 2026 is a year about answering your calling.

Saturn moving into your sign supports you in this pursuit only if you're dedicated and disciplined, in addition to determined.

February is a big month not only because of Saturn shifting signs; it also includes the first eclipse of the year. Eclipses are wily transits which stimulate growth through scrutiny. The first eclipse of the year is a solar eclipse in Aquarius which is exact on February 17. As mentioned in your Horoscope last month, there's lots of energy centring around the company you keep. This eclipse functions as an audit of those circles and if there's reciprocity in these relationships. The next day the Sun enters Pisces, which is your annual spotlight on mental health and wellness. If possible, take time out of your week for the next four weeks to ground yourself and get out of your head. The first Mercury retrograde period occurs just a few days later on the 26th: herein lies your prompt from the universe to intentionally budget time to give your mind (ruled by Mercury) a rest.

March

Best Days Overall: 20-22; 29-30
Most Stressful Days Overall: 1-4
Best Days for Love: 6-10
Best Days for Money: 5-8
Best Days for Career: 25-28
Power Word: Embody

It's almost your birthday, Aries! March begins with your planetary ruler, Mars, entering compassionate Pisces on the 2nd. This, combined with the lunar eclipse in Virgo on the 3rd, orients you towards prioritizing health and wellness this month. Be especially mindful of inflammatory foods or behaviours. The Sun finds harmony with Jupiter on the 5th and Venus shifts into your sign on the 6th, gently supporting you. This astrology supports carving out time for pleasure during the weekend of the 7th. If you've been meaning to write or lean into any form of communication, Mercury finds harmony with Jupiter on the 9th supporting you in these pursuits.

The New Moon in Pisces occurs on the 18th, working with you to plant seeds around boosting your mental health. What routines do you wish you had in place which would bolster your ability to manage existing anxieties or even lessen them? The theme of this lunation is adopting behaviours which promote long-lasting peace. Right after the New Moon, the Sun shifts into your sign, heralding the start of spring and Aries season on the 20th! It's time for you to set out upon a new trip around the Sun. Identify three words you seek to embody this year and incorporate them into your existing spiritual, journalling or self-empowerment practices. I wish you the best year yet!

Possibly as a birthday present, the universe ends the existing Mercury retrograde period on the first day of Aries's season. Yay! Remember, Mercury takes some time to ramp up to normal speed so communication, transport and technology may be a little wonky for the next week or so. The Sun meets up with Neptune in your sign on the 22nd, inspiring you to dream big, and then conjoins with Saturn on the 25th reminding you that it takes lots and lots of little steps forward to make a giant leap. The month ends with Venus moving into Taurus and drawing your focus towards finances. This is an astrological invitation to check in on your budgeting practices and identify if short-term or long-term frugality is a necessary addition to your life.

April

Best Days Overall: 9-13
Most Stressful Days Overall: 19-22; 25-26
Best Days for Love: 1-3; 28-29
Best Days for Money: 22-25
Best Days for Career: 13-17
Power Word: Fiery

The cosmic weather this month starts off with a bright Full Moon in Libra illuminating partnership for you, Aries. Regardless of your partnership status, the emotional focus around this date will be your closest one-to-one relationships. If you're single, this is an ideal time to put yourself out there if you're looking for a partner. If you're partnered already, it is strongly advised to put quality time on the calendar to spend with your significant other. This is especially the case because the kinetic energy is really going to ramp up for you this month, starting on the 9th when your planetary ruler, Mars, enters your sign. Mercury follows suit on the 14th meaning there will be *five* planets in your sign until Taurus season begins on the 19th (the Sun, Mercury, Mars, Saturn and Neptune). Anticipate everyone responding to all this fiery energy in their own ways.

The New Moon in Aries on the 17th is a transformational New Moon that encourages taking big risks, as Mars – the ruler of this lunation – is harmoniously aligned to Pluto. On the same day, Mercury will conjoin with Neptune, which inspires daydreaming and the potential to see things through rose-tinted glasses! So, if you are going to take a risk, make sure it isn't done hastily (plan ahead). Taurus's season begins on the 19th, which is your annual spotlight on all things financial. The 19th also features Mars meeting up with the ruler of restriction and slowdowns, Saturn. For a kinetic fire sign like yourself, you'll likely find yourself frustrated by an inability to go-go-go. Remember, your productivity is not a benchmark of your worth.

The weekend of the 25th features one noteworthy annual transit and one long-awaited major shift in energy. Firstly, the Sun squares off with Pluto, which makes the overarching vibe angsty. For you, Aries, this is also financial in nature, so the encouragement to consider some form of frugality from last month needs to be reiterated here. Aside from this transit, Uranus, the planet of innovation and instability, enters nimble Gemini. Uranus in Gemini affects us all on the societal level by revolutionizing how we learn and communicate. For you, you're entering a seven-year period where your patterns of communication are up for review and due to change.

May

Best Days Overall: 7-11
Most Stressful Days Overall: 24-28
Best Days for Love: 13-16
Best Days for Money: 16-20
Best Days for Career: 1-4
Power Word: Ground

Happy May, Aries! Yet again this month kicks off with another Full Moon, this time in Scorpio. The Full Moon in Scorpio illuminates fears and anxieties that have kept you stifled and must be confronted. This lunation, paired with Mercury squaring off with Pluto on the 5th, means the first week of May is probably going to feel extra angsty. If you've struggled with co-dependency or with boundaries, these types of transits tend to activate this behaviour. Prioritize self-care and self-compassion. Also, resist the urge for grandiose reactions, given that your planetary ruler Mars will also be squaring off with Jupiter on the 5th. Taurus is a Venus-ruled sign focused on values as a means to root itself. Identify the values which will best support you amid a possibly heavy first week of the month. Also, Taurus's season gives you the cue to use somatic work, like breathwork or mindfulness, to get out of your head and into your body.

The New Moon in Taurus on the 16th typically opens the possibility of introducing or exploring new streams of income, or other forms of entrepreneurial pursuits. Mercury enters Gemini the next day – especially supporting endeavours involving leaning into communication or storytelling. However, your planetary ruler, Mars, leaves your sign and enters Taurus on the 18th. This shift in energy usually invites you to slow down and take stock of the abundance you've already cultivated. In general, the combination of these transits still supports the creation of new incomes, but only if done so in a methodical, well-thought-out way. Look before you leap, Aries.

Gemini's season kicks off on the 20th, signalling your annual spotlight on communication. The month ends with a couple of tense transits as Mars squares off with Pluto and Venus squares off with Saturn. It is advised not to spread yourself too thin during this last week of May and to prioritize mental health. This month's second 'Blue' Full Moon in Sagittarius is a lunation inviting you to lean into your spirituality as a means to ground yourself during this time. The Full Moon in Sagittarius also supports using exercise as a supportive coping mechanism for stress.

June

Best Days Overall: 7–10
Most Stressful Days Overall: 27–30
Best Days for Love: 10–13
Best Days for Money: 25–28
Best Days for Career: 14–17
Power Word: Reflect

After a chaotic end to May, June starts off pretty neutrally with Mercury moving into Cancer. Mercury in Cancer directs your attention towards home and family dynamics. This is important because Mercury will turn retrograde in the sign at the end of the month. Mercury joins Venus and Jupiter, both of which are at the tail ends of their transits through the cardinal water sign now. Venus and Jupiter meet up on the 10th, which is a great day to devote quality time to loved ones in the comfort of your own home. Venus enters radiant Leo on the 13th, supporting creative self-expression and romance for you, Aries. Prioritize play and recreation around this date.

The New Moon occurs in Gemini on the 14th. This lunation happens just as Venus forms several aspects with the outer planets, finding harmony with Uranus on the 16th and Neptune on the 17th and then finding tension with Pluto on the 18th. New Moons are always the start of a new emotional cycle and this lunation strongly encourages identifying strategies to interrupt or prevent excessive overthinking. On the 19th, for the first time in about 50 years, Chiron enters Taurus. Chiron is associated with confronting and healing our deep-seated wounds. Now classified as a minor planet rather than as an asteroid, Chiron has an irregular orbit and spent extra time in your sign. Chiron will dip back into your sign later this year, but this is a significant moment to pause and reflect on your growth/healing journey over the last eight years.

Cancer's season begins on June 21, followed by Venus finding harmony with Saturn on the 25th which further reinforces the importance of incorporating more play or recreation into your schedule this month. Mars enters Gemini on the 28th, boosting social butterfly tendencies and indicating that this Mercury retrograde period is one to reconnect with those you've lost touch with. Mercury turns retrograde on the 29th. The month ends with a Full Moon in Capricorn, having you contemplate your career and what you want your legacy to be. Lastly, Jupiter moves into Leo for the first time in 12 years this month. For Aries, this is an incredibly creative transit which supports growing your endeavours along these lines, and your relationships with children/the younger generation.

July

Best Days Overall: 15–19
Most Stressful Days Overall: 15; 2830
Best Days for Love: 6–9
Best Days for Money: 23–26
Best Days for Career: 25–28
Power Word: Transform

If there was one month astrologers would point to this year for noteworthy astrology, it's July! This month starts off with your planetary ruler, Mars, getting very busy forming aspects with all three outer planets (Uranus on the 4th, Neptune and Pluto on the 5th). Mars and Uranus conjoining is explosive, literally and figuratively, so be especially careful if you're handling fireworks or anything flammable on or around the 4th. Moreover, know that tempers can flare more easily than normal, so do your best to not react to any provocations. These aspects are incredibly productive for you, Aries, as they involve your planetary ruler harmoniously linked to the planets associated with life-altering shifts.

Venus leaves Leo and enters Virgo on the 9th, gently encouraging you to stay on top of your physical wellness routines. The New Moon in Cancer occurs on July 14 and is incredibly fertile for you as well, especially in the realm of home and domestic life. I would strongly encourage you to reorganize or redecorate your space on or just after this lunation to revitalize its energy. Productive energy follows with Mars finding harmony with Uranus on the 19th. This transit also supports spontaneity and adventures.

The noteworthy astrology begins on July 20 with Jupiter finding harmony with Neptune as it opposes Pluto. The next day, Jupiter also finds harmony with Uranus. Given how slowly these planets move, this kind of confluence of interactions does not happen too often! These transits are more noticeable in how they affect the macroenvironment, so anticipate observing societal shifts unfold this month and over the coming months. On the personal level, these transits pertain to your life path and how your convictions or beliefs inform who you're becoming. These transits also occur right before Leo's season, which begins on July 22. This Leo season roars as the Sun, newly in the sign, then forms the same aspects that Jupiter just made. Leo's season is all about confronting your ego and shedding old identities which no longer serve who you seek to become. The month ends with the Sun conjoining with Jupiter just as the Moon becomes full. This Full Moon in Aquarius is a surprisingly emotional time, especially in the realm of friendship. Spend time with those who support the person you're becoming, sweet Ram.

August

Best Days Overall: 15-19
Most Stressful Days Overall: 24-29
Best Days for Love: 6-10
Best Days for Money: 10-14
Best Days for Career: 7-10
Power Word: Evolve

Partnership becomes a focal point at the start of April for Aries as Venus shifts into your polar sign, Libra. Venus will now begin to slow down and will be retrograde later this year in Scorpio and Libra. The Sun finds harmony with Saturn on the 7th, making the weekend of the 8th a productive one if you have a long to-do list to get through. Mercury enters fiery Leo on the 9th after an extended stay in Cancer, so expect communication to universally become more expressive over the next few weeks.

Eclipse season is back, with the first eclipse in this series of two occurring on the 12th. Expect strong energy in the week leading into the eclipse as Mercury follows Jupiter and the Sun by tensely opposing Pluto and harmonizing with Uranus and Neptune. These aspects occur the same day as the eclipse and the following one, spreading out the vibes a little bit longer. This eclipse could revolve around one of a few areas of life for Aries: creative self-expression, romance or children. Remember, eclipses are evolutionary transits, so even if you're feeling tense, trust that you're also growing. Eclipses in Leo also have a lot to do with how you either allow your heart to guide you or ignore its desires.

Virgo's season begins on the 22nd, which functions as your annual spotlight on physical wellness and the routines which keep you organized. Which routines have fallen by the wayside given how frenetic this summer has been? It's vital to get into a regime as the second eclipse, occurring on the 28th, has a significant mental health focus for Aries. In general, this eclipse is noteworthy because it occurs on the same day the Sun and Moon are squaring off with Uranus. Uranus is associated with frenetic energy. Having self-care and wellness routines in place already will help mitigate the restless or anxious energy that is likely to abound. Thankfully, the month concludes with Jupiter, which rules growth and expansion, harmoniously aligning with Saturn, which rules discipline and is currently in your sign. This closing transit rewards the diligent effort you've been putting into achieving long-term goals.

September

Best Days Overall: 11–15
Most Stressful Days Overall: 17–18; 23–26
Best Days for Love: 5–9
Best Days for Money: 26–30
Best Days for Career: 28–30
Power Word: Communicate

The energy of the last eclipse at the end of August seeps into the first week of September. A new leaf is turned with the New Moon on the 10th. This New Moon occurs just as Mercury enters Libra, encouraging rectification or amelioration of relationships which may have been stressed during summer. The cosmic weather continues to point you towards brushing up and maintaining your physical wellness routines. Productive energy for completing a slew of mundane or domestic tasks comes when the Sun finds harmony with Mars on the 14th. Neptune and Pluto find harmony on the 15th, supporting changes or efforts you've made this summer towards accomplishing major feats or goals. Chiron re-enters your sign one last time on the 17th, encouraging one last pass at healing deep-seated wounds and transmuting them into your purpose.

Libra's season begins on the 22nd, which is your annual spotlight on partnership and intimate one-to-one relationships. Speaking of spotlights, the Full Moon in your sign shines brightly on the 26th. This Full Moon is loaded emotionally for you as it's in your sign and represents the culmination of an emotional cycle. It's OK to feel your feelings, sweet Ram. Communication in partnership is a heavy focus for the remainder of the month as the Sun in Libra forms a grand air trine, a super-harmonious aspect, with Uranus in Gemini and Pluto in Aquarius. If you're partnered, this is an opportune time to address anything you feel needs to be brought up or use this astrology as an opportunity to express your profound gratitude for all the ways your partner supports you. If you're single or casually dating, this cosmic weather supports branding, marketing and playing the field.

Get ready to roar, Aries. The month ends with your planetary ruler, Mars, entering fiery Leo. Mars in Leo ignites your passions and brings them to the fore. Carve out time to get creative or just allow yourself the space to play. There can be a childlike excitement associated with this transit, so for the next six weeks, lean into making your inner child happy.

October

Best Days Overall: 27–31
Most Stressful Days Overall: 1–5
Best Days for Love: 25–28
Best Days for Money: 23–26
Best Days for Career: 6–9
Power Word: Values

There's not one but two planetary retrogrades to be aware of this month, Aries. October begins with Venus turning retrograde in your fellow Mars-ruled sign, Scorpio, on the 3rd. Venus's retrograde is a values and relationships audit for everyone, but for Aries it also has financial implications. This Venus retrograde pushes you to investigate how your money is tied up with or dependent upon other people. This retrograde starts off with a bang as your planetary ruler, Mars, tensely opposes Pluto on this day. The few days before and after this event are likely to be tense, as this is a transit notorious for highlighting uneven power dynamics. Thankfully, Mars finds harmony with Neptune at this time, indicating that the outlet for all the angst is either a leaning into spirituality or being of service to those in need. The first week rounds out with the Sun tensely opposing Saturn. This transit can heighten a 'never enough' mentality, so it's important you don't spread yourself too thin this first week of the month.

The New Moon in Libra occurs on the 10th and typically encourages planting new seeds around partnership and collaboration. However, given the fact that the lunation is ruled by Venus, which is very much retrograde, this lunation would actually support reinforcing existing partnerships or collaborations. If you're single, this would pertain to carving out quality time with those you consider 'best friends'. Venus tensely squares off with Mars on the 11th, setting up the weekend to be one where you likely will need to revisit and conquer some long-standing anxieties you've been grappling with.

Speaking of which, Scorpio's season begins on the 23rd and is your annual spotlight on what shadows you need to confront to further your growth. The next day, Mercury joins Venus by turning retrograde as well. Mercury retrograde periods invite reflection on patterns of thought and communication. Venus re-enters Libra on the 25th and the Moon becomes full on the 26th. The Full Moon in Taurus is in a tense alignment with Pluto, meaning this Full Moon will have you on edge. There is also a financial flair to this lunation for Aries, so briefly adopting a more frugal approach would benefit you at this time.

November

Best Days Overall: 16-17; 22-25
Most Stressful Days Overall: 10-11; 18-21
Best Days for Love: 13-17
Best Days for Money: 9-13
Best Days for Career: 27-30
Power Word: Goals

Dig deep within yourself this November, Aries. The cosmic weather for the month kicks off on the 9th with the New Moon in Scorpio. This lunation encourages introspection and asking yourself thought-provoking questions around what you truly desire. With both Mercury and Venus still retrograde at this time, this is also an ideal time to pause and reflect on how you navigated this year. Don't forget to pat yourself on the back for all the things you've accomplished! Mercury and Venus both end their retrograde periods on the same day, November 13. They'll be moving forwards slowly for the first week or so, but the energy will pick up by the end of the month.

Your planetary ruler, Mars, conjoins with buoyant Jupiter on the 16th. Consider this the first jump start of energy revving things back up. Mars rules drive, ambition and assertion. This transit is the ideal time to look ahead to 2027 and start setting your goals. Has your big dream changed since the start of the year? Identify what steps you want to take in 2027 to get yourself closer to achieving whatever it is. That said, remember that haste makes waste. With the Sun squaring off with Mars on the 20th, it's important you don't act impulsively this week.

The Sun moves into visionary Sagittarius on the 22nd. Sagittarius season is your annual spotlight on spirituality and what goals you're chasing. Sagittarius typically embodies the archetypes of the preacher, teacher or cheerleader. Do your best to embody one or more of these archetypes for yourself over the next four weeks. The Full Moon in Gemini on the 24th is full of surprises as it is conjoined with Uranus. Expect the unexpected to come to light with this lunation. Do your best not to overreact if others are especially volatile around this date. Patience is a virtue, Aries! Mars enters Virgo the next day, bringing your physical wellness back into focus. Sagittarius is an indulgent sign, and with it being Sagittarius season, do your best to enjoy yourself, but also show a little restraint when tempted to overindulge.

December

Best Days Overall: 15-19
Most Stressful Days Overall: 4-8
Best Days for Love: 10-14
Best Days for Money: 6-10
Best Days for Career: 23-26
Power Word: Self-regulate

It's the last month of the year, Aries! November's explosive vibes spill over into the start of December with your planetary ruler, Mars, squaring off with Uranus on the 5th. This aspect is typically associated with volatility with both emotions and behaviour. Aries is particularly affected by this because your ruling planet is involved. Learning or reinforcing breathwork practices or behaviours that can help you self-regulate and ground yourself are essential at this time. The New Moon in Sagittarius on the 8th is visionary and promotes further immersing yourself into your spiritual practices. Moreover, this New Moon could very well inspire a trip or voyage of some kind. This is especially applicable if there are spiritual undertones to this sojourn.

Self-care is very important this month as Venus squares off one more time with Pluto on the 9th (this is the third time in a short span due to Venus's retrograde period in October and November). Venus squaring Pluto can often bring up feelings of unworthiness or existing self-esteem issues which may lie buried deep within. Given that Chiron, the wounded healer, is making its final swing through your sign, this is an apt time to work on making headway in healing the root causes of these tough feelings. It is also important to be sure you're surrounding yourself with people who fill up your cup as much as you fill up theirs – i.e. that there's reciprocity in your relationships.

Thankfully the vibes lighten in the middle of the month as Venus finds harmony with Mars. This is great dating, romance and play energy. Lean into this and prioritize pleasure at this time. December 21 is the start of Capricorn season. Capricorn season is your annual spotlight on career and legacy. The Full Moon follows two days later and asks the question: 'What do you want to be remembered for, Aries?' Mercury enters Capricorn on the 25th, supporting you to consider in more detail the goals you'll be seeking to accomplish in 2027. Take it easy this last week of the year though; Mercury and Saturn find tension on the 31st, which won't make it conducive to do much work anyway during the last few days of the year.

Taurus

THE BULL

Birthdays from
April 21 to
May 20

Personality Profile

TAURUS AT A GLANCE

Element – Earth

Ruling Planet – Venus
   Career Planet – Saturn
   Love Planet – Mars
   Money Planet – Mercury
   Planet of Health and Work – Venus
   Planet of Home and Family Life – Sun
   Planet of Spirituality and Mental Health – Mars
   Planet of Travel, Education, Religion and Philosophy – Saturn

Totem – the Carpenter

Colours – earth tones, yellow

Colours that promote love, romance and social harmony – red-violet, violet

Colours that promote earning power – yellow, yellow-orange

Gems – coral, emerald

Metal – copper

Scents – bitter almond, rose, vanilla, violet

Quality – fixed (= stability)

Quality most needed for balance – flexibility

Strongest virtues – endurance, loyalty, patience, stability, a harmonious disposition

Deepest needs – comfort, material ease, wealth

Characteristics to avoid – rigidity, stubbornness, a tendency to be overly possessive and materialistic

Signs of greatest overall compatibility – Virgo, Capricorn

Signs of greatest overall incompatibility – Leo, Scorpio, Aquarius

Sign most helpful to career – Aquarius

Sign most helpful for emotional support – Leo

Sign most helpful financially – Gemini

Sign best for marriage and/or partnerships – Scorpio

Sign most helpful for creative projects – Virgo

Best Sign to have fun with – Virgo

Signs most helpful in spiritual matters – Aries, Capricorn

Best day of the week – Friday

Understanding a Taurus

Taurus is the most earthy of all the Earth signs. If you understand that Earth is more than just a physical element, that it is a psychological attitude as well, you will get a better understanding of the Taurus personality.

A Taurus has all the power of action that an Aries has. But Taurus is not satisfied with action for its own sake. Their actions must be productive, practical and wealth-producing. If Taurus cannot see a practical value in an action they will not bother taking it.

Taurus's forte lies in their power to make real their own or other people's ideas. They are generally not very inventive but they can take another's invention and perfect it, making it more practical and useful. The same is true for all projects. Taurus is not especially keen on starting new projects, but once they get involved they bring things to completion. Taurus carries everything through. They are finishers and will go the distance, so long as no unavoidable calamity intervenes.

Many people find Taurus too stubborn, conservative, fixed and immovable. This is understandable, because Taurus dislikes change – in the environment or in their routine. They even dislike changing their minds! On the other hand, this is their virtue. It is not good for a wheel's axle to waver. The axle must be fixed, stable and unmovable. Taurus is the axle of society and the heavens. Without their stability and so-called stubbornness, the wheels of the world (and especially the wheels of commerce) would not turn.

Taurus loves routine. A routine, if it is good, has many virtues. It is a fixed – and, ideally, perfect – way of taking care of things. Mistakes can happen when spontaneity comes into the equation, and mistakes cause discomfort and uneasiness – something almost unacceptable to a Taurus. Meddling with Taurus's comfort and security is a sure way to irritate and anger them.

While an Aries loves speed, a Taurus likes things slow. They are slow thinkers – but do not make the mistake of assuming they lack intelligence. On the contrary, Taurus people are very intelligent. It is just that they like to chew on ideas, to deliberate and weigh them up. Only after due deliberation is an idea accepted or a decision taken. Taurus is slow to anger – but once aroused, take care!

Finance

Taurus is very money-conscious. Wealth is more important to them than to many other signs. Wealth to a Taurus means comfort and security. Wealth means stability. Where some zodiac signs feel that they are spiritually rich if they have ideas, talents or skills, Taurus only feels wealth when they can see and touch it. Taurus's way of thinking is, 'What good is a talent if it has not been translated into a home, furniture, car and holidays?'

These are all reasons why Taurus excels in estate agency and agricultural industries. Usually a Taurus will end up owning land. They love to feel their connection to the Earth. Material wealth began with agriculture, the tilling of the soil. Owning a piece of land was humanity's earliest form of wealth: Taurus still feels that primeval connection.

It is in the pursuit of wealth that Taurus develops intellectual and communication ability. Also, in this pursuit Taurus is forced to develop some flexibility. It is in the quest for wealth that they learn the practical value of the intellect and come to admire it. If it were not for the search for wealth and material things, Taurus people might not try to reach a higher intellect.

Some Taurus people are 'born lucky' – the type who win any gamble or speculation. This luck is due to other factors in their horoscope; it is not part of their essential nature. By nature they are not gamblers. They are hard workers and like to earn what they get. Taurus's innate conservatism makes them abhor unnecessary risks in finance and in other areas of their lives.

Career and Public Image

Being essentially down-to-earth people, simple and uncompli-cated, Taurus tends to look up to those who are original, uncon-ventional and inventive. Taurus people like their bosses to be creative and original – since they themselves are content to perfect their superiors' brainwaves. They admire people who have a wider social or political consciousness and they feel that someday (when they have all the comfort and security they need) they too would like to be involved in these big issues.

In business affairs Taurus can be very shrewd – and that makes them valuable to their employers. They are never lazy; they enjoy working and getting good results. Taurus does not like taking unnecessary risks and they do well in positions of authority, which makes them good managers and supervisors. Their managerial skills are reinforced by their natural talents for organization and handling details, their patience and thoroughness. As mentioned, through their connection with the earth, Taurus people also do well in farming and agriculture.

In general a Taurus will choose money and earning power over public esteem and prestige. A position that pays more – though it has less prestige – is preferred to a position with a lot of prestige but lower earnings. Many other signs do not feel this way, but a Taurus does, especially if there is nothing in his or her personal birth chart that modifies this. Taurus will pursue glory and prestige only if it can be shown that these things have a direct and immediate impact on their wallet.

Love and Relationships

In love, the Taurus-born likes to have and to hold. They are the marrying kind. They like commitment and they like the terms of a relationship to be clearly defined. More importantly, Taurus likes to be faithful to one lover, and they expect that lover to reciprocate this fidelity. When this doesn't happen, their whole world comes crashing down. When they are in love Taurus people are loyal, but they are also very possessive. They are capable of great fits of jealousy if they are hurt in love.

Taurus is satisfied with the simple things in a relationship. If you are involved romantically with a Taurus there is no need for lavish entertainments and constant courtship. Give them enough love, food and comfortable shelter and they will be quite content to stay home and enjoy your company. They will be loyal to you for life.

Make a Taurus feel comfortable and – above all – secure in the relationship, and you will rarely have a problem.

In love, Taurus can sometimes make the mistake of trying to control their partners, which can cause great pain on both sides. The reasoning behind their actions is basically simple: Taurus people feel a sense of ownership over their partners and will want to make changes that will increase their own general comfort and security. This attitude is OK when it comes to inanimate, material things – but is dangerous when applied to people. Taurus needs to be careful and attentive to this possible trait within themselves.

Home and Domestic Life

Home and family are vitally important to Taurus. They like children. They also like a comfortable and perhaps glamorous home – something they can show off. They tend to buy heavy, ponderous furniture – usually of the best quality. This is because Taurus likes a feeling of substance in their environment. Their house is not only their home but their place of creativity and entertainment. The Taurus's home tends to be truly their castle. If they could choose, Taurus people would prefer living in the countryside to being city-dwellers. If they cannot do so during their working lives, many Taurus individuals like to holiday in or even retire to the country, away from the city and closer to the land.

At home a Taurus is like a country squire – lord (or lady) of the manor. They love to entertain lavishly, to make others feel secure in their home and to encourage others to derive the same sense of satisfaction as they do from it. If you are invited for dinner at the home of a Taurus you can expect the best food and best entertainment. Be prepared for a tour of the house and expect to see your Taurus friend exhibit a lot of pride and satisfaction in his or her possessions.

Taurus people like children but they are usually strict with them. The reason for this is they tend to treat their children – as they do most things in life – as their possessions. The positive side to this is that their children will be well cared for and well supervised. They will get every material thing they need to grow up properly.

On the down side, Taurus can get too repressive with their children. If a child dares to upset the daily routine – which Taurus loves to follow – he or she will have a problem with a Taurus parent.

Horoscope for 2026

When building a house, the first part of the home that is constructed are the foundations. In a similar vein, this year your totem is 'the Carpenter', as you're meant to inspect the sturdiness of existing structures and relationships – plus there's ample opportunity to build new ones. A lot of themes of this year revolve around the concepts of past and future for you, Taurus. This year will mark the first time in 12 years when Jupiter, the planet of growth and expansion, enters your home and family sector. This area of your chart rules your past and this event will serve as a referendum on the last 12 years and how you've got to where you're at today. Familial relationships and relationships within the home are heightened and will be further explored in that section of this annual Horoscope.

In the same year that Jupiter brings growth and expansion to the area of your chart which represents your past, Pluto, the planet of transformation, plants itself firmly in your career and legacy sector, which represents your future. Pluto is joined by the north node mid-year which is preceded by an eclipse in this area of your chart early in 2026. Eclipses are evolutionary transits that catalyse advancement through scrutiny and shake-ups. If you've been intending to make moves towards being more public facing, the astrology of this year supports your efforts. That being said, the astrology of 2026 also highlights the importance of balancing social and solo time. With your totem being the Carpenter, it's a good idea to view 2026 as a year to build the life you desire.

Speaking of building, 2026 is a noteworthy year as Uranus, the planet of innovation, instability and individuality, enters and stays in Gemini until 2033. Uranus briefly entered Gemini last year but quickly dodged back into your sign for one last trip through it (it has been travelling through your sign since 2019). This is important because this wild-card planet makes this shift in April, when it enters your finances sector. Uranus brings with it unpredictability and opportunity. This is one of the profound transits of the year for you, Taurus. More will be explored in the finances section of this Horoscope.

As stated above, when a carpenter begins building a house, they start first with the foundations. One major area of life which is under scrutiny this year is mental health and the wellness routines which either support or detract from it. Saturn, the planet of discipline, endurance and hard work, enters your mental health sector early in 2026, where it'll stay for the rest of the year. In order to have the stamina to build the life that you desire, you need to have routines in place which keep you grounded and focused.

For a quarterly view of the year ahead, the first quarter features a focus around mental health and career pursuits. The second quarter of 2026 continues the focus on mental health and also adds finances as an additional area of importance. The third quarter features astrology centred around home and family matters. The final quarter of the year brings the focus to routines and relationships.

Health (1st/6th/12th houses)

(Please note that this is an astrological perspective on health and not a medical one. Any health-related symptoms should be evaluated by a qualified healthcare professional.)

Mental health and wellness are a major area of focus in 2026 for Taurus. Your mental health sector gets occupied by two slow-moving, potent planetary bodies: Saturn and Neptune. Saturn rules restriction, hard work and isolation. With it occupying your mental health sector from February onwards, it's critical you quickly strike a balance between your external responsibilities and the responsibility you have to recharge your energy away from the public. It's equally critical you do not spread yourself too thin among a laundry list of unnecessary commitments. There's a difference between being productive and just being busy for the sake of not slowing down. Neptune rules dissolution of the ego and this is an important time for you to confront the ways your ego prevents you from living authentically. Your mental health planet is Mars who will not enter a retrograde period this year. Moreover, Mars will be in your own sign from May 19 to June 29, supporting the adoption of routines centred around grounding and mental wellness.

Your physical health planet is your planetary ruler, Venus. This is a relatively neutral area of life for the majority of the year until Venus turns retrograde in October. Venus will be retrograde from October 3 to November 13 and will split its retrograde across two signs: Scorpio and Libra. Venus's retrograde in Scorpio centres around how your physical wellness is tied up in partnership or your one-to-one relationships. Do you forgo your own health or holistic wellness for the sake of taking care of or appeasing others? When Venus re-enters Libra on October 25, the focus shifts to scrutinizing the routines you have in place which either support or detract from your physical health. Take the Venus retrograde period as an invitation to re-evaluate your physical health routines and put some new ones in motion come November 14.

Here are the specific areas of the body to focus on this year:

- Neck and throat: this is a perennial area of focus for Taurus as your sign rules this part of the body in medical astrology. With Uranus entering the sector of your chart which rules this part of the body mid-year, it's especially important to take care of both the neck and throat this year. Learning proper stretching techniques and being mindful around supporting the vocal cords through diet and maintenance is strongly recommended.
- The sexual organs: your planetary ruler and physical health planet, Venus, turns retrograde in Scorpio, the sign which rules this part of the body. Venus's retrograde occurs from the start of October through to mid-November. If you're due for an annual or routine physical examination to check on the health and wellness of your body, it is recommended to do so prior to the retrograde period (though anytime this year works). Supporting this area of the body through proper procedures is also recommended.
- Skin: Venus will also be retrograde in Libra during its retrograde period, and Libra rules this part of the body.

Skincare is especially important for Taurus this year at all times, but even more so just after the summer. Wearing sunscreen routinely, in addition to a morning and night skincare regime, is very important for Taurus this year.

Love and Social Life (5th/7th/11th houses)

February–March and October–November are noteworthy times for love and romance this year, Taurus. Firstly, it's important to note you have one planet which rules romance and a different planet which explicitly rules partnership. Your romance planet is Mercury, which first turns retrograde this year at the end of February, staying that way until March 20. Mercury's retrograde periods are not meant to be feared. Rather, they're times to re-evaluate how we communicate. In your case, Taurus, this retrograde period is an ideal time to reflect on whether you're communicating your needs for romance and affection. This reflection applies to all Taureans, regardless of partnership status (as it is your romance planet, not your partnership planet, which is retrograde). Moreover, March features an eclipse in the romance sector of your chart. Remember, eclipses are evolutionary transits which catalyse growth through shake-ups. If you're partnered, this eclipse would be the ideal time to introduce some much-needed spontaneity into your relationship if the dynamic has grown passive or even stale. If you're single, the spring eclipse season is the ideal time to say yes to putting yourself out there.

Your partnership planet, Mars, does not turn retrograde in 2026. However, your planetary ruler Venus will retrograde through the partnership sector of your chart this autumn. Venus, the planet of love and intimacy, will be retrograde from October 3 to November 13. For you, Taurus, it will be retrograde in your partnership sector from October 25 to November 13. It will then stay in your partnership sector until early December. Venus's retrograde period in your partnership sector is a referendum on values alignment in partnership. If you're in a relationship, this applies to the existing partnership. If you're single, this applies to the values you prioritize when pursuing a relationship.

Social life is relatively neutral this year, with the slow-moving planets Saturn and Neptune exiting this sector of your chart early in the year. Your social life planet, Jupiter, makes a loud and triumphant transition from Cancer to Leo on June 30. Leo rules the heart in medical astrology and Jupiter in this sign prompts you to surround yourself with those who fill your heart with glee. Jupiter in Leo is an auspicious time to expand groups of friends and social networks as well. This is especially the case in August when Jupiter harmoniously aligns with Saturn.

Career and Finances (10th/2nd/8th houses)

This year features a marked shift as the north node moves into your career sector for the first time in 18 years. Where the north node (and the south node) transit, they bring eclipses to these areas of the chart. The first eclipse in your career sector is actually the first eclipse of 2026, which occurs on February 17. Eclipses make ripples which last long after the lunation ends. This, combined with your career planet, Saturn, shifting signs four days prior, underscores how career is a major area of focus in 2026. More specifically, assuming greater responsibility and actively shedding identities which no longer serve you in this realm are two important sub-themes of Taurus's astrology this year. The north node technically doesn't shift into your career sector until July 27, so use the first part of 2026 to consider the big moves you'll make and then leverage the energy of this shift to take your first steps.

Your finance planet, Mercury, will be retrograde in the three water signs this year. This highlights the importance of not spending money impulsively this year. Take it upon yourself to bone up on your financial IQ through research or by consulting an expert. Mercury's overlapping retrograde period with Venus's retrograde in October and November signal these are two months in particular to especially monitor flagrant spending.

Home and Domestic Life (4th house)

This area of life receives a massive boost this year with Jupiter, the planet of growth and expansion, entering your home and domestic life sector on June 30. Jupiter moving into Leo makes a move or an expansion of your current home ripe with possibility. The sign of Leo rules the heart in medical astrology, so Jupiter in Leo beseeches you to make your home more heartfelt. There's a concept in Scandinavian cultures called *hygge*, which means setting up your home in a way that facilitates a cosy or especially comfortable environment. Your Jupiter-in-Leo homework/home-work assignment is to make your living space more *hygge*. This should be accomplished any time after June 30.

With the Sun being your planet of the home, there's a higher chance of shake-ups or scrutiny in the familial dynamics around the two eclipse seasons this year (February/March and August). Don't worry though; eclipses are evolutionary, so more likely than not these are conversations that have needed to happen for some time. Moreover, knowing this, it's especially important to respond thoughtfully instead of reacting when provoked during the eclipse seasons. Harmonious times of the year for the Sun are when the Sun is in fire signs (March 21–26, July 27–August 1, November 23–28).

Self-improvement (3rd/5th/9th houses)

Your spirituality and higher education planet is Saturn, which, as mentioned earlier in this Horoscope, will begin occupying Aries for the next two and a half years from February 13. Saturn rules discipline and restriction, so there's a marked shift in energy for you given that this planet is going from watery, compassionate Pisces to fiery, pioneering Aries. 'Pioneering' is a good verb to embody in 2026 in all your pursuits surrounding self-improvement. Don't be afraid to try to better yourself in ways you've never attempted before. This is especially supported earlier in the year since Saturn will form aspects with Neptune (February 20) and Pluto (March 28). Embody your 2026 totem of the Carpenter and build out your future brick by brick.

Month-by-month Forecasts

January

Best Days Overall: 3-7
Most Stressful Days Overall: 20-23
Best Days for Love: 10-13
Best Days for Money: 13-17
Best Days for Career: 23-26
Power Word: Spirituality

Happy New Year, Taurus! The cosmic weather of 2026 kicks off with the Full Moon in Cancer lighting up your communication sector on the 3rd. This lunation represents an emotional culmination around patterns of communication. Any self-effacing behaviours related to communication, like unnecessarily censoring yourself or having hypercritical self-talk, are likely to come to light around this date. Between the 6th and the 9th, your planetary ruler, Venus, gets busy – first by conjoining with the Sun on the 6th and then by opposing Jupiter on the 9th. These transits support leaning into your spirituality as a means to ground yourself at the start of this year. This is important because the 10th features a build-up of aspects which can make the overarching energy kinetic and chaotic. The Sun conjoins with Mars, which rules drive, ambition, assertion and conflict. The two planets then both find tension with Jupiter which amplifies the energy of other planets it aspects. You can assume the few days before these transits are exact – and the few days after these transits are exact – to be most like an energetic powder keg.

The New Moon in Capricorn on the 18th ushers in a new emotional cycle for you around spirituality and/or higher education. If you have found that you don't have spiritual practices to lean on to ground yourself with, this is an opportune time to explore and educate yourself in order to develop a sustainable system around spirituality. This lunation also centres around studying or seeking additional certification in an academic area you desire more expertise in. The next day, it's Aquarius season!

Aquarius's season is your annual spotlight on career and legacy. This will be a major theme this year for you as there are noteworthy transits occurring all year in this chart sector for Taurus.

Beware of hypervigilant behaviour during the weekend of and the week that follows the 20th. The Sun, Mercury and Venus all conjoin with Pluto between the 20th and the 23rd with Mars following suit on the 27th. Transits involving Pluto tend to bring to light issues which have been purposely or subconsciously buried. Be gentle with yourself this week. One of the most notable transits of 2026 occurs on January 26 as Neptune formally enters Aries, staying until 2032/2033. Prioritizing mental health and wellness is a major focal point of the year for Taurus in 2026.

February

Best Days Overall: 2-6
Most Stressful Days Overall: 20-24
Best Days for Love: 16-19
Best Days for Money: 10-13
Best Days for Career: 21-25
Power Word: Community

February's astrology starts off on the 1st with the Full Moon in Leo illuminating home and domestic life for you. This is an opportune time to organize, rearrange and prioritize getting your house in order (literally and figuratively). Mercury finds tension with Uranus on the 5th, making it tough to keep a filter on your tongue when speaking. Venus follows suit on the 8th making the energy of this week a little frenetic. Expect the unexpected, Taurus! Saturn finally and formally moves into Aries where it'll stay for about two and a half years. Saturn joining Neptune in Aries only further highlights the importance prioritizing mental health is for you this year.

The first eclipse of the year occurs on the 17th. Remember, eclipses are evolutionary transits which stimulate growth through scrutiny and shake-ups. This eclipse centres around career for Taurus, so be open to shifts and changes which come in the weeks that follow. If you've been itching for a change in this area of life, this eclipse will only augment these feelings. Saturn meets up at the exact degree Neptune is occupying on the 20th, which is helpful for getting clear about the path you need to take to achieve your dreams.

Pisces's season begins the 18th! Pisces season is your annual spotlight on groups of friends and organizations you immerse yourself in. Venus finds harmony with Jupiter on the 22nd, which is lovely energy for surrounding yourself with people you care about or for doing something romantic with a special someone. However, Mercury turns retrograde for the first time this year on the 26th. This Mercury retrograde implores you to examine the reciprocity of your friendships and to be intentional about giving your time to those who equally value and uplift you. Mercury's retrograde starts off a little rockily as Mars finds tension with Uranus on the 27th, making you and those around you more reactive. Remember, Mercury's retrogrades are times when you're prompted to rethink and re-evaluate *how* you communicate.

March

Best Days Overall: 10–14
Most Stressful Days Overall: 3–8
Best Days for Love: 28–30
Best Days for Money: 21–25
Best Days for Career: 24–28
Power Word: Breathe

The second eclipse of 2026 kicks off the cosmic weather of March on the 3rd. This eclipse centres around the circles of friends and communities you immerse yourself in. This eclipse occurs as Mercury's retrograde is encouraging you to check in with yourself about whether these relationships consistently contain mutual support and appreciation. Your planetary ruler, Venus, enters fiery Aries on the 6th. With Venus quickly conjoining with Neptune and Saturn on the 7th and 8th respectively, it's advised you don't spread yourself too thin. Venus meeting up with Saturn typically has a sobering vibe to it, even in pioneering Aries.

The New Moon in Pisces is a beautiful opportunity to spend time with loved ones and express your gratitude. This lunation also promotes seeking out new communities to immerse yourself in, especially if there is a spiritual or service orientation to them. Aries's season begins on the 20th, meaning it's the start of a new year astrologically! Mercury also turns direct and ends its retrograde period on this day. Aries's season starts off with the Sun meeting up with Neptune and Saturn. As mentioned in earlier months, there's a recurring theme for you in 2026, Taurus, focused on prioritizing your mental health. The cosmic weather of the first week of Aries season is in keeping with this theme. The Sun meeting up with Neptune and Saturn may make you feel like there's so much to do, when really the most important thing for you right now is just to 'be'. Breathe, sweet Taurus.

Saturn finds harmony with Pluto on the 28th which is very supportive of productivity, especially in the realm of career. Your planetary ruler Venus enters your sign on the 30th. This is a joyous transit for you which promotes intentionally carving out time for pleasure or splendour over the next few weeks (Venus leaves your sign on April 24). Venus in Taurus is associated with sensuality and the five senses. Book yourself a massage, light some fragrant candles, or find some other way to honour your planetary ruler entering your sign.

April

Best Days Overall: 26–30
Most Stressful Days Overall: 1–5
Best Days for Love: 13–17
Best Days for Money: 24–27
Best Days for Career: 6–9
Power Word: Embody

It's almost your season, Taurus! The Full Moon in Libra kicks off the astrology of this month. This lunation centres around physical health and wellness for you. Make sure you're on top of your routines this month. Mars and Mercury both enter Aries, on the

9th and 13th respectively. This leads to a major build-up of Aries energy – and when the New Moon in Aries occurs on the 17th there will be five planets in that one sign on this day. Aries is very pioneering energy, so everyone will be feeling a little extra bold and brash. For Taurus, as mentioned earlier, this energy also pertains to the importance of regulating mental health. Exercise is one great way to lean into this fiery energy and support your holistic wellness.

On the 19th, it's finally your season! Identify three words you seek to embody this year and create a mantra for yourself, or journal about why you seek to embody them. Just because Taurus season has begun, doesn't mean you need to rush – Mars conjoins with Saturn on this day, telling you to slow down. This transit can cause feelings of restlessness, so do your best to embrace the slow pace. Your planetary ruler Venus meets up with Uranus just before shifting into Gemini on the 24th. This is creative energy that should be tapped into. You may not be known for it but be open to spontaneity on or around this day as well. The Sun finds tension with Pluto on the 25th, encouraging you to shed aspects of your identity which no longer serve you. This transit may also remind you what parts of your career you'd like to see changed or transformed this year.

After roughly eight years of being in your sign, Uranus finally moves out of Taurus and into Gemini. Uranus in Gemini will change the landscape of how society communicates and learns. For Taurus, the next six or seven years are some of the most significant, financially speaking. Uranus is associated with breakthroughs and breakdowns. If you don't feel financially savvy, it is imperative you educate yourself. And even if you are significantly financially literate, plan to devote more time to tracking how you spend your cash and where your money goes.

May

Best Days Overall: 16–20
Most Stressful Days Overall: 4–5; 26–29
Best Days for Love: 1–3; 22–23
Best Days for Money: 18–22
Best Days for Career: 9–13
Power Word: Slack

Taurus's season continues this month, and there is a Full Moon on the 1st in your polar sign, Scorpio. This Full Moon directs your emotional focus to partnership. If you're partnered, this lunation provides ideal energy for deepening the intimacy in this relationship. Scorpio is known for its investigative prowess, so consider asking your partner a few questions about him or herself you actually don't know the answers to. If you're single, this lunation supports putting yourself out there or asking yourself thought-provoking questions related to your attitude around seeking partnership. The period from the 4th to the 6th is a tense time as Mercury (in your sign) finds tension with Pluto and Mars finds tension with Jupiter. Do your best to cut yourself some slack during this time if you find you're being too hard on yourself.

Mercury in your sign finds harmony with Jupiter on the 13th, which is a great way to round out the last week of Taurus season. This transit supports communication and expressing yourself. The New Moon in your sign occurs on the 16th and ushers in a new emotional cycle around how you treat yourself. Given that you are just starting a new trip around the Sun, this is the ideal time to set a new standard of how you support yourself. The next day, Mercury moves into Gemini and conjoins with Uranus. Monitor your spending around this date and be mindful of unanticipated expenses.

On May 20, it's officially Gemini's season, which marks Taurus's annual spotlight on finances. This is augmented a bit more this year by Uranus being co-present in this sign. Be mindful of rose-tinted glasses around your finances, or of meeting new people around this date as Venus squares off with Neptune on the 20th. This energy is actually baked into all of Gemini season. The month concludes with an angst-inducing couple of transits as Mars squares off with Pluto and Venus squares off with Saturn. Remember the advice about the New Moon in your sign given above, and support yourself, Taurus. While Mars squaring Pluto does typically evoke strong reactions from others, it is also very supportive of feats of perseverance. Pace yourself and push through, sweet Bull.

June

Best Days Overall: 10-13
Most Stressful Days Overall: 18-21
Best Days for Love: 24-28
Best Days for Money: 3-7
Best Days for Career: 13-17
Power Word: Budget

June kicks off on the heels of a bright Full Moon in Sagittarius. This lunation illuminates fears and anxieties you need to confront, so plan for it being a little extra emotional than normal. Sagittarius is a visionary sign, so the goal is to get you to be able to move beyond what keeps you constrained so that you can dream even bigger. Mercury enters Cancer on the 1st which supports speaking your truth. Your planetary ruler, Venus, meets up with Jupiter on the 10th which facilitates lovely buoyant energy. Surround yourself with your loved ones and prioritize play at this time. Venus enters Leo on the 13th, which supports childlike wonder and intentionally cultivating more warmth in your home.

The New Moon in Gemini occurs on the 14th. This New Moon ushers in a new emotional cycle around finances and budgeting. Developing new and more advanced systems for tracking your finances is strongly advised, with Uranus also being a financial influence now for Taurus. Your planetary ruler Venus gets very busy from the 16th to the 18th, finding harmony with Uranus on the 16th and Neptune on the 17th, while finding tension with Pluto on the 18th. Expect the energy to feel busy during this week and don't spread yourself too thin. On the 19th, Chiron, the minor planet related to healing deep-seated wounds, briefly enters your sign for the first time since 1983. Chiron will only spend three months in your sign this year, before formally re-entering it for four years in 2027. A major goal for this summer is a focus on holistic healing.

On June 21, Cancer's season officially begins. Cancer's season is your annual spotlight on all things communication. Venus forms a supportive aspect with Saturn, encouraging you to integrate pleasure into your calendar over the next few weeks. Examples of this could be creating a recurring reminder to pause your typical hustle and bustle to have some uninterrupted rest, or it could be to actively seek out more opportunities to laugh. Mercury turns retrograde in Cancer on the 29th. This retrograde forces you to confront the ways your patterns of communication limit you or keep you stifled.

July

Best Days Overall: 23-26
Most Stressful Days Overall: 3-4; 28-30
Best Days for Love: 7-10
Best Days for Money: 16-19
Best Days for Career: 18-22
Power Word: Changes

You're halfway through 2026, Taurus! Jupiter, the planet of growth and conviction, shifts into Leo for the second half of the year. Jupiter spends about 12 months in any one sign, so the last time it was in Leo was mid-2014 to mid-2015. This shift functions as the first major check-in in the 12-year cycle around accumulating wisdom and making a mark you entered three years ago! Actively seek opportunities and positions over the next 12 months which will help you become wiser and bolder. July's first week astrologically has a high-paced energy to it as Mars meets up with Uranus and finds harmony with Neptune and Pluto between the 4th and the 5th. As I'm telling every sign this year, be extra careful if you plan to handle any form of fireworks, explosives or flammable agents on or around the 4th, as Mars and Uranus together are literally (and figuratively) associated with explosions and accidents.

Your planetary ruler, Venus, enters Virgo on the 9th, encouraging you to intentionally seek out opportunities to be of service and give back. The next week, Venus finds tension with Uranus, on the 14th, making you feel a little more frenetic than usual. If you have established practices you use to ground yourself, be diligent with those during this week. If you haven't established ways to ground yourself, this is the opportune time to identify and begin to implement them.

July contains the most noteworthy astrology of the year as the slow-moving outer planets, Uranus, Neptune and Pluto, all exactly aspect each other between the 15th and the 18th. This is arguably more notable on how it influences the world at the societal level, but your journey of chasing personal goals undergoes a transformation this month, and into August. Moreover, Jupiter follows suit between the 20th and the 21st and aspects all three outer planets. July is the most important month of 2026 to study collective shifts. Leo's season is officially here on the 22nd, and the Sun in Leo follows the trend and forms powerful aspects with Uranus, Neptune and Pluto. The energy of the first week of Leo season is loud. This is especially the case as these planetary alignments are augmented by the Full Moon in Aquarius on the 29th. This is your annual Full Moon centred around your career and legacy. Be open to what shifts and growth await you in this area of life this summer.

August

Best Days Overall: 6-10
Most Stressful Days Overall: 13-17
Best Days for Love: 1-4
Best Days for Money: 29-31
Best Days for Career: 3-7
Power Word: Frenetic

Happy August, Taurus! After a July chock-full of cosmic weather, the first week of August allows for the astrological tide to ebb and flow uninterrupted. The first big update astrologically occurs on the 6th when your planetary ruler, Venus, enters Libra. On the plus side, Venus loves being in Libra as much as it loves being in your sign. However, Venus will now begin to slow down and prepare for its retrograde in a few months. On the 7th, the Sun finds harmony with Saturn, setting the first week of the month up to be a productive one. Whip out your to-do list and get to work. Venus finds harmony with Pluto on the 10th, which is a positive relational transit for getting to know others or asking yourself important questions.

The energy changes the week of the 12th as the third eclipse of the year is exact on that date. The solar eclipse in Leo spotlights home and domestic matters for you. Does your house feel like a home? You're being directed to ensure your home feels as much like a sanctuary as possible. Mercury also forms aspects with the three slow-moving outer planets on this day and the 13th, making the energy feel busier. The pace for the rest of this month picks up, so don't allow yourself to get too worked up or caught up in the hustle and bustle of it all.

August 22 starts off Virgo's season and indicates the transition into autumn. After a busy summer, schedule some time out to nest, rest or reflect during Virgo season. This Virgo season features the final eclipse of the year, in Pisces. This eclipse centres around community for you, further reinforcing the importance of balancing social and solo time. This eclipse is more frenetic than typical as it finds tension with Uranus. August's astrology ends on the

final day of the month with Jupiter and Saturn harmoniously aligning. This is a wonderful transit for taking big steps in achieving
long-term goals you've been pursuing since 2020. Think back to
what your focus was that year and take a moment to celebrate how
far you've come since then.

September

Best Days Overall: 22–26
Most Stressful Days Overall: 16–20
Best Days for Love: 4–8
Best Days for Money: 12–15
Best Days for Career: 1–3
Power Word: Wellness

August's eclipse energy lasts until the New Moon in Virgo on
September 10. This lunation ushers in a new emotional cycle
around creative self-expression and romance for you. Sing, dance,
paint or lean into whatever form of creativity fuels your soul. The
10th also features your planetary ruler Venus shifting into Scorpio
– the sign it will turn retrograde in next month. Venus in Scorpio is
an incredibly relationship-oriented transit for you and the cosmic
weather is now shifting to make partnership a more prominent
theme throughout the autumn. The 10th also features Mercury
shifting in Libra. This is the first astrological transit of the year
which centres on physical health and wellness – another prominent theme for Taurus this autumn. Mercury aspects Uranus,
Neptune and Pluto between the 12th and 13th. With Neptune
finding tension with Mercury, be mindful of the added likelihood of
seeing things through rose-tinted glasses when meeting new
people around this date.

September 15 to the 17th features multiple astrological transits of note for Taurus. Firstly, on the 15th, Neptune finds
harmony with Pluto, again serving as a check-in to all the moves
you made this summer. On the 16th, Venus finds tension with
Pluto, meaning the week of the 16th is one you'll likely feel a little
more on edge. Being hypervigilant or battling with self-esteem

are two common signs of this transit, so be gentle with yourself. Chiron, the wounded healer, exits Taurus for one last trip through Aries. This only adds to the mounting overarching astrology that centres around prioritizing your mental health and wellness this year.

On the 22nd, the Sun moves out of Virgo and into Libra. Libra season is your annual spotlight on all things concerned with physical wellness and kicks off with a bright Full Moon in Aries on the 26th. This lunation brings an emotional focus to the link between physical and emotional health. It is advised to reread the health section of your annual Horoscope for more information. On the 27th, Mars enters Leo, encouraging you to tackle lingering repairs or to fix things in the home. This transit could potentially provoke in-fighting within the home as well, so do your best to actively listen and respond collaboratively if riled.

October

Best Days Overall: 7–10
Most Stressful Days Overall: 19–21; 25–27
Best Days for Love: 23–26
Best Days for Money: 2–5
Best Days for Career: 8–12
Power Word: Partnership

October starts off with your planetary ruler, Venus, turning retro-grade on the 3rd. Venus's retrogrades universally feature some sort of audit around existing or past relationships, but that's especially the case for you, Taurus. This Venus retrograde period will have you reflecting on the existing values that inform how you partner and conduct yourself in one-to-one relationships. Venus will be retrograde this entire month and half of November, so anticipate this being a central theme of October for you. The 3rd also features Mars opposing Pluto, a transit which will have everyone being more kinetic and explosive. This transit also centres around career for Taurus, so don't spread yourself too thin at work. This is only augmented by the Sun finding tension with Saturn on the 4th – a transit which is often met with the feeling that overworking is the only way to succeed.

The New Moon in Libra on the 10th focuses you on the importance of physical health and wellness. You're invited to endeavour to slightly alter your weekly schedule for a six-month period to include one additional way to improve your diet or physical fitness. This should be a small, manageable step that will pay dividends if adhered to long-term. This should not be overly ambitious though, because the goal for this month is to not overextend yourself.

Scorpio's season begins on the 23rd, which is your annual spotlight on relationships. Speaking of which, Mercury turns retrograde in Taurus's partnership sector the next day. Now Venus and Mercury are both in retrograde motion. It's recommended not to launch any new initiatives until after these retrograde periods conclude in November. Venus re-enters Libra from Scorpio, pulling more focus towards staying organized and on top of your daily/weekly routines. The month concludes with the Full Moon bright in your sign on the 26th. This lunation finds tension with Pluto, pushing you to shed aspects of your identity which no longer serve you. If you haven't carved out time for self-care during the last week of October, definitely do so around this date.

November

Best Days Overall: 27-30
Most Stressful Days Overall: 1-5
Best Days for Love: 25-29
Best Days for Money: 13-16
Best Days for Career: 18-22
Power Word: Surprises

The focus on partnership grows at the start of November with the New Moon in Scorpio occurring on the 9th. If you're single, this is an ideal lunation for putting yourself out there over the next few days. Venus's retrograde will end on the 13th, freeing you up even more to explore and meet prospective partners. If you're not single, this lunation is an ideal time to spend quality time with your significant other. This is an inquisitive New Moon, so make sure this quality time affords ample conversation. On the 13th, both Mercury and Venus end their retrograde periods and turn direct again. Remember, they will still be slow for the rest of the month, so anticipate a little bit of wonkiness with communication and technology.

Mars conjoins with Jupiter on the 16th which encourages you to go-go-go. This transit has a home and domestic life focus to it for Taurus, so channel this productive energy into your home or familial relationships. With the two planets being in close proximity to the south node, this is also an excellent time to do a deep clean of your living space. However, don't bite off more than you can chew, given that the Sun finds tension with Mars a few days later.

Sagittarius's season begins on the 22nd and functions as your annual spotlight on joint finances. Do you know exactly how your money is influenced or intertwined with others? Finances are a big focus for the end of this month with the Full Moon in Gemini occurring two days later. It is recommended to adopt a frugal mindset towards the end of this month as this lunation will be tightly conjoined with Uranus, which tends to cause unexpected surprises. Surprises abound this final week of the month as the Sun also faces off with Uranus on the 26th. The month ends with Uranus finding harmony with Pluto, supporting your efforts around freeing yourself from fear and anxiety. If you've been considering working with a specialist to navigate doing so, this transit would support seeking this type of support.

December

Best Days Overall: 12–16
Most Stressful Days Overall: 5–9
Best Days for Love: 3–7
Best Days for Money: 20–24
Best Days for Career: 15–19
Power Word: Courage

December begins with Venus moving back into Scorpio after ending its retrograde period last month. Venus in Scorpio is a heavily relational transit for Taurus and Venus will be in the sign all month, drawing your focus towards partnership regardless of your relationship status. Being grounded and controlled is the name of the game at the start of this month, with Mars squaring off with Uranus on the 5th and Mercury entering Sagittarius on the 6th. When Mars and Uranus find tension with one another, people tend to knee-jerk reactions instead of thoughtfully responding to situations which arise. Leaning into breathwork, mindfulness or journalling is recommended to support staying grounded and controlled.

The final New Moon of the year is in Sagittarius on the 8th. This lunation centres around the theme introduced last month of confronting and dismantling long-standing fears or anxieties which have held you back or prevented you from pursuing some sort of dream. End 2026 courageously, sweet Bull! Your planetary ruler, Venus, squares off with Pluto on the 9th, bringing fears and insecurities in partnership to the surface. Surround yourself with those you can be 100 per cent authentically yourself with. A couple of days later, Mercury finds harmony with Saturn, supporting efforts with writing and communication. Moreover, Venus finds harmony with Mars on the 12th, which lightens the heavier vibes of earlier in the week. This is ideal energy to go on a spontaneous adventure with a special someone.

Capricorn's season begins on the 21st and is your annual spotlight on spirituality and higher education. The Full Moon illuminates these areas of life for you and encourages you to explore how you can integrate them more into 2027. If you've been considering any sort of voyage or travel, this lunation supports building in some sort of spiritual or educational component to it. This travel could also be more local if it fits the brief of having a spiritual or educational component to it. The vibes for the final week of the year are slow, with Mercury finding tension with Saturn on the 31st. Nesting and resting is recommended to get ready for a productive 2027. Happy New Year, Taurus!

Gemini

♊

THE TWINS

Birthdays from
May 21
to June 20

Personality Profile

GEMINI AT A GLANCE

Element – Air

Ruling Planet – Mercury
   Career Planet – Jupiter
   Love Planet – Jupiter
   Money Planet – Moon
   Planet of Health and Work – Mars
   Planet of Home and Family Life – Mercury

Totem – the Innovator

Colours – yellow, yellow-orange

Colour that promotes love, romance and social harmony – sky blue

Colours that promote earning power – grey, silver

Gems – agate

Metal – quicksilver

Scents – lavender, lilac, lily of the valley, storax

Quality – mutable (= flexibility)

Quality most needed for balance – thought that is deep rather than superficial

Strongest virtues – great communication skills, quickness and agility of thought, ability to learn quickly

Deepest need – communication

Characteristics to avoid – gossiping, hurting others with harsh speech, superficiality, using words to mislead or misinform

Signs of greatest overall compatibility – Libra, Aquarius

Signs of greatest overall incompatibility – Virgo, Sagittarius, Pisces

Sign most helpful to career – Pisces

Sign most helpful for emotional support – Virgo

Sign most helpful financially – Cancer

Sign best for marriage and/or partnerships – Sagittarius

Sign most helpful for creative projects – Libra

Best Sign to have fun with – Libra

Signs most helpful in spiritual matters – Taurus, Aquarius

Best day of the week – Wednesday

Understanding a Gemini

Gemini is to society what the nervous system is to the body. It does not introduce any new information but is a vital transmitter of impulses from the senses to the brain and vice versa. The nervous system does not judge or weigh these impulses – it only conveys information. And it does so perfectly.

This analogy should give you an indication of a Gemini's role in society. Geminis are the communicators and conveyors of information. To Geminis the truth or falsehood of information is irrelevant, they only transmit what they see, hear or read about. Thus they are capable of spreading the most outrageous rumours as well as conveying truth and light. Geminis sometimes tend to be unscrupulous in their communications and can do both great good or great evil with their power. This is why the sign of Gemini is symbolized by twins: Geminis have a dual nature.

Their ability to convey a message – to communicate with such ease – makes Geminis ideal teachers, writers and media and marketing people. This is helped by the fact that Mercury, the ruling planet of Gemini, also rules these activities.

Geminis have the gift of the gab. And what a gift this is! They can make conversation about anything, anywhere, at any time. There is almost nothing that is more fun to Geminis than a good conversation – especially if they can learn something new as well. They love to learn and they love to teach. To deprive a Gemini of conversation, or of books and magazines, is cruel and unusual punishment.

Geminis are almost always excellent students and take well to education. Their minds are generally stocked with all kinds of information, trivia, anecdotes, stories, news items, rarities, facts and statistics. Thus they can support any intellectual position that they care to take. They are awesome debaters and, if involved in politics, make good orators. Geminis are so verbally smooth that even if they do not know what they are talking about, they can make you think that they do. They will always dazzle you with their brilliance.

Finance

Geminis tend to be more concerned with the wealth of learning and ideas than with actual material wealth. As mentioned, they excel in professions that involve writing, teaching, sales and journalism – and not all of these professions pay very well. But to sacrifice intellectual needs merely for money is unthinkable to a Gemini. Geminis strive to combine the two. Cancer is on Gemini's solar 2nd house of money cusp, which indicates that Geminis can earn extra income (in a harmonious and natural way) from investments in residential property, restaurants and hotels. Given their verbal skills, Geminis love to bargain and negotiate in any situation, and especially when it has to do with money.

The Moon rules Gemini's 2nd solar house. The Moon is not only the fastest-moving planet in the zodiac but actually moves through every sign and house every 28 days. No other heavenly body matches the Moon for swiftness or the ability to change quickly. An analysis of the Moon – and lunar phenomena in general – describes Gemini's financial attitudes very well. Geminis are financially versatile and flexible; they can earn money in many different ways. Their financial attitudes and needs seem to change daily. Their feelings about money change also: sometimes they are very enthusiastic about it, at other times they could not care less.

For a Gemini, financial goals and money are often seen only as means of supporting a family; these things have little meaning otherwise.

The Moon, as Gemini's money planet, has another important message for Gemini financially: in order for Geminis to realize their financial potential they need to develop more of an understanding of the emotional side of life. They need to combine their awesome powers of logic with an understanding of human psychology. Feelings have their own logic; Geminis need to learn this and apply it to financial matters.

Career and Public Image

Geminis know that they have been given the gift of communication for a reason, that it is a power that can achieve great good or cause unthinkable distress. They long to put this power at the service of the highest and most transcendental truths. This is their primary goal, to communicate the eternal verities and prove them logically. They look up to people who can transcend the intellect – to poets, artists, musicians and mystics. They may be awed by stories of religious saints and martyrs. A Gemini's highest achievement is to teach the truth, whether it is scientific, inspirational or historical. Those who can transcend the intellect are Gemini's natural superiors – and a Gemini realizes this.

The sign of Pisces is in Gemini's solar 10th house of career. Neptune, the planet of spirituality and altruism, is Gemini's career planet. If Geminis are to realize their highest career potential they need to develop their transcendental – their spiritual and altruistic – side. They need to understand the larger cosmic picture, the vast flow of human evolution – where it came from and where it is heading. Only then can a Gemini's intellectual powers take their true position and he or she can become the 'messenger of the gods'. Geminis need to cultivate a facility for 'inspiration', which is something that does not originate in the intellect but which comes through the intellect. This will further enrich and empower a Gemini's mind.

Love and Relationships

Geminis bring their natural garrulousness and brilliance into their love life and social life as well. A good talk or a verbal joust is an interesting prelude to romance. Their only problem in love is that their intellect is too cool and passionless to incite ardour in others. Emotions sometimes disturb them, and their partners tend to complain about this. If you are in love with a Gemini you must understand why this is so. Geminis avoid deep passions because these would interfere with their ability to think and communicate. If they are cool towards you, understand that this is their nature.

Nevertheless, Geminis must understand that it is one thing to talk about love and another actually to love – to feel it and radiate it. Talking about love glibly will get them nowhere. They need to feel it and act on it. Love is not of the intellect but of the heart. If you want to know how a Gemini feels about love you should not listen to what he or she says, but rather observe what he or she does. Geminis can be quite generous to those they love.

Geminis like their partners to be refined, well educated and well travelled. If their partners are more wealthy than they are, all the better. If you are in love with a Gemini you had better be a good listener as well.

The ideal relationship for the Gemini is a relationship of the mind. They enjoy the physical and emotional aspects, of course, but if the intellectual communion is not there they will suffer.

Home and Domestic Life

At home the Gemini can be uncharacteristically neat and meticulous. They tend to want their children and partner to live up to their idealistic standards. When these standards are not met they moan and criticize. However, Geminis are good family people and like to serve their families in practical and useful ways.

The Gemini home is comfortable and pleasant. They like to invite people over and they make great hosts. Geminis are also good at repairs and improvements around the house – all fuelled by their need to stay active and occupied with something they like to do. Geminis have many hobbies and interests that keep them busy when they are home alone.

Geminis understand and get along well with their children, mainly because they are very youthful people themselves. As great communicators, Geminis know how to explain things to children; in this way they gain their children's love and respect. Geminis also encourage children to be creative and talkative, just like they are.

Horoscope for 2026

What a big year this is for you, Gemini! Uranus, the planet of inno-vation, instability and individuality, enters and stays in your sign until 2032/2033. Uranus entering your sign is a once-in-a-life-time astrological event for you, as the planet takes 84 years to traverse the zodiac! Uranus in your sign ushers in a year of major reinvention and breakthroughs for you. While common for a frenetic energy to underlie this period, Uranus brings break-throughs. Now, it's important to note that Uranus did briefly dip into your sign last year. However, it quickly retreated back into Taurus to prepare for its more noteworthy debut this year. Uranus makes this move on April 25 and will stay solely in your sign for the next six years.

This is why your totem for 2026 is 'the Innovator'. Astrologically, you're being called on to liberate yourself from the chains of what-ever (or whoever) is stifling your growth. In its place, you must innovate a new way of being. Having grounding practices in place leading up to Uranus's shift into Gemini will be helpful, as the planet is not known to 'walk on eggshells' and will disrupt the status quo without qualms about the upheaval. If you're born early in Gemini's season (a May Gemini), this is especially potent as Uranus will be in close proximity to your natal Gemini Sun. Regardless, over the next six years, all Geminis will go through some sort of profound reinvention. My best piece of advice for navi-gating this transit is to 'be your own anchor' and not depend on others to centre or be assured of yourself.

Aside from this once-in-a-lifetime astrological transit, another big theme for 2026 centres around a topic Gemini is strongly asso-ciated with: communication. Gemini is often referred to as the narrator, the storyteller or the messenger. Being the air sign ruled by Mercury, the planet of communication, Gemini almost always has something to say. In 2026, Jupiter, the planet of conviction and growth, enters your communication sector at the end of June. Jupiter augments whatever area of the horoscope it's transiting, so anticipate an increase in how often you open your mouth.

Remember, communication is a two-way street, so growing as an active listener is a smart way to leverage the energy of Jupiter in your communication sector. This is especially true for relationships as Jupiter is your relationship planet.

For a quarterly view of your year ahead, the first quarter of 2026 centres around finances and social life. The second quarter is when Uranus enters your sign, so self-improvement is paramount. The third quarter features Jupiter newly in your communication sector, bringing communication to the forefront. The final quarter of the year centres around physical wellness, creativity and romance.

Health (1st/6th/12th houses)

(Please note that this is an astrological perspective on health and not a medical one. Any health-related symptoms should be evaluated by a qualified healthcare professional.)

In line with what is shared above in the introductory section of this yearly Horoscope, Uranus shifting from Taurus into Gemini is also noteworthy for you from a health lens, as Uranus will no longer be traversing the mental health sector of Gemini's chart. Many modern astrologers attribute anxiety to Uranus. The past six to seven years have been a noteworthy mental health journey for you, especially in the realm of navigating anxiety. Uranus shifting out of your mental health sector, of course, does not rid you of the very human lifelong relationship we all have with anxiety, but it does begin a new chapter in how you navigate this relationship. Your mental health planet, Venus, remains neutral for most of the year, until it turns retrograde in October. This retrograde, which occurs from October 3 to November 13, functions as an audit on the routines you have in place to manage and support your mental health. Venus will actually spend the first half of this retrograde period in your physical health sector, which only further highlights the link between physical and mental health. Utilizing exercise and diet as the means to support mental health is strongly recommended.

Venus will be retrograde in your physical health sector from October 3 to the 25th. October 3 is noteworthy because it's the only time in 2026 when Mars, your physical health planet, will oppose Pluto, the planet of transformation. It's strongly advised to not overwork or overburden yourself towards the end of September leading into this transit, through to around October 25 if possible. If, for whatever reason, you must assume additional responsibilities or spread yourself thin, it is vital to keep up physical wellness habits like diet and exercise. Mars will harmoniously aspect Jupiter just as Venus's retrograde period ends in mid-November, supporting the resumption of your personal hustle and bustle.

Here are the specific areas of the body to focus on this year:

- Arms and hands: this is a perennial area of focus for Gemini as these parts of the body are ruled by the sign in medical astrology. Jupiter will also be entering the sector of your chart related to this part of the body, placing greater emphasis on it. Proper stretching and physical maintenance are strongly recommended.
- Lungs: these is the other part of the body which Gemini rules, and this area is strongly emphasized this year due to the overarching focus on communication in 2026. Breathwork would be especially useful to learn and adopt as a means of centring and grounding yourself this year. Supporting this part of the body through diet, especially in the autumn during Venus's retrograde period, is recommended.
- Ankles: Saturn, planet of consequences and restriction, enters the sector of your chart which rules the ankles early in the year. Doing your due diligence to stretch and support this area of the body on a routine basis would pay dividends on your overall physical growth and development this year. This planetary shift also places an emphasis on strengthening this part of the body. Consider consulting an expert if you're unfamiliar with how to properly support your ankles this year.

Love and Social Life (5th, 7th, 11th houses)

Social life is an area of life with substantial focus this year, Gemini, as Saturn and Neptune both enter your social life sector early in 2026. Saturn rules discipline, responsibility and hard work and will enter your social life sector when it shifts into Aries on February 13. The astrology of 2026 would support becoming a leader or assuming additional responsibility/power within an organization you're part of. Saturn in this area of your chart also requires you to take a hard look at the reciprocity of your friendships. Hold those who believe in you closer this year. Saturn will stay in this sector for Gemini until 2028, which means there's also the option to not rush into assuming this sort of power and instead to make moves to support yourself in taking on additional responsibility next year.

Neptune rules dreams, compassion and illusion. Neptune is the second-slowest planet to orbit the zodiac, so it will stay in your social life sector until 2039. Neptune in this area of Gemini's chart signifies the growing importance of surrounding yourself with those who align with or uplift your personal expression of spirituality. Making more of a concerted effort to immerse yourself in groups that can support you in getting deeper in touch with your spiritual value system is strongly recommended. However, it is important to note that Neptune is the planet that rules deception or illusion, and a completely different signification for this astrological event is to be careful not to be deceived by some sort of network or circle.

Your partnership planet is Jupiter, which, as mentioned earlier in this Horoscope, shifts from Cancer to Leo on June 30. If you're single, look to July and August as months ripe with partnership opportunities. Jupiter will form aspects with all three outer planets (Uranus, Neptune and Pluto) between July 20 and the 21st. Jupiter will then harmoniously realign with Neptune at the end of August. If you're partnered, July and August are the months most likely for growth or a change in dynamics. Jupiter in Leo is a heart-centred childlike energy, so honour it through play with your significant other. The same advice applies for those single Geminis putting themselves out there on dates during this time. Love, partnership and romance undergo a bit of an audit or re-evaluation during Venus's retrograde period, October 3 to November 13. Do not fear retrograde periods, but rather lean into the prompting to slow down and check in with yourself.

Career and Finances (10th/2nd/8th houses)

Going into 2026, career pursuits have been under scrutiny for some time thanks to Saturn occupying this domain for the last three years and Neptune occupying this chart sector since 2011. All that changes in 2026 when both planets shift out of your career sector and into the social life sector. It is important to note, however, that tension in this area will be felt mildly when Mercury enters its retrograde period in this chart sector from the end of February to mid-March.

In addition, it'll be important for you to track how your career planet, Jupiter, interacts with the other planets, especially Saturn and the generational planets (Uranus, Neptune and Pluto). Noteworthy times of abundance would be when Jupiter harmoniously aligns with Saturn during the last week of August, and when it harmoniously aligns with the minor planet Chiron, the wounded healer, during the first week of December. The greatest amount of energy around Jupiter occurs in the height of summer when the planet aspects all three generational planets over the course of two days, July 20–21. With Saturn and Neptune no longer occupying this sector for Gemini from mid-February onwards, you'll have more licence to embody your totem, the Innovator. This is an auspicious year to start new projects or career pursuits.

Financially speaking, 2026 is a year of 'what you put in, you'll get out'. This summer features Jupiter exiting the financial sector of your chart (to enter the communication sector) in July and Mercury undergoing its second retrograde period in this sector. Mercury's retrogrades are times to review and revise, so it is strongly recommended to revisit and, if necessary, rethink your budgeting and/or investment practices. This retrograde period occurs from June 29 to July 23. However, it is important to note that Mercury retrograde periods aren't like a light switch that just flips on and off: the effects of the retrograde period can be felt a couple weeks before and after the range given.

Home and Domestic Life (4th house)

This is the area of life with the least astrological activity in 2026 for you, Gemini. One noteworthy astrological transit would be the lunar eclipse in Virgo which occurs on March 3. Remember, eclipses are evolutionary transits which stimulate growth through shake-ups and scrutiny. This eclipse has the potential to make you aware of an overdue repair needed on your home or a much-needed shift in family dynamics. Your home and domestic life planet is Mercury, which turns retrograde three times this year. All three Mercury retrograde periods (February 25 to March 20, June 29 to July 23 and October 24 to November 13) are times when you could be called to revisit conversations you ought to have with family members (or those who reside in the home) in order to establish greater harmony in this area of life.

Self-improvement (3rd/5th/9th houses)

As mentioned earlier on, the reason why 2026 is so profound for you, Gemini, is because Uranus will be moving into and staying in your sign for the next six to seven years. The astrology of 2026 strongly aligns with self-improvement through reinventing your-self or your goals. This is supported by noteworthy astrological activity occurring in your higher education and spirituality sector, including an eclipse on February 13. Pluto, the planet of transfor-mation, stays in this sector all year long. If you've been feeling the urge to go back to college or to get a professional certification or qualification, do it.

The other major area related to self-improvement is communi-cation. With Jupiter entering your communication sector mid-year, you'll be goaded into speaking and sharing more. As a result, being intentional about word choice (i.e. having a filter) will be important this year. Moreover, using different way to broadcast what you have to say (whether it's through vlogging, blogging, podcasting, etc.) is another way to capitalize on this exciting astrology and improve yourself.

Month-by-month Forecasts

January

Best Days Overall: 2–6
Most Stressful Days Overall: 19–23
Best Days for Love: 15–19
Best Days for Money: 1–4
Best Days for Career: 22–26
Power Word: Transform

Happy New Year, Gemini! The cosmic weather for 2026 kicks off with your planetary ruler, Mercury, entering Capricorn. This transit imbues you with a goal-oriented, yet realistic, point of view for the next few weeks. Good energy to start the year with! The Full Moon in Cancer shines bright and illuminates personal finances for you. Starting the year off with a thorough budget and insight into how you spend your money is strongly recommended. Eclipse season starts next month and will also have financial implications, so it's best to get a head start on setting yourself up for success in this arena. The Sun conjoins with Venus on the 6th, which is a lovely practical energy to start your year off productively.

The New Moon in Capricorn occurs on the 18th. This New Moon ushers in a new emotional cycle around how your fears, insecurities or anxieties influence your reticence to chase your goals. The next day, it officially becomes Aquarius season! Aquarius season is your annual spotlight on spirituality and higher education. With Pluto now firmly ensconced in this sign, it's strongly advised to lean into your preferred spiritual routines as a means to ground yourself when navigating your anxiety. Mercury follows the Sun's lead and enters Aquarius, where it occupies the sign with Venus and Pluto as well.

This build-up of Aquarian energy is likely to create a heavier, edgier vibe initially, as the Sun, Mercury and Venus all meet up with transformative Pluto between the 20th and the 23rd. Shedding aspects of your identity which no longer serve you is the universe's prompt at this time. Mars joins the Aquarius party on the 23rd bringing the total number of planets in the air sign up to five. Wow! The month rounds out with a significant shift in energy as Neptune moves into Aries, where it will stay until 2039. Neptune in Aries will affect the world on a societal level through emphasizing the importance of individuality in spirituality. A societal shift towards individual needs over that of the collective is also expected. For you, Gemini, this transit will slowly mould and shape the groups and networks you immerse yourself in towards ones which better reflect your spiritual values system.

February

Best Days Overall: 13–16
Most Stressful Days Overall: 4–6; 26–27
Best Days for Love: 20–23
Best Days for Money: 9–12
Best Days for Career: 1–4
Power Word: Expression

Happy February, Gemini! A bright Full Moon in Leo starts off the astrology of this month, highlighting your patterns of communication. Leo is a sign known for being able to speak its truth: do you feel comfortable doing so? This Full Moon will likely embolden you in all forms of communication, so think before you speak. This is especially the case because a few days later, on the 5th, Mercury will square off with Uranus. As a Mercury-ruled person yourself, this transit is absolutely associated with forgetting any filter and communicating in a knee-jerk fashion instead of thoughtfully. The next day, Mercury moves into creative and compassionate Pisces. This is an opportune time to lean more into creative self-expression (singing, dancing, journalling, painting, etc.).

On the 13th, Saturn formally moves into Aries after oscillating to and from the sign last year. Saturn in Aries is a 2½-year transit which could very well inspire you to seek more responsibility in professional organizations you are a part of. Saturn in Aries influences your friend groups by providing you with a realistic view of how supportive and sustainable they truly are. Relationships predicated on reciprocity will only be bolstered for you during this time, and those that no longer serve you will slowly (or quickly) crumble. Your planetary ruler, Mercury, finds harmony with Jupiter on the 16th, supporting all forms of communication for you.

The first eclipse of 2026 occurs on the 17th with a solar eclipse in Aquarius. This eclipse centres around the role spirituality and higher education play in your life. Shifts and changes in these areas are likely this year. Moreover, this eclipse could also inspire you to take a voyage which will provide you with important insights into what next steps you should take. Bon voyage, Gemini! The next day, Pisces's season begins – your annual spotlight on career and legacy. Mercury turns retrograde for the first time this year on the 26th, having you reconsider what goals you seek to accomplish in 2026. If you haven't actually written out these goals, it is strongly recommended to do so to help structure the rest of your year ahead. Take new action once the retrograde period ends next month.

March

Best Days Overall: 7–12
Most Stressful Days Overall: 1–5
Best Days for Love: 11–14
Best Days for Money: 20–24
Best Days for Career: 3–7
Power Word: Surround

March begins with the second eclipse of the year, this time in Virgo. This eclipse occurs on the 3rd and centres around changes in home or domestic life for Gemini. Keeping an organized home is crucial at this time, given the scrutinizing properties of eclipses. If you haven't begun spring cleaning yet, this would be an opportune time to do so. Family dynamics are also being examined at this time. Venus enters Aries on the 6th and then conjoins with Neptune and Saturn on the 7th and 8th respectively. These transits encourage you to surround yourself with friends who support all the ways you are uniquely yourself. Your planetary ruler Mercury rounds out the first part of the month by finding harmony with Jupiter, again supporting efforts in all forms of communication. However, be mindful that Mercury is still retrograde so it's important you approach critical conversations thoughtfully.

The New Moon in Pisces ushers in a new emotional cycle around career and legacy on the 18th. New Moons are powerful transits for planting seeds, and with Mercury ending its retrograde period a couple of days later, capitalize on this energy by checking lingering items off your to-do list. On the 20th, Mercury turns direct as the Sun enters Aries. Happy New Astrological Year! The Sun conjoins with Neptune and Saturn on the 22nd and 25th respectively, setting this month up as an important one for surrounding yourself with community.

On the 28th Saturn finds harmony with Pluto. This transit further encourages you to pursue additional responsibility in groups or organizations you are a part of. On the last day of the month, Venus enters Taurus. This transit begins to shift the over-arching cosmic focus towards prioritizing mental wellness over the next few months. Especially considering that you have just navigated the first eclipse season of the year, make sure you are carving out intentional time to nest, rest and rejuvenate over the next few weeks. Venus in Taurus supports leaning into the five senses as a means to relax – so get that bubble bath ready, eat some yummy food or get some bodywork done!

April

Best Days Overall: 3-7
Most Stressful Days Overall: 19-23; 25-26
Best Days for Love: 1-2; 28-30
Best Days for Money: 16-20
Best Days for Career: 26-29
Power Word: Balance

April's cosmic weather begins with a bright Full Moon in Libra on the 1st. This lunation centres around creative self-expression and/or romance for you, Gemini. If you've been meaning to put yourself out there or be seen in some creative medium, this lunation encourages you to do so. Remember, Full Moons function as emotional culminations, so you may want to spend a few days exploring how you seek to be seen in this new light. Mars enters Aries on the 9th, which typically provides a kinetic productive energy. That being said, the first 10 days of this transit feature Mars getting slowed down by Neptune and Saturn, so don't be shocked if restless feelings arise mid-month.

The New Moon in Aries occurs on the 17th and only adds to the mounting energy around immersing yourself in supportive communities and seeking responsibilities in organizations you are proud to be a part of. Taurus's season begins on the 19th, bringing your annual spotlight on mental health and wellness. Do you feel like you have a good balance between social and solo time, Gemini? The next four weeks are all about striving to secure this type of balance in your life. Taurus season starts off slowly, with Mars exactly conjoining with Saturn on the 19th as well.

On the 24th, Venus enters your sign, followed by slow-moving Uranus formally doing so on the 26th. Uranus did oscillate in and out of your sign briefly last year. Nonetheless, this is one of the most important energetic shifts for you as Uranus takes 84 years to go around the zodiac, so it hasn't fully stayed in your sign for a monumental amount of time. On the collective level, Uranus in Gemini will revolutionize how technology is interwoven into communication and learning in ways you can't even predict. On the individual level, you're beginning to embark upon a personal liberation. Uranus in Gemini encourages break-ups, breakdowns and breakthroughs as a means to course correct you on your life path. This transit is relevant for all Geminis, but May Geminis will begin to feel this most intensely over the next couple of years.

May

Best Days Overall: 20–24
Most Stressful Days Overall: 2–6
Best Days for Love: 18–21; 30–31
Best Days for Money: 17–22
Best Days for Career: 13–16
Power Word: Persevere

There's not one Full Moon this month, Gemini, but two! The cosmic weather of May begins with the Full Moon in Scorpio on the 1st. This lunation brings an emotional focus to physical health and wellness for you just before the start of your solar season. Your planetary ruler, Mercury, enters Taurus on the 2nd and then finds tension with Pluto which peaks on the 5th. If a Full Moon in the sign of Scorpio wasn't angst-inducing enough, Mercury squaring off with Pluto only builds on this energy. Do your best to quieten your inner critic which could spike during this time. Lean into self-compassion and self-care routines you already have in place. Mars finds tension with Jupiter on the 5th, making those around you on edge as well, so don't add fuel to the fire.

Fortunately, Mercury finds harmony with Jupiter for the third time this year on the 13th, bringing some much-needed relief to the tense air. The New Moon in Taurus on the 16th supports integrating new components into your routine which support emotional or mental health. This could be a journalling practice, reducing your screen time, or some other small way you can contribute to your overarching wellbeing. Mercury enters your sign on the 17th providing you with mental and verbal acuity over the next few weeks. On the 18th, Venus enters Cancer, supporting efforts you're taking to save or grow your finances.

Happy birthday! Gemini season begins on the 20th, with Venus and Neptune squaring off. This could imbue you with rose-tinted glasses when meeting new people over this season. The vibes get a little tenser or more severe towards the end of the month as Mars finds tension with Pluto. Though this transit is edgy, it also supports feats of perseverance so if you've been tackling a large goal, this could provide a much-needed boost. The month concludes with a second Full 'Blue' Moon in Sagittarius, illuminating partnership for you. Sagittarius is an expansive, spontaneous sign, so be open to this energy in the realm of partnership at the start of June.

June

Best Days Overall: 14-18
Most Stressful Days Overall: 26-30
Best Days for Love: 25-28
Best Days for Money: 10-13
Best Days for Career: 1-4
Power Word: Shift

Gemini season continues with your planetary ruler, Mercury, entering Cancer on the 1st. Mercury will begin to slow down over the next few weeks to prepare for its next retrograde period at the end of the month. On the 4th, Mercury in Cancer finds tension with Neptune in Aries; be mindful around your spending at this time and if you need to sign a contract, have a trusted ally read it over as well. On the 10th Venus conjoins with Jupiter, which is a wonderful transit for spending time with loved ones. For Gemini, this transit is also an ideal time to invest or to identify additional streams of income. Venus enters Leo on the 13th, inviting you to express your love and gratitude for those who support you through thick and thin.

The New Moon in Gemini occurs on the 14th. This lunation ushers in a new emotional cycle around how you navigate life and how you talk to yourself. This is a year of substantial energetic shifts, which requires you to be able to support yourself amid these transitions. Over the next six months, actively root out the self-effacing ways you communicate with yourself. This is especially important in this month as Venus finds tension with Pluto on the 18th – a transit notorious for stirring up self-esteem issues or insecurities. Self-care is crucial during the middle of this month.

The Sun moves into Cancer and initiates Cancer's season on the 21st. Cancer season is your annual spotlight on finances. A major theme of this season will actually be reviewing and revising your existing budget, as Mercury will turn retrograde in Cancer in a few days. Mercury's retrograde periods are all about reflecting and revisiting, with this one having a financial focus for you, Gemini. The Full Moon in Capricorn lights up your joint finances sector, bringing to your attention the ways in which your money is influenced by or interwoven with others. The month concludes with Jupiter, the planet of growth and expansion, entering radiant Leo on the 30th. This transit brings abundance to and fully supports speaking, writing and other forms of communication for you over the next 12 months.

July

Best Days Overall: 22–26
Most Stressful Days Overall: 2–6
Best Days for Love: 19–23
Best Days for Money: 20–24
Best Days for Career: 9–13
Power Word: Important

The astrology of July gets going on the 4th with Mars forming several aspects to the slow-moving planets, Uranus, Neptune and Pluto. Mars conjoining with Uranus is literally and figuratively explosive, so be especially careful if handling fireworks or anything flammable around this date. Mars is the planet of assertion and conflict, so under scrutiny from the three slow-moving planets, these themes are likely to be hot topics and an emotional focus for the start of the month. There is a frenetic energy also associated with these transits, so do your best to dispel this energy through productive movement.

July's astrology is arguably the most noteworthy of the year as several planets aspect the three slow-moving outer planets and these planetary bodies also align with each other. Given how slowly Uranus, Neptune and Pluto move, it is very rare for the three to align with each other in such a short time span. That's what makes 2026 such a special year! Uranus harmonizes with Neptune on the 15th and with Pluto on the 18th. More impactful on the micro level (vs the societal level) is Jupiter, newly in Leo, forming aspects to all three planets between the 20th and 21st. Communication for Gemini is extremely prominent at this time. Moreover, these transits highlight the vital importance of you following your heart in the decisions you make for the rest of the year.

Leo's season begins on the 21st and Mercury ends its retrograde period on the 23rd. Leo season starts off a little noisily as the Sun faces off with Pluto on the 27th. This transit can force you to confront aspects of your identity you've outgrown, or patterns of behaviour which no longer serve you. Lean into spirituality if you're feeling on edge as the Full Moon in Aquarius lights up this area of life for Gemini. If you weren't ready to go on a voyage during Aquarius's season a few months ago, this Full Moon inspires you to do so now. The month concludes with the Sun meeting up with Jupiter on the 29th, a day which supports appeasing your inner child.

August

Best Days Overall: 22-25
Most Stressful Days Overall: 10-14
Best Days for Love: 2-5
Best Days for Money: 6-10
Best Days for Career: 27-31
Power Word: Frugal

It's eclipse season again, Gemini! After an eventful July, the summer stays busy in August. Venus starts off the cosmic weather of the month by moving into Libra on the 6th. This transit inspires prioritizing pleasure and play over the next few weeks. If you've been seeking to deepen your connection with a special someone, Venus will find harmony with Pluto a few days later, on the 10th. This transit also supports a makeover or an aesthetic transformation if you've been seeking to do one. That being said, Mars enters Cancer on the 11th – so don't overspend; it is wise to adopt a sense of frugality this month, given the financial implications of this transit for Gemini. Mars isn't associated with being conservative with money.

The first eclipse of the month is a solar eclipse in Leo on the 12th. This eclipse occurs as Mercury finds harmony with Uranus and Neptune, and finds tension with Pluto, all on the same day. All of which is to say, the week of the 12th is a busy, albeit chaotic one energetically. Eclipses in Leo tend to elicit verbose emotional responses in others (and possibly yourself), so be prepared. This eclipse encourages you to lean into your authenticity and to shed limiting beliefs which impact your ability to take pride in your uniqueness.

Virgo's season begins on the 22nd and is your annual spotlight on home and family dynamics. Mercury moves into Virgo on the 25th bringing your focus a bit more towards domestic matters over the next few weeks. The final eclipse of the year is a lunar eclipse in Pisces and is the most powerful of all four of them as it tightly squares off with Uranus. This eclipse may feel a bit like a lightning strike as a result, and it would benefit you to prepare for the possibility of sudden lifestyle shifts in the few weeks leading up to and in the wake of this lunation. There is also a career orientation to this lunation, which should build on the growth in your career since last year (eclipses also occurred in Pisces in 2025).

September

Best Days Overall: 27–30
Most Stressful Days Overall: 11–15
Best Days for Love: 22–26
Best Days for Money: 15–19
Best Days for Career: 6–10
Power Word: Address

September starts with Venus entering its pre-shadow retrograde period. A pre-shadow period is the time before a planet officially turns retrograde when it begins to slow down. As a result, the vibe for this month will start to feel 'retrograde-y'. More will be shared in next month's Horoscope on the specifics of how this retrograde affects you. On the 10th, a slow Venus enters Scorpio, bringing physical health and wellness as more of a focus area this autumn. It would be helpful for you to conduct an internal check-in with yourself now on how strict you've been with your physical wellness routines (there will be an astrological audit of this next month).

The New Moon in Virgo also occurs on the 10th and signifies a more formal end to the summer eclipse season. This lunation ushers in a new emotional cycle around home and family dynamics. If you've needed to have a heart to heart with any loved ones, this lunation is a fertile time to do so. Home reorganizing is a common way for Gemini especially to work with this lunation. The Sun finds harmony with Mars on the 14th, making the few days after the New Moon the most opportune time for home improvements. The middle of the month also features Venus squaring off with Pluto, which can ramp up your inner critic or bring up issues revolving around self-esteem.

The Sun moves into your fellow air sign Libra on the 22nd. Libra season is your annual spotlight on creative self-expression and romance. This year's Libra season is a little different as the ruler of this sign, Venus, will turn retrograde in a few weeks. Re-evaluating the role creative self-expression plays in your life, and whether you should seek to incorporate it more into your lifestyle, is a big topic of focus this autumn. The same type of reconsideration applies to how you approach romance. The month ends with a bright Full Moon in Aries on the 26th. This lunation strongly encourages you to immerse yourself in those social circles which uplift you and honour your unique individuality.

October

Best Days Overall: 10-15
Most Stressful Days Overall: 20-25
Best Days for Love: 26-31
Best Days for Money: 6-11
Best Days for Career: 8-12
Power Word: Routine

October's astrology starts off with Venus turning retrograde in Scorpio. Venus will be retrograde for the next six weeks and it will regress back into Libra, meaning its retrograde period will encompass a Scorpio section and a Libra section. Venus's retrogrades always function as audits of values and relationships. For Gemini, this Venus retrograde also features a focus on physical health and wellness. Venus is not like Saturn in that it doesn't necessarily pertain to consequences and harsh realities, but a Venus retrograde period centring around physical fitness could have you feeling like you need to take a hard look in the mirror and consider how strict (or not) you are with yourself. Be gentle with yourself though, sweet Gemini; Mars will find tension with Pluto on the 3rd, making the vibes extra edgy.

The New Moon in Libra on the 11th is a beautiful lunation centring around romance and creative self-expression. Over the next two weeks, lean into whatever form of creativity provides you with the most fulfilment. Venus follows Mars's lead and finds tension with Pluto on the 20th. If there was ever a time this month to lean into activities that uplift you, it would be around this date.

Scorpio's season is officially here on the 23rd. The Sun moving into Scorpio only augments the spotlight on physical wellness and routines for Gemini. The next day, Mercury joins Venus by turning retrograde. As mentioned in your annual forecast at the start, this is the third and final Mercury retrograde, all of which have been completely in water signs. Be open to getting in touch with your emotional needs over the next three weeks. The Full Moon in Taurus illuminates mental health and wellness on the 26th. Prioritize nesting and resting on or around the couple of days following this lunation. This lunation features an aspect which relates to shedding aspects of your identity which no longer serve you, or confronting aspects of your identity you've buried and need to unearth and address. The Full Moon in Taurus isn't all emo though – it is actually an ideal time to pamper yourself using your five senses.

November

Best Days Overall: 26–30
Most Stressful Days Overall: 11–15
Best Days for Love: 23–27
Best Days for Money: 29–30
Best Days for Career: 1–5
Power Word: Kinetic

The New Moon in Scorpio starts off the notable astrology of November on the 9th. This lunation functions as a check-in on the themes of Venus's and Mercury's retrograde periods surrounding physical health and wellness. New Moons usher in new beginnings, so this is the opportune time to implement changes or additions to your weekly routines which will support your holistic wellbeing. The vibes substantially shift on the 13th as Mercury and Venus both turn direct again on the same day. Remember, both planets will still be slow for the rest of the month, so please anticipate things taking a little more time where technology, transport and communication are concerned – they could be a bit wonky.

The kinetic energy picks up as Mars conjoins with Jupiter in Leo on the 16th. This is expansive energy to either get productive or expend energy through fitness. Mars and Jupiter conjoined has the potential to make people seemingly brash, so do your best to thoughtfully respond and not have a knee-jerk reaction if provoked around this date. The energy may feel like it's picking up a bit too much around the 20th as the Sun squares off with Mars. It is important to schedule some nesting or resting time around this date.

Sagittarius's season is finally here on the 22nd. The Sun in Sagittarius is your annual spotlight on partnership and intimate one-to-one relationships. As you know, any partnership contains the equally important relationship of you to yourself. This is what gets illuminated by the Full Moon in your sign on the 24th. If you're partnered, this Full Moon highlights specific needs you have which could be met better by either yourself or your partner. If you're single, don't be surprised if your attitude or emotions around prospective partnership are heightened by this lunation. This lunation finds harmony with Neptune and inspires you to dream big in this area of life as well. Regardless of your partnership status, allow yourself to ponder what dynamics, settings or behaviours in partnership would make you truly happy. The month finishes on a productive note with the Sun finding harmony with Saturn. The last few days of the month are ideal for checking items off your to-do list.

December

Best Days Overall: 10–14
Most Stressful Days Overall: 27–31
Best Days for Love: 1–3; 6–8
Best Days for Money: 21–24
Best Days for Career: 11–15
Power Word: Blossom

You've made it to the end of another year, Gemini! The cosmic weather for December kicks off with Venus entering Scorpio once again on the 4th and Mars finding tension with Uranus on the 5th. Venus in Scorpio encourages you to not hold back from asking questions of yourself or others. Mars and Uranus squaring off creates an air of volatility, so double down on grounding practices for the start of this month. Mercury enters Sagittarius on the 6th, followed by the New Moon in Sagittarius on the 8th. This new moon ushers in a new emotional cycle around partnership for you. Regardless of your partnership status, there is fertile energy to build on existing dynamics or to plant the seeds for future partnerships to blossom. If you're single, this lunation affords an opportune time to put yourself out there.

However, the most important relationship at the start of December is the one you have with yourself. On the 9th, Venus squares off with Pluto, which can heighten insecure feelings or feelings related to worthiness. Carve out some time for some much-needed TLC and show yourself some love to mitigate the angst from this transit. Thankfully, your planetary ruler Mercury finds harmony with Saturn on the 11th. This transit is great for wrapping up projects at the end of the year. If you have a long holiday to-do list, this is also a transit ripe with productive energy. Venus rounds out the middle of the month by finding harmony with Mars. This is a snuggly and fun transit, so lean into the bubbly vibes this transit yields.

Speaking of snuggly, the 18th features harmony between the Sun in Sagittarius and Jupiter in Leo. This is a great astrological transit to connect with a significant other or bring your relationship to the next level. If you're single, this is great energy to mingle. The Sun moves into Capricorn on the 21st. Capricorn season is your annual spotlight on joint finances. Do you know how your money is influenced by or intertwined with others? The Full Moon in Cancer on the 23rd is a good time to invest your money or seek out a business collaboration. The last week of 2026 does not feature the most productive astrology, so it's best if you take it easy and journal about your goals for 2027.

Cancer

THE CRAB

Birthdays from
June 21
to July 20

Personality Profile

CANCER AT A GLANCE

Element – Water

Ruling Planet – Moon
  Career Planet – Mars
  Love Planet – Saturn
  Money Planet – Sun
  Planet of Fun, Entertainment, Creativity and Pleasure – Mars
  Planet of Good Fortune – Jupiter
  Planet of Health and Work – Jupiter
  Planet of Home and Family Life – Venus
  Planet of Spirituality and Mental Health – Mercury

Totem – the Commander

Colours – blue, puce, silver

Colours that promote love, romance and social harmony – black, indigo

Colours that promote earning power – gold, orange

Gems – moonstone, pearl

Metal – silver

Scents – jasmine, sandalwood

Quality – cardinal (= activity)

Quality most needed for balance – mood control

Strongest virtues – emotional sensitivity, tenacity, the urge to nurture

Deepest need – a harmonious home and family life

Characteristics to avoid – over-sensitivity, negative moods

Signs of greatest overall compatibility – Scorpio, Pisces

Signs of greatest overall incompatibility – Aries, Libra, Capricorn

Sign most helpful to career – Aries

Sign most helpful for emotional support – Libra

Sign most helpful financially – Leo

Sign best for marriage and/or partnerships – Capricorn

Sign most helpful for creative projects – Scorpio

Best Sign to have fun with – Scorpio

Signs most helpful in spiritual matters – Gemini, Pisces

Best day of the week – Monday

Understanding a Cancer

In the sign of Cancer the heavens are developing the feeling side of things. This is what a true Cancerian is all about – feelings. Where Aries will tend to err on the side of action, Taurus on the side of inaction and Gemini on the side of thought, Cancer will tend to err on the side of feeling.

Cancerians tend to mistrust logic. Perhaps rightfully so. For them it is not enough for an argument or a project to be logical – it must feel right as well. If it does not feel right a Cancerian will reject it or chafe against it. The phrase 'follow your heart' could have been coined by a Cancerian, because it describes exactly the Cancerian attitude to life.

The power to feel is a more direct – more immediate – method of knowing than thinking is. Thinking is indirect. Thinking about a thing never touches the thing itself. Feeling is a faculty that touches directly the thing or issue in question. We actually experience it. Emotional feeling is almost like another sense which humans possess – a psychic sense. Since the realities that we come in contact with during our lifetime are often painful and even destructive, it is not surprising that the Cancerian chooses to erect barriers – a shell – to protect his or her vulnerable, sensitive nature. To a Cancerian this is only common sense.

If Cancerians are in the presence of people they do not know, or find themselves in a hostile environment, up goes the shell and they feel protected. Other people often complain about this, but one must question these people's motives. Why does this shell disturb them? Is it perhaps because they would like to sting, and feel frustrated that they cannot? If your intentions are honourable and you are patient, have no fear. The shell will open up and you will be accepted as part of the Cancerian's circle of family and friends.

Thought processes are generally analytic and dissociating. In order to think clearly we must make distinctions, comparisons and the like. But feeling is unifying and integrative.

To think clearly about something you have to distance yourself from it. To feel something you must get close to it. Once a Cancerian has accepted you as a friend, he or she will hang on to you. You have to be really bad to lose the friendship of a Cancerian. If you are related to Cancerians they will never let you go no matter what you do. They will always try to maintain some kind of connection even in the most extreme circumstances.

Finance

The Cancer-born has a deep sense of what other people feel about things and why they feel as they do. This faculty is a great asset in the workplace and in the business world. Of course, it's also indispensable in raising a family and building a home, but it has its uses in business. Cancerians often attain great wealth in a family business. Even if the business is not a family operation, they will treat it as one. If the Cancerian works for somebody else, then the boss is the parental figure and the co-workers are brothers and sisters. If a Cancerian is the boss, then all the workers are his or her children. Cancerians like the feeling of being providers for others. They enjoy knowing that others derive their sustenance because of what they do. It is another form of nurturing.

With Leo on their solar 2nd money house cusp, Cancerians are often lucky speculators, especially with residential property or hotels and restaurants. Resort hotels and nightclubs are also profitable for the Cancerian. Waterside properties attract them. Though they are basically conventional people, they sometimes like to earn their livelihood in glamorous ways.

The Sun, Cancer's money planet, represents an important financial message: in financial matters Cancerians need to be less moody, more stable and fixed. They cannot allow their moods – which are here today and gone tomorrow – to get in the way of their business lives. They need to develop their self-esteem and feelings of self-worth if they are to realize their greatest financial potential.

Career and Public Image

Aries rules the 10th solar career house cusp of Cancer, which indicates that Cancerians long to start their own business, to be more active publicly and politically and to be more independent. Family responsibilities and a fear of hurting other people's feelings – or getting hurt themselves – often inhibit them from attaining these goals. However, this is what they want and long to do.

Cancerians like their bosses and leaders to act freely and to be a bit self-willed. They can deal with that in a superior. They expect their leaders to be fierce on their behalf. When the Cancerian is in the position of boss or superior he or she behaves very much like a 'warlord'. Of course, the wars they wage are not egocentric but in defence of those under their care. If they lack some of this fighting instinct – independence and pioneering spirit – Cancerians will have extreme difficulty in attaining their highest career goals. They will be hampered in their attempts to lead others.

Since they are so parental, Cancerians like to work with children and make great educators and teachers.

Love and Relationships

Like Taurus, Cancer likes committed relationships. Cancerians function best when the relationship is clearly defined and everyone knows his or her role. When they marry it is usually for life. They are extremely loyal to their beloved. But there is a deep little secret that most Cancerians will never admit to: commitment or partnership is really a chore and a duty to them. They enter into it because they know of no other way to create the family that they desire. Union is just a way – a means to an end – rather than an end in itself. The family is the ultimate end for them.

If you are in love with a Cancerian you must tread lightly on his or her feelings. It will take you a good deal of time to realize how deep and sensitive Cancerians can be. The smallest negativity upsets them. Your tone of voice, your irritation, a look in your eye or an expression on your face can cause great distress for the Cancerian. Your slightest gesture is registered by them and reacted to. This can be hard to get used to, but stick by your love – Cancerians make great partners once you learn how to deal with them. Your Cancerian lover will react not so much to what you say but to the way you are actually feeling at the moment.

Home and Domestic Life

This is where Cancerians really excel. The home environment and the family are their personal works of art. They strive to make things of beauty that will outlast them. Very often they succeed.

Cancerians feel very close to their family, their relatives and especially their mothers. These bonds last throughout their lives and mature as they grow older. They are very fond of those members of their family who become successful, and they are also quite attached to family heirlooms and mementos. Cancerians also love children and like to provide them with all the things they need and want. With their nurturing, feeling nature, Cancerians make very good parents – especially the Cancerian woman, who is the mother *par excellence* of the zodiac.

As a parent the Cancerian's attitude is 'my children right or wrong'. Unconditional devotion is the order of the day. No matter what a family member does, the Cancerian will eventually forgive him or her, because 'you are, after all, family'. The preservation of the institution – the tradition – of the family is one of the Cancerian's main reasons for living. They have many lessons to teach others about this.

Being so family-orientated, the Cancerian's home is always clean, orderly and comfortable. They like old-fashioned furnishings but they also like to have all the modern comforts. Cancerians love to have family and friends over, to organize parties and to entertain at home – they make great hosts.

Horoscope for 2026

Cancer is one the four cardinal signs of the zodiac which are associated with heralding the start of a new season. Though you may not be as known for initiating change or for trailblazing as much as your fellow cardinal signs Aries and Capricorn, this innate quality is interwoven into your personality. That being said, 2026 is the year you embody 'the Commander'. Your totem is the Commander primarily because Saturn, the planet of discipline and responsibility, and Neptune, the planet of dreams and the collective, both enter your career sector early in the year. Moreover, both Saturn and Neptune will stay and occupy this sector for several years (Saturn until 2028 and Neptune until 2032/2033).

The confluence of these two energies occupying the same chart sector is truly intriguing because at their core, these two planets are the antitheses of one another. Saturn very much rules reality and consequences while Neptune rules aspirations and viewing things through rose-tinted glasses. These two planets set up 2026 as a year where only hard work towards your dreams will pay off, but it will pay off with major dividends. This journey formally starts in February when the two planets conjoin on the 20th, and is reinforced because Jupiter, the planet of growth and expansion, will still be in your sign, occupying the self-improvement sector of your chart.

Aside from career and self-improvement, another area of life that is noteworthy in 2026 for Cancer is finances. This is primarily because buoyant Jupiter moves out of your self-improvement sector and into your finances sector mid-year. Though traditionally described as a 'benefic', Jupiter really brings a 'more is more' type vibe to the chart sector it occupies. Therefore, if your budgeting and/or investment practices have been on point thus far, this is an auspicious transit centred around abundance. If, however, you've been financially profligate and careless, this transit could cause your behaviour to spiral out of control, so proceed with caution.

For a quarterly view of your year ahead, the first quarter of 2026 centres around career and self-improvement. The second quarter continues these themes and also includes mental health and wellness as a focus. The third quarter brings finances into focus, in addition to overarching career pursuits. The final quarter of the year has a substantial focus on romance and family dynamics.

Health (1st/6th/12th houses)

(Please note that this is an astrological perspective on health and not a medical one. Any health-related symptoms should be evaluated by a qualified healthcare professional.)

Your mental health planet is Mercury, which will turn retrograde in all three water signs over the course of this year. Water is the element associated with emotion and intuition. The astrology of 2026 strongly points to the value of talking about your feelings with an expert. This is especially true over the summer when Mercury is retrograde in your own sign. Mercury's retrograde in Cancer will occur from June 29 to July 23. Mental health is also more of a focal point this year as Uranus, the planet of individuality and instability, enters your mental health sector. Uranus in this chart sector prompts you to approach emotional regulation in new and innovative ways. Uranus in Gemini has strong ties to technology, so monitor how technology influences your mental/emotional wellbeing.

Your physical health planet is Jupiter, which spends the first part of 2026 in your sign. As stated above, Jupiter brings 'more is more' energy and rules growth, so if you've been on top of your physical wellness through diet and exercise, Jupiter brings abundance and splendour. If you've been ignoring physical wellness, however, Jupiter in your sign amplifies the effects of this negligence. The diet component of wellness is especially important as Jupiter has strong associations with indulgence. This of course doesn't mean you should be hypervigilant, but simply be mindful of how the food you consume affects your body.

Here are the specific areas of the body to focus on this year:

- Stomach, breasts and lymphatic system: this is a perennial area of focus for you as Cancer rules these parts of the body in medical astrology. These parts of the body are further emphasized by the fact that Jupiter, your physical health planet, will be occupying your sign for the first half of 2026. In addition to diet and exercise, consult an expert about supportive practices for these areas of the body.
- Heart: at the end of June, Jupiter, your health planet, leaves your sign and enters Leo. Leo rules the heart in medical astrology, so it's especially recommended to adopt heart-healthy routines like cardio workouts and eating food supportive of heart health, with the approval of an expert to do so.
- Digestive system: Venus will be retrograde in the area of your chart related to this part of the body this year. Retrograde periods are times to reflect, review and readjust. Consider how your routines are either supporting or detracting from your digestive health this year.

Love and Social Life (5th/7th/11th houses)

While there are no transits through your relationship sector, your relationship planet, Saturn, encounters a noteworthy amount of activity through both changing signs and aspecting other planets this year. Saturn is a slow-moving planet that takes about 28 to 29years to orbit the zodiac. As a result, Saturn spends about two and a half years in every sign. Saturn will enter and stay in Aries starting on February 13. Saturn entering Aries also signifies a new holistic cycle for the planet as it leaves the last sign of the zodiac (Pisces) and enters the first (Aries).

With it starting a new cycle, Saturn in Aries prompts you to prioritize your needs in partnership. If there is a lack of reciprocity in one-to-one relationships, Saturn moving into Aries will act as an audit and demand you advocate for yourself. If you're single, Saturn in Aries will ask you to reflect on your relationship to relationships and, if you're seeking one, what you need to embody in order to be open to receiving one. Essentially, the name of the love game in

2026 is centred around identifying your needs and holding yourself accountable for getting them met. Noteworthy periods of time in 2026 are the weeks of February 13, when the shift for Saturn from Pisces to Aries occurs; February 20, when Saturn conjoins with dreamy Neptune; March 28, when Saturn finds harmony with transformative Pluto; and August 31, when buoyant Jupiter aligns with Saturn. Whether partnered or single, all of these weeks provide energy which emphasizes leaning into partnership. If possible, schedule some time with your special someone or to put yourself out there.

Your social life planet, Venus, will turn retrograde towards the end of the year in your romance sector. If you're single, this indicates there's the potential for a romantic connection within groups and circles you're already a part of. It is best advised to work with the retrograde period to identify these potential flames and then pursue them after Venus is moving in direct motion once again, i.e. after November 13. Venus finds tension with Pluto during its retrograde (specifically around October 20), so bookmark the latter half of that month as a time of heightened potential turbulence with romantic and social life endeavours.

Career and Finances (10th/2nd/8th houses)

As stated in the introduction to this year's Horoscope, this year your totem is the Commander because of all the activity occurring in your career sector in 2026. Saturn, the planet of structure, responsibility and reality, enters this sector and will stay there for two and a half years. Moreover, Neptune, the planet of dreams, spirituality and idealism also enters this sector but will stay until 2032/2033.

The combination of these planetary energies occupying your career sector is significant for several reasons. Very similar to the way Rocky Balboa had to train for his big fight in an ultra-regimented and disciplined way, a person is typically called on to undergo the same type of hard work in the area of life related to the chart sector Saturn occupies. This means, in order to achieve your big career goals it's time to get serious and get to work. With

Neptune thrown into the mix, it'll be even more paramount to maintain this level of discipline, because Neptunian energy is associated with procrastination and even escapist tendencies as a means of avoiding facing reality. In addition, Saturn and Neptune together throw a work-life balance off kilter. As a result, it'll be vital for you to intentionally carve out time to restore this balance and ensure you keep the career flame alive while not burning out completely. Moreover, the combination of Saturn and Neptune can also bring shifts in career desires, as they call into question how your career benefits or impacts society at large. One of the primary causes of a career change with these two planetary energies in this chart sector would be as a means to ensure you'll be leaving a legacy you'd be proud of. Ask yourself now, before these energies take full hold, what you want to be remembered for – and then do so again at the end of this year.

This year is also a noteworthy year financially speaking for Cancers, with Jupiter transiting this chart sector for the last six months of 2026. Jupiter is like a magnifying glass, so your relationship with money will be amplified for better or worse. It's strongly advised to take steps towards creating a more responsible and beneficial relationship with finances prior to Jupiter's shift into this chart sector on June 30.

Home and Domestic Life (4th house)

This is a relatively neutral area of life this year as there are no outer planets entering or transiting this sector and no eclipses in this chart sector for Cancer. When this happens, the energy surrounding this chart sector is very much 'what you put in, you get out'. Your home and domestic life planet is Venus, which will undergo a retrograde period from October 3 to November 13. Venus will be retrograde in two chart sectors: first in the sector related to creativity, romance and children (from October 3 to October 25) and then in the home and domestic life sector from October 25 until it turns direct again on November 13. For you, Cancer, the first part of this retrograde centres around how home or family life impacts your ability to be creative. For those Cancers with children, there's an additional layer centred around those relationships and working through any underlying relationship dynamics that need to be addressed. The second part of this retrograde period doubles down on home and family dynamics. Venus's retrograde periods are not to be feared, but rather viewed as opportunities to re-evaluate or reconfigure existing relationship dynamics.

Self-improvement (1st/3rd/5th/9th houses)

Self-improvement for Cancer this year can be organized into two categories: communication and spirituality. Your communication planet is Mercury, which happens to be the planet that rules thinking and communication. This year, Mercury will spend especially long periods of time in each of the three water signs as it will retrograde three times (one retrograde period per water sign), adding up to 202 days this year spent in the element of water. With over half the year spent in water signs, you can anticipate communication to have a noteworthy emotional bent this year. Learning how to navigate and be comfortable with vulnerability is an important way Cancer can grow this year. Moreover, learning how to speak earnestly and with emotion, without losing candour, is another important focus area for Cancer this year.

Your spirituality planet is Jupiter, which rules belief and conviction in traditional astrology. Jupiter will start the year in your sign, encouraging you to get comfortable with taking up space and making your presence known. Reading and studying philosophers who centre their work around cultivating an innate sense of belonging is recommended. Being aware of which spaces welcome you in, versus which merely tolerate you, will drastically broaden your sense of figuring out where to spend your time this year.

Month-by-month Forecasts

January

Best Days Overall: 2–6
Most Stressful Days Overall: 8–12
Best Days for Love: 1–3; 17–18
Best Days for Money: 23–26
Best Days for Career: 20–24
Power Word: Shed

Happy New Year, Cancer! The astrology of 2026 starts off with a bright Full Moon in your sign on the 3rd. This lunation centres around personal transformation and how that pertains to your goals for this year. Jupiter is still in your sign for six more months, so work with that expansive energy and dream big. The Sun conjoins with Venus a few days later on the 6th, making it a great day for you to prioritize pleasure or play with a significant other or a special someone. Relationship dynamics are an emotional focus for Cancer this month as Venus in Capricorn opposes Jupiter in your sign on the 9th and the Sun and Mars in Capricorn follow suit on the 10th. Mars opposite Jupiter is a transit associated with an increase in kinetic assertive energy. Work with these transits to progress existing relationship dynamics or pursue prospective partners. However, do your best to stay grounded as this energy is often associated with overexerting oneself.

The New Moon in Capricorn ushers in a new emotional cycle around partnership on the 18th. Capricorn is a goal-oriented sign, so this is the ideal lunation to set goals around partnership, regardless of your partnership status. If you are partnered, you may want to set goals with your partner. These should be goals you seek to achieve by the Full Moon in Capricorn in six months' time. The next day, the Sun moves into Aquarius meaning it's officially Aquarius season! Aquarius season is your annual spotlight on joint finances and how your money is intertwined with or influenced by others. Venus conjoins with Pluto in Aquarius on the 20th. This transit may spike your fears or insecurities, but it only unearths these feelings for you to confront and move beyond them. Be gentle with yourself around this date.

The Sun and Mercury follow suit conjoining with Pluto on the 22nd and 23rd. The week of the 18th to the 24th is an ideal time to shed what beliefs, thoughts or behaviours you've brought into this year from 2025 which no longer serve you or are stifling your ability to chase your 2026 goals. Free yourself, sweet Crab! After spending 2025 oscillating between two signs, Neptune formally moves into Aries on the 26th, where it'll stay until 2039. Neptune in Aries ushers in a 13-year period of you placing a higher value on emotional or spiritual fulfilment in your career.

February

Best Days Overall: 6-10
Most Stressful Days Overall: 15-19
Best Days for Love: 10-14
Best Days for Money: 1-5
Best Days for Career: 20-24
Power Word: Discipline

February starts off spotlighting finances for you, Cancer, as January ends with Mars conjoining with Pluto. Frugality is the name of the game this month. The Full Moon in Leo draws your emotional focus more so to finances. If you haven't identified or implemented budgetary practices yet this year, this lunation is an ideal time to start. Given how financially oriented the overarching astrology is this year for Cancer, you may want to consult a financial planning expert if possible, or to educate yourself more on matters related to financial literacy.

Just like Neptune oscillated back and forth between Pisces and Aries last year, so did Saturn, who formally enters the fire sign on the 13th. Saturn is the planet of responsibility, discipline and hard work. Saturn in Aries scrutinizes your existing career, career goals and the steps you are taking (or haven't taken yet) to achieve these goals. Saturn in Aries demands discipline from you in this area of life in 2026. Thankfully, Saturn rules consequences, and positive consequences are rewards. Embrace the climb, Cancer!

The first eclipse of 2026 occurs on the 17th when a solar eclipse in Aquarius occurs. Remember, eclipses are evolutionary transits which stimulate growth through scrutiny and tension. This eclipse has the potency to build on the Venus/Pluto transit last month which started to unearth fears and insecurities for you to address and overcome. This eclipse also is financial in nature for Cancer, especially around investments and joint ventures with others. If you have contracts to sign around this date, absolutely have a trusted ally review the contract with you.

On the 18th, it's officially Pisces's season. Pisces's season is your annual spotlight on spirituality and higher education. The build-up of Pisces energy over the next few weeks also encourages planning a voyage or trip which would support spiritual enlighten-ment or a necessary shift in perspective. The month concludes with the first Mercury retrograde period of the year. The next three weeks centre around reviewing and revising how you approach communication with yourself and others.

March

Best Days Overall: 22-26
Most Stressful Days Overall: 1-5
Best Days for Love: 25-28
Best Days for Money: 6-10
Best Days for Career: 27-30
Power Word: Productive

The astrology of March kicks off with the second eclipse of the year – a lunar eclipse in Virgo. This eclipse forces you to confront self-effacing patterns of communication. Your voice should not limit you, Cancer. Venus enters Aries a few days later on the 6th, where it conjoins with Neptune and Saturn on the 7th and 8th respectively. These transits and the astrology of the next several weeks will focus more on career and legacy. What do you want to be remembered for, Cancer? Mercury harmonizes with Jupiter on the 9th, supporting efforts around education for you.

The New Moon in Pisces occurs on the 18th and ushers in a new emotional cycle around spirituality and higher education. With Mercury's retrograde period also touching on this area of life, in what ways could you integrate spiritual practices more into your weekly routines? Aries's season kicks off on the 20th, providing your annual spotlight on career and legacy. Mercury ends its retrograde period on this day, freeing you to move forward in pursuing goals which were delayed by the retrograde. However, Mercury takes a couple of weeks to get back up to full speed, so don't feel like you need to rush to accomplish your entire to-do list immediately.

The Sun conjoins with Neptune on the 22nd, which inspires and supports dreaming big, and is followed by a meeting with Saturn on the 25th which takes these big-picture ideas and encourages fleshing them out with small actionable steps to achieve your goals. The astrology of the end of March supports a heads-down productivity. Saturn in Aries finds harmony with Pluto in Aquarius on the 28th – this is an auspicious financial transit for Cancer. This transit builds upon the financial energy of last month which supported investments or identifying new streams of income. The month ends with Venus moving into Taurus. This transit encourages you to get social. Surround yourself with those who uplift you. The spring is a social time for Cancer, so make sure you are actively maintaining and strengthening the relationships which matter most to you.

April

Best Days Overall: 7–12
Most Stressful Days Overall: 1–4
Best Days for Love: 24–27
Best Days for Money: 26–29
Best Days for Career: 15–19
Power Word: Endeavour

April's cosmic weather leads with the annual Full Moon in Libra on the 1st. This lunation lights up the home and family sector of your chart. Libra is the sign of harmony and collaboration, so this Full Moon centres your emotional focus on familial relationships or relationships inside your home. Mars enters one of the signs it's most comfortable in, fiery Aries, on the 9th. Mars in Aries is a career and public perception transit for you, Cancer, which brings a much-needed burst of kinetic energy to this area of life. Moreover, anticipate more direct, less filtered communication in your day-to-day life as Mercury follows suit and joins Mars in Aries on the 14th. If you've been meaning to launch any new endeavours, this build-up of Aries energy is an opportune time to do so.

No lunation is more supportive in the pursuit of something new than the New Moon in Aries, which occurs on the 17th. You have a full week to work with the fertile energy of the New Moon and, given that Mars meets up with Saturn on the 19th, it is recommended you wait towards the end of this week-long period before fully immersing yourself in launching this new initiative. Seven days later, on the 24th, Venus meets up with Uranus at the final degree of Taurus, supporting spontaneous adventures with friends. Venus then moves into Gemini later that day, drawing some attention to your emotional and mental health.

The Sun squares off with Pluto on the 25th, further reinforcing the importance of prioritizing your mental health. After oscillating between Taurus and Gemini, Uranus formally moves into Gemini on the 25th as well, where it will stay until 2032/2033. Uranus in Gemini changes the societal landscape through accelerating the way technology is interwoven into how we collectively communicate and learn. For Cancer, this transit also initiates a six- to seven-year period where you're tasked with approaching mental wellness in new and innovative ways. This could be as simple as seeking out a meditation or mindfulness practice if you've never attempted to do so before, or working with a mental health counsellor for the first time.

May

Best Days Overall: 16–20
Most Stressful Days Overall: 1–2; 28–31
Best Days for Love: 18–22
Best Days for Money: 2–5
Best Days for Career: 23–26
Power Word: Community

With the Moon being your ruling luminary, the fact that there are two Full Moons this month speaks to how eventful May is likely to be for you, Cancer. The month begins with the Full Moon in Scorpio on the 1st. While typically a moody lunation, this Full Moon also centres around creative self-expression and romance for Cancer. Utilize creativity as a means to ground yourself if you're feeling particularly highly strung around this date. This is important to keep in mind as Mercury finds tension with Pluto and as Mars finds tension with Jupiter on the 5th. These transits will likely make you feel especially restless. Do your best to focus on what is in your control and channel whatever frenetic energy you're experiencing into achieving goals within that domain.

The New Moon in Taurus occurs on the 16th and supports you with immersing yourself in new communities. If you've been meaning to get involved with a new professional organization or to increase your responsibilities in one you're already in, this lunation is a green light to do so. Two days later, Venus enters your sign. Venus in your sign promotes prioritizing pleasure and play over the next few weeks. Moreover, Venus in Cancer encourages you to make your living situation more conducive to your mental health.

This is important as the energy over the next six weeks or so will start to focus more on mental and emotional wellness, Cancer.

Gemini's season begins on the 20th and is your annual spotlight on exactly this: mental health. Mars finds tension with Pluto on the 26th, which is a transit which will likely have everyone a little on edge. Be kind to yourself during this time. If you have routines which support grounding yourself, now is the time to lean into them. The month concludes with a Blue Moon, a second Full Moon, this time in Sagittarius. This Full Moon centres around physical health and the link between your body and mind/emotions. Through regulating your body, you can regulate the mind.

June

Best Days Overall: 22-26
Most Stressful Days Overall: 15-19
Best Days for Love: 5-8
Best Days for Money: 13-16
Best Days for Career: 1-4
Power Word: Heal

It's almost your season, Cancer! Mercury joins Venus by entering your sign on the 1st. Mercury moving into Cancer indicates that the planet will turn retrograde in a few weeks as its entire retrograde period this summer will be in your sign. Keep that in the back of your mind this month. The vibes leading into the 10th are buoyant as Venus and Jupiter conjoin in your sign. As mentioned last month, Venus in your sign is a time to prioritize pleasure. With Jupiter ruling growth and expansion, this prompt from the universe is at its strongest around this date. Arguably, this is also a good time financially to identify lucrative opportunities and build more abundance for yourself. Venus stays in your sign until the 13th when it moves into Leo. This creates a notable shift in energy as the planet prepares to tensely oppose Pluto over the next week (the exact hit is on the 18th).

Before this opposition completely occurs, the New Moon in Gemini ushers in a new emotional cycle around mental health and

wellness on the 14th. You are being tasked with being more intentional around how the environments you immerse yourself in and
the company you keep impact your emotional wellness. (You will
be able to reflect upon the changes in this area of life at the Full
Moon in Gemini in December.) Venus in Leo then forms aspects to
Uranus, Neptune and Pluto between the 16th and 18th. Self-care
is paramount during this week. On the 19th, Chiron, the minor
planet associated with transmuting wounds into purpose, finally
exits Aries and moves into Taurus. Chiron will oscillate between
the two signs this year, ushering in a six-year period centred
around deepening your value system as a means to further ongoing
efforts to heal deep-seated wounds.

Happy birthday! On the 21st, it's officially your solar season,
Cancer. With Jupiter, the planet of growth and expansion, in the
final degree of your sign, now is an auspicious time to identify two
or three words you seek to embody and grow into this year. You
may want to journal or discuss with a friend why you are choosing
these specific words to embody this year. Mercury turns retrograde
on the 29th, supporting your need to reflect on the past in order to
best navigate the present moment. The month concludes with a
partnership-oriented Full Moon on the 29th and Jupiter entering
Leo for the first time in 12 years on the 30th. Full information
around Jupiter in Leo can be found at the start of this annual
Horoscope.

July

Best Days Overall: 6–10
Most Stressful Days Overall: 27–31
Best Days for Love: 19–22
Best Days for Money: 1–4
Best Days for Career: 24–28
Power Word: Important

Congratulations Cancer, July is actually the month with the most
noteworthy astrology of 2026. This means (in varying degrees
based on when your actual birthday is) the astrology of this month

will influence your entire next trip around the Sun. First things first; July's astrology begins on the 4th with Mars and Uranus conjoining. Here's a public service announcement: this transit is notorious for surprises and is often, literally and figuratively, associated with explosions; if you're handling fireworks or anything flammable around this date, please be extra cautious. Venus enters Virgo on the 9th, encouraging you to be extra communicative and chatty over the next few weeks.

The slow-moving outer planets, Uranus, Neptune and Pluto, all take extremely long times to orbit the zodiac. Uranus takes approximately 84 years, Neptune 160 years and Pluto 250 years. As a result, it's very rare for them to all align with each other. On the 15th, however, that begins to happen, with Uranus finding harmony with Neptune. On the 18th, Uranus and Pluto do the same. These transits arguably have a more collective level of effect and signify overarching shifts in how technology is radically transforming the fabric of society. On the micro-level, this month's astrology really questions your life's calling and whether you feel as though you're on the proper path. Two days later, on the 20th, Jupiter finds harmony with Uranus and Neptune but finds tension with Pluto. These transits only augment the sentiment around getting in touch with your life's calling.

On the 22nd the Sun leaves your sign and enters Leo. Leo's season provides your annual spotlight on finances and budgeting. It's best to adopt a frugal approach at the start of Leo season as the Sun follows Jupiter and finds tension with Pluto on the 27th. The Full Moon in Aquarius shines brightly on the 29th as it dances with Jupiter. This lunation centres around two themes for Cancer. Firstly, it beseeches you to be sure you're informed how your money is influenced by or interwoven with others. Secondly, it draws out anxieties you need to conquer to progress forward in achieving the goals you've set for yourself this year.

August

Best Days Overall: 1-5
Most Stressful Days Overall: 11-15; 28
Best Days for Love: 14-18
Best Days for Money: 22-25
Best Days for Career: 7-10
Power Word: Push

After an astrologically eventful July, the trend continues as this month is the second eclipse season of the year. Before the eclipses occur, however, there's some astro-weather to discuss. On the 6th, Venus enters Libra and invites you to spend this month prioritizing nesting and resting. Balancing social and solo time is the name of the game this month, Cancer. The next day, the Sun finds harmony with Saturn, a softer financial transit that reminds you that if you spend a little, you should save a little. Mars, the planet of drive, ambition and assertion, enters your sign on the 11th. Mars in your sign adds some much-needed fuel in your tank for the next six weeks. However, remember Cancer, amid the kinetic and frenetic energy this month, it's important to strive for balance.

The first eclipse of the month is a solar eclipse in Leo on the 12th. As a reminder, eclipses push us to grow through tension. This eclipse is financial for Cancer and a big reason why it is recommended you adopt a frugal mindset this solar season. Even though Mercury is direct, it would be better to hold off on business deals until after eclipse season, if possible. You may also hear your inner critic more loudly at this time. Once again, balance and taking care of your emotional wellness are your priorities this summer.

Virgo's season begins on the 22nd and is your annual spotlight on patterns of communication. This Virgo season features the Sun moving into your sign immediately after conjoining with the south node. This Virgo season is a little different because you're being tasked to shed old patterns of communication which negatively impact existing relationships. On the 28th, the second eclipse of the month and final eclipse of 2026 occurs, in Pisces. This is the most volatile eclipse of the four with the eclipse very tightly finding tension with Uranus. For Cancer, this eclipse encourages an evolution around your spiritual values system or spiritual practices to better support you in maintaining balance and equilibrium in your day-to-day life. Pisces is the sign associated with compassion, so take extra effort to be kind to yourself, sweet Crab.

September

Best Days Overall: 11-15
Most Stressful Days Overall: 26-30
Best Days for Love: 3-7
Best Days for Money: 1-4
Best Days for Career: 20-23
Power Word: Organize

In typical Virgo season fashion, the astrology of the start of September promotes checking items off your to-do list, Cancer. On the last day of August, Jupiter and Saturn harmoniously conjoined in fire signs. Jupiter and Saturn finding harmony supports steps you're taking to grow in your career or in personal projects you want to be part of your legacy. On the 10th of this month, Venus enters fellow water sign Scorpio. Venus is now slowing down as it will turn retrograde at the beginning of next month. Venus in Scorpio is a transit which promotes play and creativity.

The New Moon in Virgo also occurs on the 10th. This lunation supports getting organized if you're feeling stuck this month. Work with this New Moon by writing out a list of small, actionable tasks which, when completed, will add up to significant productivity. That being said, remember that you should not confuse productivity with worthiness. Speaking of checking items off your to-do list, the Sun finds harmony with Mars on the 14th which is great for putting your head down and doing exactly this. Chiron re-enters Aries for one final tour through the sign on the 17th. The last eight years have been significant in how you've morphed and changed in your career. Take time to pause and reflect on this journey.

Libra's season begins on the 22nd and is your annual spotlight on home and domestic life. The Full Moon in Aries shines brightly on the 26th and is surprisingly visionary given its proximity to Neptune. Now that you've taken time to pause and reflect on your career journey thus far, this lunation supports you in dreaming big about what's next. Mars enters Leo on the 27th where it'll stay for close to two months. This transit can feel like a hole is burning in your wallet, so continuing to adopt a frugal mindset is recommended. Mercury enters Scorpio on the 30th and will slow down soon as it prepares to turn retrograde one more time next month. Mercury in Scorpio supports not stifling yourself if you feel compelled to ask questions of others, and also encourages you to be willing to ask yourself questions you've been avoiding.

October

Best Days Overall: 8-12
Most Stressful Days Overall: 24-28
Best Days for Love: 27-31
Best Days for Money: 11-15
Best Days for Career: 22-26
Power Word: Certainty

October's astrology kicks off with Venus turning retrograde in Scorpio on the 3rd. Venus will be retrograde in both Scorpio and Libra over the next six weeks. Venus is the planet of values, intimacy and pleasure. Every Venus retrograde period functions like a values audit, especially of interpersonal relationships. That being said, the vibe of each retrograde is influenced by which sector of the chart Venus is currently in as it retrogrades. Venus retrograde in Scorpio will have many people confronting their relationship to and desire for certainty. The impermanence of all things in life is a concept Venus in Scorpio often grapples with. For Cancer, this retrograde also corresponds to your relationship with creativity. Do you allow yourself to be creative or play on a routine basis?

The weekend of October 3 also features Mars finding tension with Pluto on the 3rd, and the Sun finding tension with Saturn on the 4th. These transits combined can have you stuck in a scarcity mindset around career or relationships. Be gentle with yourself, Cancer. The New Moon in Libra occurs on the 10th. This lunation supports creating the atmosphere at home which would best support emotional regulation. Whether that means investing in organizational tools or making your living space cosier, take time to make your home reflect how you'd like to feel.

The Sun moves into Scorpio a couple of days after Venus squares off with Pluto for the second time. The Venus retrograde prompt around grappling with certainty is highlighted by this astro-weather. Moreover, your relationship with co-dependency is also up for review at this time with Mercury turning retrograde in Scorpio on the 24th. Venus re-enters Libra on the 25th and will be retrograde for close to three more weeks. Venus in Libra prompts audits on values and relationships to family dynamics and to those relationships occurring within the home. The Full Moon in Taurus squares off with Pluto, making this a more emotional Full Moon. This Full Moon supports surrounding yourself with friends with whom you can be vulnerable and authentically yourself.

November

Best Days Overall: 17–21
Most Stressful Days Overall: 23–26
Best Days for Love: 15–19
Best Days for Money: 16; 28–30
Best Days for Career: 1–3; 29
Power Word: Reflect

Mercury and Venus will be retrograde for almost two more weeks, Cancer – how are you doing? Mercury and Venus have overlapping retrograde periods for a second year in a row. Think back to March 2025; what themes of values, relationships and communication were present during that time? With Mercury being retrograde in Scorpio and Venus being retrograde in Libra, your patterns of behaviour in relationships are especially up for review at this time. November's astrology, especially in the first two weeks with this double retrograde period, strongly encourages reflection, whether that be through journalling, talking with a close friend, or even working with a counsellor.

The New Moon in Scorpio occurs on the 9th and ushers in a new emotional cycle in Cancer's creativity and children sector. Sometimes in astrology, areas of life that don't necessarily overlap are in the same sector of the chart. For some Cancers, their relationship to creative self-expression and how they utilize it as a tool for emotional regulation is the focus of this lunation. For others, their relationship to children, the younger generation, or possibly even having children is the emotional focus here. On the 13th, both Mercury and Venus end their retrograde periods and turn direct – yay! Remember, the two planets will take a few weeks to be back up and running directly at full speed.

On the 22nd, the Sun moves into visionary Sagittarius. The Full Moon in Gemini highlights the link between physical wellness and emotional/mental wellbeing. Sagittarius's season is always your annual spotlight on physical wellbeing and the routines you keep which either support or detract from this wellness. Be mindful of what you consume and how you treat your body around this lunation. On the 29th, two slow-moving outer planets, Uranus and Pluto, once again harmoniously align. Doing a financial end-of-year retrospective check or analysis of how your finances have changed this year is recommended around this date. The month ends with the Sun finding harmony with Saturn, a productive transit for checking items off your to-do list which were delayed by the retrograde periods. The Sun finding harmony with Saturn is also an opportune time to pause and congratulate yourself for accomplishments you may not have given yourself proper kudos for this month or year.

December

Best Days Overall: 15–19
Most Stressful Days Overall: 8–12
Best Days for Love: 12–14; 21–22; 25
Best Days for Money: 1–4
Best Days for Career: 3–7
Power Word: Health

It's the last month of the year, Cancer! December begins with Venus once again entering Scorpio on the 4th. Venus in Scorpio now nudges you to prioritize quality time for the interpersonal relationships in your life where you've already cultivated intimacy. Intimacy in this context means that you trust you can safely be vulnerable in the presence of the other person. The next day, Mars and Uranus find tension, making people quicker to 'fly off the handle'. You don't need to walk on eggshells, but just remember that people may be a little more volatile than usual. Mercury in Sagittarius rounds off the first week of December by finding harmony with Neptune – a dreamy transit supporting creative writing and daydreaming.

On the 8th, the New Moon in Sagittarius encourages you to identify three small, actionable steps you can integrate into your physical wellness routines now that you'll be able to maintain for at least the next six months (until the Full Moon in Sagittarius next year). Consistent small steps will have far more of an impact than big steps which fizzle out quickly. Also, if you've been avoiding any annual check-up or seeing any sort of medical specialist, this lunation nudges you to book that appointment. Sagittarius is a wily fire sign and the volatile energy from the 5th is still pervasive as Mercury also finds tension with Uranus on this date. Venus squares off one final time with Pluto on the 9th, which can have you and others feeling hypervigilant or self-deprecating around this date. Lean into Sagittarius's natural cheerleader energy and direct that pep talk inwards.

Capricorn's season begins on the 21st, which is your annual spotlight on partnership. The Full Moon in your sign has you reflecting on your relationship with yourself this year. Have you been a supportive partner to yourself this year? If not, cultivating more self-compassion should be high on your 2027 goal list. The last week of the year features energy which slows you down. Don't be hard on yourself if you can't be as productive as you'd like. Happy New Year, Cancer!

Leo

♌

THE LION

Birthdays from
July 21
to August 21

Personality Profile

LEO AT A GLANCE

Element – Fire

Ruling Planet – Sun
  Career Planet – Venus
  Love Planet – Saturn
  Money Planet – Mercury
  Planet of Health and Work – Saturn
  Planet of Home and Family Life – Mars

Totem – the Crusader

Colours – gold, sienna

Colours that promote love, romance and social harmony – black, indigo, ultramarine blue

Colours that promote earning power – yellow, yellow-orange

Gems – amber, chrysolite, yellow diamond

Metal – gold

Scents – bergamot, frankincense, musk, neroli

Quality – fixed (= stability)

Quality most needed for balance – humility

Strongest virtues – leadership ability, self-esteem and confidence, generosity, creativity, love of joy

Deepest needs – fun, elation, the need to shine

Characteristics to avoid – arrogance, vanity, bossiness

Signs of greatest overall compatibility – Aries, Sagittarius

Signs of greatest overall incompatibility – Taurus, Scorpio, Aquarius

Sign most helpful to career – Taurus

Sign most helpful for emotional support – Scorpio

Sign most helpful financially – Virgo

Sign best for marriage and/or partnerships – Aquarius

Sign most helpful for creative projects – Sagittarius

Best Sign to have fun with – Sagittarius

Signs most helpful in spiritual matters – Aries, Cancer

Best day of the week – Sunday

Understanding a Leo

When you think of Leo, think of royalty – then you'll get the idea of what the Leo character is all about and why Leos are the way they are. It is true that, for various reasons, some Leo-born do not always express this quality – but even if not they should like to do so.

A monarch rules not by example (as does Aries) nor by consensus (as do Capricorn and Aquarius) but by personal will. Will is law. Personal taste becomes the style that is imitated by all subjects. A monarch is somehow larger than life. This is how a Leo desires to be.

When you dispute the personal will of a Leo it is serious business. He or she takes it as a personal affront, an insult. Leos will let you know that their will carries authority and that to disobey is demeaning and disrespectful.

A Leo is king (or queen) of his or her personal domain. Subordinates, friends and family are the loyal and trusted subjects. Leos rule with benevolent grace and in the best interests of others. They have a powerful presence; indeed, they are powerful people. They seem to attract attention in any social gathering. They stand out because they are stars in their domain. Leos feel that, like the Sun, they are made to shine and rule. Leos feel that they were born to special privilege and royal prerogatives – and most of them attain this status, at least to some degree.

The Sun is the ruler of this sign, and when you think of sunshine it is very difficult to feel unhealthy or depressed. Somehow the light of the Sun is the very antithesis of illness and apathy. Leos love life. They also love to have fun; they love drama, music, the theatre and amusements of all sorts. These are the things that give joy to life. If – even in their best interests – you try to deprive Leos of their pleasures, good food, drink and entertainment, you run the serious risk of depriving them of the will to live. To them life without joy is no life at all.

Leos epitomize humanity's will to power. But power in and of itself – regardless of what some people say – is neither good nor evil. Only when power is abused does it become evil. Without power even good things cannot come to pass. Leos realize this and are uniquely qualified to wield power. Of all the signs, they do it most naturally. Capricorn, the other power sign of the zodiac, is a better manager and administrator than Leo – much better. But Leo outshines Capricorn in personal grace and presence. Leo loves power, whereas Capricorn assumes power out of a sense of duty.

Finance

Leos are great leaders but not necessarily good managers. They are better at handling the overall picture than the nitty-gritty details of business. If they have good managers working for them they can become exceptional executives. They have vision and a lot of creativity.

Leos love wealth for the pleasures it can bring. They love an opulent lifestyle, pomp and glamour. Even when they are not wealthy they live as if they are. This is why many fall into debt, from which it is sometimes difficult to emerge.

Leos, like Pisceans, are generous to a fault. Very often they want to acquire wealth solely so that they can help others economically. Wealth to Leo buys services and managerial ability. It creates jobs for others and improves the general wellbeing of those around them. Therefore – to a Leo – wealth is good. Wealth is to be enjoyed to the fullest. Money is not to be left to gather dust in a mouldy bank vault but to be enjoyed, spread around, used. So Leos can be quite reckless in their spending.

With the sign of Virgo on Leo's 2nd money house cusp, Leo needs to develop some of Virgo's traits of analysis, discrimination and purity when it comes to money matters. They must learn to be more careful with the details of finance (or to hire people to do this for them). They have to be more cost-conscious in their spending habits. Generally, they need to manage their money better. Leos tend to chafe under financial constraints, yet these constraints can help Leos to reach their highest financial potential.

Leos like it when their friends and family know that they can depend on them for financial support. They do not mind – and even enjoy – lending money, but they are careful that they are not taken advantage of. From their 'regal throne' Leos like to bestow gifts upon their family and friends and then enjoy the good feelings these gifts bring to everybody. Leos love financial speculations and – when the celestial influences are right – are often lucky.

Career and Public Image

Leos like to be perceived as wealthy, for in today's world wealth often equals power. When they attain wealth they love having a large house with lots of land and animals.

At their jobs Leos excel in positions of authority and power. They are good at making decisions – on a grand level – but they prefer to leave the details to others. Leos are well respected by their colleagues and subordinates, mainly because they have a knack for understanding and relating to those around them. Leos usually strive for the top positions even if they have to start at the bottom and work hard to get there. As might be expected of such a charismatic sign, Leos are always trying to improve their work situation. They do so in order to have a better chance of advancing to the top.

On the other hand, Leos do not like to be bossed around or told what to do. Perhaps this is why they aspire so for the top – where they can be the decision-makers and need not take orders from others.

Leos never doubt their success and focus all their attention and efforts on achieving it. Another great Leo characteristic is that – just like good monarchs – they do not attempt to abuse the power or success they achieve. If they do so this is not wilful or intentional. Usually they like to share their wealth and try to make everyone around them join in their success.

Leos are – and like to be perceived as – hard-working, well-established individuals. It is definitely true that they are capable of hard work and often manage great things. But do not forget that, deep down inside, Leos really are fun-lovers.

Love and Relationships

Generally, Leos are not the marrying kind. To them relationships are good while they are pleasurable. When the relationship ceases to be pleasurable a true Leo will want out. They always want to have the freedom to leave. That is why Leos excel at love affairs rather than commitment. Once married, however, Leo is faithful – even if some Leos have a tendency to marry more than once in their lifetime. If you are in love with a Leo, just show him or her a good time – travel, go to casinos and clubs, the theatre and discos. Wine and dine your Leo love – it is expensive but worth it and you will have fun.

Leos generally have an active love life and are demonstrative in their affections. They love to be with other optimistic and fun-loving types like themselves, but wind up settling with someone more serious, intellectual and unconventional. The partner of a Leo tends to be more political and socially conscious than he or she is, and more libertarian. When you marry a Leo, mastering the freedom-loving tendencies of your partner will definitely become a life-long challenge – and be careful that Leo does not master you.

Aquarius sits on Leo's 7th house of love cusp. Thus if Leos want to realize their highest love and social potential they need to develop a more egalitarian, Aquarian perspective on others. This is not easy for Leo, for 'the king' finds his equals only among other 'kings'. But perhaps this is the solution to Leo's social challenge – to be 'a king among kings'. It is all right to be regal, but recognize the nobility in others.

Home and Domestic Life

Although Leos are great entertainers and love having people over, sometimes this is all show. Only very few close friends will get to see the real side of a Leo's day-to-day life. To a Leo the home is a place of comfort, recreation and transformation; a secret, private retreat – a castle. Leos like to spend money, show off a bit, entertain and have fun. They enjoy the latest furnishings, clothes and gadgets – all things fit for kings.

Leos are fiercely loyal to their family and, of course, expect the same from them. They love their children almost to a fault; they have to be careful not to spoil them too much. They also must try to avoid attempting to make individual family members over in their own image. Leos should keep in mind that others also have the need to be their own people. That is why Leos have to be extra careful about being over-bossy or over-domineering in the home.

Horoscope for 2026

What or who are you fighting for, Leo? This is the big question for 2026 and why your totem for the year is 'the Crusader'. For the first time in 12 years, Jupiter, the planet of beliefs and conviction, enters your sign. In addition to beliefs and conviction, Jupiter also rules growth and expansion, so pencil that into your 2026 plans. Jupiter in your sign motivates you to get clear on your message and your calling. Given it's the planet which rules belief systems, having routine spiritual practices as a means to ground and centre yourself will be integral in 2026. And this is especially true for Leo as Saturn, the planet of discipline and hard work, and Neptune, the planet of dreams and spirituality, both enter your spirituality sector at the start of the year (and will stay there all year). Saturn will stay in this sector until 2028, and Neptune will stay there until 2032/2033.

In addition to spirituality, another area of life with a heavy emphasis in 2026 is love and partnership. Pluto, the planet of transformation, has already begun its 19-year journey through this chart sector for Leo. In 2026, the north node also enters and spends 18 months co-present with Pluto, come the end of July. Where the north node goes, it brings increase. It also brings eclipses, which are evolutionary transits that stimulate growth through scrutiny and shake-ups. How to navigate all this cosmic energy is detailed below in the love and social life section of this Horoscope.

Uranus, the planet of innovation, instability and individuality, leaves Leo's career sector and enters its social life and friendship sector on April 25th. Uranus loves surprises, so be open to new friendship circles or professional networks popping into your orbit. Also, be open to new mediums for immersing yourself in circles or groups. Jupiter in your sign auspiciously aligns with Uranus on July 21st making the summer the ideal time for expanding social circles this year. As the Crusader, a necessary way to temperature-test new circles or groups is being intentional about vetting for an alignment of values early on.

For a quarterly view of the year ahead, the first quarter features a heavy focus on spirituality, higher education and relationships. The second quarter brings social life and groups of friends to the forefront. The third quarter focuses on self-image and self-improvement, while the final quarter of 2026 features the overarching theme of identifying purpose, and also has a focus on home and family dynamics.

Health (1st/6th/12th houses)

(Please note that this is an astrological perspective on health and not a medical one. Any health-related symptoms should be evaluated by a qualified healthcare professional.)

Your physical health planet, Saturn, is very busy this year, changing signs early in 2026 and then forming aspects with several other planets over the course of the year. Saturn moving from watery Pisces to fiery Aries is very noteworthy by itself in relation to physical health. Be mindful of inflammation this year as the Mars-ruled sign of Aries has associations with it. This is a year to be more diligent around sticking to an anti-inflammatory, gut-friendly diet. Saturn in Aries absolutely calls you to improve your exercise regime or how you approach fitness in general. Consider incorporating a martial art or some form of dynamic, movement-based exercise into your weekly exercise routines. Though Saturn isn't known for being the planet which rules fun, being in a Mars-ruled sign encourages staying kinetic, so have fun with this. That being said, Mars is not a planet to be wary of its limits, so take the advice of an expert or professional.

Your mental health planet is the Moon, the ruler of all things emotional. With the eclipses shifting into your sign this year, it's important you don't bottle up or hide your feelings. Routines which support emotional regulation, whether it be breathwork, journalling, yoga, etc., are highly recommended, especially during the eclipse seasons this year (February/March and August). Keeping a 'Moon Journal' and tracking how your mood is influenced by the lunar phases is also recommended.

Here are the specific areas of the body to focus on this year:

- Heart: this is a perennial area of focus for Leo as your sign rules this part of the body in medical astrology. Leo season starts off this year with your planetary ruler, the Sun, facing off with transformative Pluto. If you've been meaning to get a medical check-up, treat Leo's season as your invitation to do so.
- Face and head: your physical health planet, Saturn, enters Aries in February, which is the sign which rules these parts of the body in medical astrology. Being diligent around a facial skincare routine is strongly recommended. Actively reducing muscle tension in the head and jaw through massage or other therapies is also recommended.
- Thighs and buttocks: your physical health planet Saturn will enter and transit the chart sector associated with this part of the body. Dynamic stretching of these areas prior to exercise, and static/cooldown stretching post-workout, are recommended.

Love and Social Life (5th/7th/11th houses)

This is an important year for relationships for Leo. Starting in February, there's a solar eclipse in your partnership sector on the 17th. As a reminder, eclipses are evolutionary transits which catalyse change through scrutiny and shake-ups. This eclipse occurs as Mars, the planet of drive, assertion and carnality, and Pluto, the planet of power and transformation, are both present in your partnership sector. Expect sparks to fly and be ready to welcome changes in this area of life this year. Regardless of your partnership status, one important aspect of this cosmic weather is forcing you to confront and reassess how you approach interpersonal conflict.

Mars and the eclipse would also support spontaneity as a means of keeping a relationship fresh, so be open to grabbing a weekend off with your significant other and taking a quick trip.

July is also a very important month in the realm of partnership for Leo for a couple of reasons. Firstly, Saturn, your partnership planet, forms aspects to Uranus, Neptune and Pluto between the 20th and 21st. Collectively, we'll feel societal shifts over the summer. For you, Leo, you can anticipate reverberations of these noteworthy transits in your relationships. The cosmic weather of July centres around reinforcing the structure of existing partnership or core values which will inform future partnership. The following week, the north node enters your partnership sector for the first time in 18 years. The north node brings an increase to the chart sector it occupies. A big part of this transit focuses around parting with aspects of your temperament or personality which no longer serve you and stifle you in relationships.

Your social life sector remains relatively neutral as Uranus exits it in April and no other slow-moving planet occupies it this year. Mars will transit this chart sector for about six weeks, from June 29 to August 12, bringing some kinetic energy to this space. Mars in your social life sector strongly supports you scheduling more time for social activities and recreation. Your social life planet, Mercury, will turn retrograde three times this year. Each Mercury retrograde period is an invitation to reflect on how you feel both during and after spending time with your various friend groups. Mercury will be retrograde from February 25 to March 20, June 29 to July 23 and October 24 to November 13.

Career and Finances (10th/2nd/8th houses)

Your career planet is Venus, which remains relatively neutral for most of the year until it turns retrograde in October. The Venus retrograde period, which occurs from October 3 to November 13, is a time to pause and reflect not only on how successful you've been in achieving your 2026 career goals, but also to assess if you're on track in carving out the legacy you want to leave. The Venus retrograde question for Leo really is, 'What do you want to be remembered for?' Venus will be retrograde in Libra for the first half of its retrograde period, highlighting the importance of collaboration and having allies in the pursuit of achieving larger career goals. After eight years of transiting your career sector (since 2018), Uranus shifts out of this area of your chart. The period of Uranus in this chart sector is usually typified by either sudden career shifts, instability or innovation in the career space. It would serve you to reflect on where you were in your career journey prior to 2018 and where you are now.

Financially, the most noteworthy time of year is late winter/early spring, given there's a lunar eclipse in this chart sector on March 3. This eclipse occurs concurrently with your finance planet, Mercury, being retrograde between February 25 and March 20. Eclipses are scrutinizing events, so it's best to be intentionally frugal going into the spring. If you've been meaning to create additional streams of income, it's recommended to do your planning work during the retrograde period and then launch the endeavour after Mercury turns direct again. Your finance planet will be retrograde two more times, from June 29 to July 23 and from October 24 to November 13. The same recommendation around launching financial endeavours applies to these retrograde periods as well.

Home and Domestic Life (4th house)

This is a more neutral area of life in 2026 as your home and domestic life planet, Mars, does not turn retrograde this year. That being said, Mars will be transiting other important chart sectors which relate back to its domain of home and family life. From January 24 to March 3, Mars will be in your partnership sector. If you've been meaning to cohabit with a partner, this astrological transit is a strong invitation to do so. If you already live with a significant other, it's important to note that Mars brings conflict and all things kinetic. In one respect, Leo is known for its roar, so it'll be important for you to respond thoughtfully and not react if provoked. In another respect, this transit functions as a potent invitation to spice up the relationship or go on an adventure together. If you're single, Mars supports forward momentum and efforts to put yourself out there.

There are no outer planets transiting this chart sector, but Mercury and Venus will both be retrograde in this sector from the end of October (from the 24th for Mercury, and from the 25th for Venus) until November 13. Retrograde periods are times for reflection and reconfiguration. Treat this as an opportunity to assess the lay out of your living space or to revisit necessary conversations with those you live with.

Self-improvement (1st/3rd/5th/9th houses)

Being open to the evolutionary energy of 2026 is a major part of Leo's self-improvement in 2026. As the north node enters Aquarius on July 27, the south node enters your own sign at the same time. The south node brings with it eclipses and the push to shed beliefs, attitudes and ways of conducting yourself that no longer serve you. August is an important month for growth in this regard as there is a solar eclipse in Leo on the 12th and Jupiter (occupying your sign) finds harmony with Saturn, which rules responsibility and structure, on the 31st. Your totem this year is the Crusader, so identifying which self-held beliefs empower you in your pursuits and which send you on false quests is a necessary task this year.

Tied to this is how you communicate. Venus is your communication planet and will be retrograde at the end of the year from October 3 to November 13. While the retrograde period of course encourages reflection on interpersonal communication, the ways in which you communicate to yourself must also be addressed during this period. Part of what the south node calls on you to shed is limiting patterns of communication with yourself. Jupiter conjoins the south node at the end of Venus's retrograde, on November 12, further prompting you to address this.

Month-by-month Forecasts

January

> Best Days Overall: 9-13
> Most Stressful Days Overall: 23-27
> Best Days for Love: 22-25
> Best Days for Money: 1-4
> Best Days for Career: 6-9
> Power Word: Regime

Happy New Year, Leo! The new year starts off in a clichéd fashion with a focus on physical health and wellness, given that Mercury enters Capricorn on the 1st. That being said, an arguably more prominent focus at the very start of the year is mental wellness, with the Full Moon in Cancer shining brightly on the 3rd. The link between physical health and mental wellbeing is a strong theme of this lunation for you. Your planetary ruler, the Sun, conjoins joyously with Venus on the 6th. This transit supports efforts you're taking to organize and plan for the year ahead. This is further emphasized by the Sun meeting up with Mars on the 10th. Don't let this energy get you too riled up though – slow and steady wins the race, sweet Lion.

The New Moon in Capricorn on the 18th is the astrological event of January to work with if you're seeking to make adjustments and changes to your diet, fitness or your overall regime. Capricorn is a sign known for its endurance, so if you are modifying or adding to this area of life, be wise about incorporating these changes in small increments so they stick. Habits take time and patience to form. The next day, the Sun moves into your polar sign, Aquarius. Aquarius season is your annual spotlight on partnership and one-to-one relationships. A concentration of energy revolving around this area of life quickly builds with Mercury, Venus and Mars all entering the sign between the 18th and the 24th.

All four of these planetary bodies conjoin with Pluto, the ruler of transformation, between the 22nd and 27th. Pluto is known for its edgy energy which catalyses growth or changes in direction. It's paramount you practise self-compassion during this period as these transits are known to heighten the inner critic. After oscillating between Pisces and Aries all last year, Neptune formally enters and stays in Aries on the 26th, where it will stay until 2039. More information on how this transit influences you on the personal level can be found in the overview of your Horoscope above.

February

Best Days Overall: 20-24
Most Stressful Days Overall: 14-18
Best Days for Love: 17-20
Best Days for Money: 2-5
Best Days for Career: 21-25
Power Word: Address

It's February, Leo! This month's cosmic weather kicks off with a brilliant Full Moon in your sign on the 1st. The emotional focus of this lunation centres around how you partner with yourself. Are you your biggest supporter or often the first detractor? Moreover, this Full Moon seeks for you to embrace all aspects of what makes your individuality. Only you are uniquely you, Leo! On the 5th, Mercury squares off with Uranus. This transit has the tendency for people to speak without a filter or without thinking. Take extra care to be intentional with your choice of words around this date. Venus follows suit, finding tension with Uranus on the 8th. Uranus rules individuality, instability and sudden changes. This transit typically inspires a level of spontaneity in partnership and further reinforces the importance of embracing what makes you unique.

Just like Neptune, Saturn spent all last year bouncing between Pisces and Aries last year. On the 13th, Saturn joins Neptune by entering Aries and will stay in the fire sign for roughly two and a half years. Saturn in Aries functions as an audit of your spirituality or guiding philosophies, which are either supporting or preventing you from achieving the major goals you're seeking to achieve. February also features the first eclipse of 2026, on the 17th. As a reminder, eclipses are evolutionary transits which shake things up through scrutiny or tension. This eclipse encourages growth around partnership for Leo, regardless of partnership status. If you're single, this eclipse will have you re-evaluating how you feel about this. If you're partnered, it's likely you'll be pushed to address or work on underlying needs you have that have currently been unaddressed.

The next day, the Sun enters Pisces. Pisces's season is your annual spotlight on joint finances. Do you know how your money is influenced by or intertwined with others? This question is a focal point of Mercury's first retrograde period, which begins on the 26th. This Mercury retrograde could also have you confronting anxieties or insecurities which are inhibiting your ability to form relationships or connect with others.

March

Best Days Overall: 5–8; 30–31
Most Stressful Days Overall: 25–29
Best Days for Love: 7–10
Best Days for Money: 18–22
Best Days for Career: 4–7
Power Word: Connect

March begins on the heels of a volatile alignment between Mars and Uranus. Doubling down on your grounding practices is vital given that this occurs in the thick of the year's first eclipse season. The second eclipse of 2026 occurs on the 3rd and is a lunar eclipse in Pisces. This eclipse is firstly financial in nature, so it's best to adopt a frugal mindset over the next few weeks. This eclipse also features a recitation of the Mercury retrograde theme around confronting insecurities in order to evolve. Be gentle with yourself if you're feeling the growing pains, Leo.

The Sun in Pisces finds harmony with Jupiter on the 5th, which is one of the most bubbly transits of the last few months. This transit encourages you to regulate your emotions through doing something kind and caring for yourself. Venus in Aries conjoins with Neptune on the 7th and with Saturn on the 8th. These transits encourage you to take time to immerse yourself in nature to ground or centre yourself. If this isn't possible, carving out time to walk around your neighbourhood, or just limiting screen time, would suffice.

The New Moon in Pisces occurs on the 18th. This lunation ushers in a new emotional cycle around utilizing spirituality to connect with others. On the 20th, Aries's season begins and gifts you the end of the first Mercury retrograde period of the year. Mercury will take a few weeks to be up and running at full steam, though, so be patient. The Sun meets up with Saturn on the 25th, making you take stock of your to-do list. Venus enters Taurus at the end of the month. Venus in Taurus is the first career-oriented transit of the year for Leo. Venus is the planet of values, so it would be wise to take stock of whether your current career aligns with your values system as upcoming transits during Taurus's season will put this under closer scrutiny. Venus in Taurus also supports appreciating and pampering your five senses to be grateful and splendorous.

April

Best Days Overall: 14–18
Most Stressful Days Overall: 23–27
Best Days for Love: 2–5
Best Days for Money: 8–12
Best Days for Career: 27–30
Power Word: Spicy

Aries's season continues on the 1st with the Full Moon in Libra. This lunation centres around communication for you, Leo. Do you feel as though you can speak your truth in your more intimate relationships? Mars enters Aries resulting in a build-up of fire energy which revs your engine. That being said, Mars will meet up with Saturn on the 19th. This transit is notorious for restless feelings. Remember Leo, your productivity does not equal your worth. Before this meeting between Mars and Saturn, Mercury only adds to the build-up of fire energy by also entering Aries, on the 14th.

The New Moon in Aries occurs on the 17th. On the day of the New Moon, the Sun, the Moon, Mercury, Mars, Saturn and Neptune will all be in Aries. Talk about spicy energy! This lunation will likely have you itching to be productive and to get things done. However, with Mars's meeting with Saturn only two days away, it'd be better to channel this energy into organizing or planning for once you get the astrological green light (in about a week or so). The New Moon also inspires dreaming big, as Mercury harmoniously aligns with Neptune on this date as well.

On the 19th, the Sun enters Taurus. Taurus season is your annual spotlight on career and legacy. Taurus season starts off with a cosmic traffic jam as Mars meets up with Saturn on this day. Mars conjoining with Saturn often has the feeling of being stuck in traffic. Don't let the restlessness get under your skin. This transit is only compounded by Mercury also meeting up with Saturn the next day. On the 24th, Venus enters Gemini, encouraging you to immerse yourself in the groups and communities which uplift you. On the 25th, Uranus formally enters Gemini, where it'll stay until 2032/2033. More information about how Uranus in Gemini defines your year can be found in your annual report above. The 25th also features the Sun squaring off with Pluto. April ends with the prompt to shed aspects of your identity which no longer serve you.

May

Best Days Overall: 18–22
Most Stressful Days Overall: 1–4; 26
Best Days for Love: 28–31
Best Days for Money: 9–13
Best Days for Career: 16–19
Power Word: Verbalize

May follows the trend of the previous months by leading with a Full Moon, this time in watery Scorpio. This Full Moon encourages nesting and resting in your home. Recharge, reset and get ready for a busy summer, Leo! Mercury finds tension with Pluto just as Mars squares off with Jupiter on the 5th. This double dose of tension actually supports putting on your detective hat and asking questions, if you're trying to get to the bottom of something. There's a lot of kinetic energy to tap into with the Mars transit, so lean in and check some items off your to-do list. On the 13th, Mercury finds harmony with Jupiter, supporting any important communication, written or verbal, you need to take care of.

On the 16th, the New Moon in Taurus ushers in a new emotional cycle around career and legacy. This lunation functions as a mid-year check-in on the goals you've set out to accomplish this year. Have you made substantial progress? Do you need to adjust either how you're approaching trying to achieve these goals or the goals themselves? Mars enters Taurus two days later, supporting career drive and ambition. Venus enters Cancer on the 18th, reminding you that even if this summer is very social, you need to balance that with some solo recharging time as well.

On the 20th, the Sun enters chatty Gemini. Gemini's season is your annual spotlight on social life. Prioritize making memories with the people you love! Mars squares off with Pluto, which is an edgy transit emphasizing your relationship with anger and conflict. Be open to what is brought to your attention. On the 31st, there's a Blue Moon (a second Full Moon) in Sagittarius. This lunation emphasizes romance, recreation or creative self-expression for you, Leo. It asks the question, 'Is the balance between work and play in your life askew towards the former?' If so, what will it take to intentionally carve out time for recreation or to enjoy a creative hobby? Lean into the social element of Gemini season and find time for adventure and fun.

June

Best Days Overall: 13-16; 30
Most Stressful Days Overall: 25-29
Best Days for Love: 5-9
Best Days for Money: 8-12
Best Days for Career: 10-13
Power Word: Patterns

Stay focused, Leo! June starts off with Mercury, freshly in Cancer, finding tension with Neptune. This transit is often associated with your head being too much in the clouds and not focused on what's in front of you. There's a celebratory alignment between Venus and Jupiter in Cancer on the 10th. This transit strongly supports rest and relaxation for you. Venus then quickly enters your sign a few days later on the 13th. Venus in Leo is a resplendent transit which supports creative or romantic endeavours for you. Venus is also the planet which rules aesthetics, so this transit is also an invitation to entertain a makeover if you've been contemplating one.

The New Moon in Gemini occurs on the 14th and is an opportune time to immerse yourself in new communities or professional organizations. If you're a writer or giving a speech, this lunation also supports efforts with communication. Venus finds harmony with Uranus, supporting spontaneous adventures with friends on the 16th. However, Venus finds serious tension with Pluto two days later. This transit can rile up feelings of unworthiness or insecurity, so double down on your self-compassion this week, Leo.

The Sun enters Cancer on the 21st, ushering in your annual spotlight on emotional wellness. Make sure you're prioritizing your peace this Cancer season. The end of June is just a preview into how busy the rest of the summer will be, astrologically speaking. On the 29th, Mercury turns retrograde again, in Cancer. This retrograde period will likely have you reflect on the patterns and behaviours you often practise which either support or detract from your mental health. Unhealthy coping mechanisms will also be scrutinized by this transit. The final piece of cosmic weather for June is also health-oriented – the Full Moon in Capricorn. This lunation draws your focus to your physical wellness over the first six months of the year. This lunation also draws attention to how organized or disorganized your weekly fitness routines currently are. With the summer being the most notable season astrologically, it's important you have your ducks in a row, Leo.

July

Best Days Overall: 19–22
Most Stressful Days Overall: 26–30
Best Days for Love: 29–31
Best Days for Money: 12–15
Best Days for Career: 5; 17–19
Power Word: Shifting

It's almost your season, Leo! July also happens to include the most noteworthy astrology of 2026, so we have a lot to discuss. The astro-weather kicks off with Mars conjoining with Uranus on the 4th. Mars and Uranus together are like a cosmic powder keg, so be mindful that others (or yourself) may fly off the handle quicker than normal. This transit is also associated with literal explosions as well, so, if you're handling anything flammable or explosive around this date, take extra precautions. Venus enters Virgo on the 9th, which is the first transit to begin a cosmic focus towards finances. More financial transits will arise over the next couple of months. Venus in Virgo supports planting proverbial seeds where your money could grow. Explore new streams of income or investment opportunities.

As mentioned in earlier monthly Horoscopes, two of the slowest-moving planets, Uranus and Neptune, both changed signs this year. These two planets harmoniously align with each other on the 15th and then Uranus does the same with Pluto (who moved into Aquarius a couple of years ago). It is very rare for all three planets to aspect each other like this! These transits speak to important societal shifts around technology and its influence on daily life. On the personal level, these aspects speak to the moments you can or should make a big shift in your own life. Jupiter, the planet of growth and conviction, follows suit and harmoniously aligns to Neptune and Uranus on the 20th and 21st respectively. As the gas giant does this, it also finds tension with Pluto. Astrology is about cycles and these transits function as personal and societal check-ins on what growth and development has taken place since 2020.

On the 22nd, your season begins! Leo season is your annual spotlight on your relationship with yourself. It is recommended you select a couple of words you seek to grow into this year and integrate them into some sort of journal or intention-setting prac-tice. The Sun mimics Jupiter and forms the same aspects to all three slow-moving planets, further emphasizing the personal metamorphosis this summer is calling you to embody.

August

Best Days Overall: 1-7
Most Stressful Days Overall: 10-15; 28-29
Best Days for Love: 14-18
Best Days for Money: 22-26
Best Days for Career: 16-20
Power Word: Eclipse

August begins on the heels of a bright Full Moon in Aquarius which brought an emotional focus to partnership. Regardless of partner-ship status, a major theme of this lunation to carry into August is the role your individuality and ability to be authentically yourself plays in whether you're content with this area of life right now. On the 6th, Venus, the planet of intimacy, moves into Libra, a sign often associated with partnership or collaboration. Libra is repre-sented by the scales and is the sign signifying balance. Balance is what you should be striving for this month, Leo, as it is eclipse season once again.

The 7th through to the 10th features a few productive transits to lean into if you have a long to-do list. Don't spread yourself too thin though, because the first eclipse of the month is a solar eclipse in your own sign on the 12th! Eclipses in your sign are often felt in the physical body. Pace yourself and intentionally prioritize wellness this month when possible. This eclipse also draws an emotional focus towards how you seek to be seen by others. Leo doesn't just seek the spotlight for the heck of it; the sign genuinely cares about being understood and the intimacy that develops through such a connection. Mercury opposes Pluto on this day, which compounds the edginess of the eclipse. With Mars transiting Leo's emotional wellness sector, it's extra important that you strive for a balance between social and solo time.

Last month, the south node moved into your sign, ushering in an 18-month universal prompt to shed aspects of your identity which no longer serve you. The first check-in of this transit occurs on the 22nd when the Sun (in the final degree of your sign) conjoins with the south node. Be open to what you let go of over the next year and a half. Virgo's season kicks off on the same day, which is your annual spotlight on finances. The month concludes with the final eclipse of the year, a lunar eclipse in Pisces. This eclipse encourages you to break away from belief systems or philosophies which fearmonger or contribute to your anxiety.

September

Best Days Overall: 26–30
Most Stressful Days Overall: 17–21
Best Days for Love: 24–28
Best Days for Money: 5–9
Best Days for Career: 12–16
Power Word: Slow

September begins with Jupiter and Saturn finding harmony with one another. This transit is ideal for launching new initiatives. On the macro-level, Jupiter and Saturn aspects correlate to news surrounding countries and their economies. This transit is arguably ubiquitously financial on the macro and individual level. With the Sun spotlighting finances for you as it is, this is the opportune time to review your existing budget and make any necessary adjustments. Conducting a financial review is also important because Venus enters Scorpio on the 10th. The reason why this is important to note is that it means Venus is slowing down in readiness for its retrograde in a few weeks. In modern astrology, Venus rules personal finances, so any Venus retrograde period would inherently be a time when spending practices are scrutinized.

The New Moon in Virgo furthers the astrological emphasis on finances for you, Leo. The ruler of this lunation, Mercury, finds tension with Neptune on the 12th, highlighting that you may not be fully aware of everything going on with your finances, or may be viewing them through rose-tinted glasses. If you've never worked with a financial planner or some kind of expert, this New Moon is an opportune time to do so. The Sun in Virgo finds harmony with Mars in Cancer on the 14th. While normally associated with productivity, for Leo this alignment actually supports rest as a means to ensure endurance or sustainability with your existing routines. On the 16th, Venus squares off with Pluto for the first of three times over the next four months. Venus and Pluto finding tension tends to rile up insecurities or your inner critic. Self-compassion is fundamental over the next few months with Venus's retrograde being imminent.

Libra's season begins on the 22nd bringing your annual spotlight on your patterns of communication. There's more to be discussed about this next month with the Venus retrograde. On the 26th, the Full Moon in Aries lights up the night sky. This Full Moon is spiritual in nature for Leo. Moreover, this Full Moon enquires if a trip or voyage could be a much-needed medium for reflection or a shift in perspective. Immersing yourself in nature is also recommended as a means to ground yourself or to combat an overactive mind.

October

Best Days Overall: 9–10; 13–17
Most Stressful Days Overall: 3–4; 26–31
Best Days for Love: 7–10
Best Days for Money: 15–18
Best Days for Career: 5–9
Power Word: Reflect

October's astrology begins with Venus turning retrograde on the 3rd. Venus will begin its retrograde in Scorpio and then re-enter Libra later this month. All Venus retrograde periods function as values and relationship audits or re-examinations. Venus's retrograde in Scorpio has a family emphasis for Leo or an emphasis on relationships within the home. Retrograde periods are reflection periods, so just be aware of what comes up in these dynamics over the next six weeks. The beginning of October will likely feel a little extra heavy, given that Mercury and Mars find tension with Pluto on the 3rd and the Sun and Saturn do the same on the 4th. It would behove you to monitor how reactive you're being during the first week or so of the month.

October 10 features the New Moon in Libra. This lunation ushers in a new emotional cycle around how you communicate with yourself. Do you struggle with being extra self-critical? This New Moon encourages you to start off on a new foot with how you speak to yourself. Venus and Mars finding tension hours after this lunation also highlights the importance of enforcing boundaries (if possible) around how family members or those living within the home communicate with you, if they speak to you in a way you don't appreciate.

Venus once again squares off with Pluto on the 20th, marking the second chapter in the story started last month about bringing to your attention lingering insecurities that are impacting your self-esteem. Be mindful of what comes up around this date and be gentle with yourself. On the 23rd, the Sun moves into Scorpio. Scorpio's season is your annual spotlight on home and domestic life. The next day, Mercury turns retrograde again, this time in

Scorpio. Communication with family and those who live within the home is the primary aspect of life up for review with this retrograde period. This is further enforced by Venus's re-entry into Libra on the 24th. The month concludes with a noticeable Full Moon in Taurus on the 26th. This lunation draws an emotional focus to career and legacy. What do you want to be remembered for, Leo?

November

Best Days Overall: 15–18; 29–30
Most Stressful Days Overall: 8–12
Best Days for Love: 24–27
Best Days for Money: 26–29
Best Days for Career: 3–6
Power Word: Energize

Hi, Leo! There are only two weeks left of both retrogrades currently going on – you got this! With both Mercury and Venus retrograde together, planning is better supported than execution. If you have any sort of endeavour to launch, it would be best to wait until after the 13th if possible. The New Moon in Scorpio occurs on the 9th and ushers in a new emotional cycle around home and domestic life. This lunation would be the opportune time to re-energize the home through redecoration or reorganization of your living space. Emotions could very well be running high with this lunation as Mars is very close to conjoining with Jupiter. This combination of astrological weather supports being careful with how you wield your words.

On the 13th, Mercury and Venus both turn direct and end their retrograde periods. Remember, just because they are no longer retrograde doesn't mean they will be functioning optimally immediately – give it a couple of weeks before you can consider the retrogrades to be completely behind you. Mars officially meets up with Jupiter on the 16th in your sign, further supporting having a filter in place when you speak. If you felt especially restless or stifled during the two retrograde periods, this week will have you feeling antsy to make up for lost time. The astrology of the middle of this month calls for patience above all else, Leo.

On the 22nd, the Sun moves into Sagittarius. Sagittarius's season is your annual spotlight on creativity and romance. The Full Moon in Gemini on the 24th encourages you to spend time with those friends who validate your emotions and accept you for who you are. Mars moves into Virgo the next day. This transit is financial for Leo and is often associated with extravagant spending. Adopting a frugal mindset for at least the next couple of weeks is recommended. November ends with a productive alignment between the Sun and Saturn. This is one of the final really productive transits of the year, so lean into this energy if you have lots more to accomplish.

December

Best Days Overall: 21–25
Most Stressful Days Overall: 6–10
Best Days for Love: 16–20
Best Days for Money: 11–15
Best Days for Career: 1–4
Power Word: Dream

It's the end of the year, Leo – happy December! The cosmic weather for the month kicks off with Venus moving back into Scorpio now that it's done with its retrograde period. This transit encourages intentionally carving out time in your schedule for quality time with family or those you live with. Moreover, this is an opportune time to make your living space warmer and more inviting. Venus rules splendour and intimacy, so in this configuration would support making your space more cosy. The 5th features an always chaotic alignment between Mars and Uranus. You can feel this transit a few days before and after it is exact as well. This transit is associated with explosive discourse. Similar to my recommendation in July, Mars and Uranus interacting is also literally associated with explosions and fire, so if you're handling anything flammable or explosive around this date, please be extra cautious.

Mercury in Sagittarius finds harmony with Neptune on the 7th and the New Moon in Sagittarius occurs on the 8th. This combination of astrological energy makes for very dreamy vibes. This is an ideal time to create a vision board or goal set for next year. Moreover, this is also creative energy to lean into any creative hobbies or outlets which bring you pleasure. Venus squares off one final time with Pluto, reinforcing the importance of prioritizing pleasure around this date. Venus then finds harmony with Mars on the 12th, which is an opportune transit for romantic endeavours. Cuddle up with your special someone or take yourself on a fun date. Venus finding harmony with Mars is also helpful for more intimate relationship building as well.

On the 21st, the Sun moves into Capricorn, starting your annual spotlight on physical health and wellness. The second Full Moon in Cancer of the year occurs on the 23rd and spotlights the link between physical wellness and emotional wellbeing. Regulate your body to regulate your mind, Leo. Mercury moves into Capricorn on the 25th, further drawing your attention to physical wellness. The last week of the year does not feature productive energy, so utilize this downtime in a way supportive of your body and mind.

Virgo

♍

THE VIRGIN

Birthdays from
August 22
to September 22

Personality Profile

VIRGO AT A GLANCE

Element – Earth

Ruling Planet – Mercury
  Career Planet – Mercury
  Love Planet – Jupiter
  Money Planet – Venus
  Planet of Home and Family Life – Jupiter
  Planet of Health and Work – Saturn
  Planet of Fun, Entertainment, Creativity and Pleasure – Saturn
  Planet of Sexuality – Mars

Totem – the Exorcist

Colours – earth tones, ochre, green

Colour that promotes love, romance and social harmony – aqua blue

Colour that promotes earning power – jade green

Gems – agate, hyacinth

Metal – quicksilver

Scents – lavender, lilac, lily of the valley, storax

Quality – mutable (= flexibility)

Quality most needed for balance – a broader perspective

Strongest virtues – mental agility, analytical skills, ability to pay attention to detail, healing powers

Deepest needs – to be useful and productive

Characteristic to avoid – destructive criticism

Signs of greatest overall compatibility – Taurus, Capricorn

Signs of greatest overall incompatibility – Gemini, Sagittarius, Pisces

Sign most helpful to career – Gemini

Sign most helpful for emotional support – Sagittarius

Sign most helpful financially – Libra

Sign best for marriage and/or partnerships – Pisces

Sign most helpful for creative projects – Capricorn

Best Sign to have fun with – Capricorn

Signs most helpful in spiritual matters – Taurus, Leo

Best day of the week – Wednesday

Understanding a Virgo

The virgin is a particularly fitting symbol for those born under the sign of Virgo. If you meditate on the image of the virgin you will get a good understanding of the essence of the Virgo type. The virgin is, of course, a symbol of purity and innocence – not naïve, but pure. A virginal object has not been touched. A virgin field is land that is true to itself, the way it has always been. The same is true of virgin forest: it is pristine, unaltered.

Apply the idea of purity to the thought processes, emotional life, physical body, and activities and projects of the everyday world, and you can see how Virgos approach life. Virgos desire the pure expression of the ideal in their mind, body and affairs. If they find impurities they will attempt to clear them away.

Impurities are the beginning of disorder, unhappiness and uneasiness. The job of the Virgo is to eject all impurities and keep only that which the body and mind can use and assimilate.

The secrets of good health are here revealed: 90 per cent of the art of staying well is maintaining a pure mind, a pure body and pure emotions. When you introduce more impurities than your mind and body can deal with, you will have what is known as 'dis-ease'. It is no wonder that Virgos make great doctors, nurses, healers and dieticians. They have an innate understanding of good health and they realize that good health is more than just physical. In all aspects of life, if you want a project to be successful it must be kept as pure as possible. It must be protected against the adverse elements that will try to undermine it. This is the secret behind Virgo's awesome technical proficiency.

One could talk about Virgo's analytical powers – which are formidable. One could talk about their perfectionism and their almost superhuman attention to detail. But this would be to miss the point. All of these virtues are manifestations of a Virgo's desire for purity and perfection – a world without Virgos would have ruined itself long ago.

A vice is nothing more than a virtue turned inside out, misapplied or used in the wrong context. Virgos' apparent vices come from their inherent virtue. Their analytical powers, which should be used for healing, helping or perfecting a project in the world, sometimes get misapplied and turned against people. Their critical faculties, which should be used constructively to perfect a strategy or proposal, can sometimes be used destructively to harm or wound. Their urge to perfection can turn into worry and lack of confidence; their natural humility can become self-denial and self-abasement. When Virgos turn negative they are apt to turn their devastating criticism on themselves, sowing the seeds of self-destruction.

Finance

Virgos have all the attitudes that create wealth. They are hard-working, industrious, efficient, organized, thrifty, productive and eager to serve. A developed Virgo is every employer's dream. But until Virgos master some of the social graces of Libra they will not even come close to fulfilling their financial potential. Purity and perfectionism, if not handled correctly or gracefully, can be very trying to others. Friction in human relationships can be devastating not only to your pet projects but – indirectly – to your wallet as well.

Virgos are quite interested in their financial security. Being hard-working, they know the true value of money. They do not like to take risks with their money, preferring to save for their retirement or for a rainy day. Virgos usually make prudent, calculated investments that involve a minimum of risk. These investments and savings usually work out well, helping Virgos to achieve the financial security they seek. The rich or even not-so-rich Virgo also likes to help his or her friends in need.

Career and Public Image

Virgos reach their full potential when they can communicate their knowledge in such a way that others can understand it. In order to get their ideas across better, Virgos need to develop greater verbal skills and fewer judgemental ways of expressing themselves. Virgos look up to teachers and communicators; they like their bosses to be good communicators. Virgos will probably not respect a superior who is not their intellectual equal – no matter how much money or power that superior has. Virgos themselves like to be perceived by others as being educated and intellectual.

The natural humility of Virgos often inhibits them from fulfilling their great ambitions, from acquiring name and fame. Virgos should indulge in a little more self-promotion if they are going to reach their career goals. They need to push themselves with the same ardour that they would use to foster others.

At work Virgos like to stay active. They are willing to learn any type of job as long as it serves their ultimate goal of financial security. Virgos may change occupations several times during their professional lives, until they find the one they really enjoy. Virgos work well with other people, are not afraid to work hard and always fulfil their responsibilities.

Love and Relationships

If you are an analyst or a critic you must, out of necessity, narrow your scope. You have to focus on a part and not the whole; this can create a temporary narrow-mindedness. Virgos do not like this kind of person. They like their partners to be broad-minded, with depth and vision. Virgos seek to get this broad-minded quality from their partners, since they sometimes lack it themselves.

Virgos are perfectionists in love just as they are in other areas of life. They need partners who are tolerant, open-minded and easy-going. If you are in love with a Virgo do not waste time on impractical romantic gestures. Do practical and useful things for him or her – this is what will be appreciated and what will be done for you.

Virgos express their love through pragmatic and useful gestures, so do not be put off because your Virgo partner does not say 'I love you' day in and day out. Virgos are not that type. If they love you, they will demonstrate it in practical ways. They will always be there for you; they will show an interest in your health and finances; they will fix your sink or repair your video recorder. Virgos deem these actions to be superior to sending flowers, chocolates or Valentine cards.

In love affairs Virgos are not particularly passionate or sponta-neous. If you are in love with a Virgo, do not take this personally. It does not mean that you are not alluring enough or that your Virgo partner does not love or like you. It is just the way Virgos are. What they lack in passion they make up for in dedication and loyalty.

Home and Domestic Life

It goes without saying that the home of a Virgo will be spotless, sanitized and orderly. Everything will be in its proper place – and don't you dare move anything about! For Virgos to find domestic bliss they need to ease up a bit in the home, to allow their partner and children more freedom and to be more generous and open-minded. Family members are not to be analysed under a micro-scope; they are individuals with their own virtues to express.

With these small difficulties resolved, Virgos like to stay in and entertain at home. They make good hosts and they like to keep their friends and families happy and entertained at family and social gatherings. Virgos love children, but they are strict with them – at times – since they want to make sure their children are brought up with the correct sense of family and values.

Horoscope for 2026

In 2026, Virgo's totem is 'the Exorcist' because one of your primary tasks this year will be confronting and clearing longstanding anxi-eties and fears which have haunted you. Saturn, the planet of responsibility and hard work, shifts into Aries for the first time in roughly 29 years. In doing so, it enters the sector of Virgo's chart which houses fears, insecurities and personal demons. Neptune, the planet of dreams and illusion, will make the same shift and be co-present in this chart sector for the first time in your lifetime. Neptune takes about 160 years to orbit the zodiac, so the last time it entered Aries was in the 1860s! These two cosmic entities work together to invite you to see through the illusion of fear. What once may have kept you safe, may now just be keeping you stuck, dear Virgo.

Mercury, Virgo's ruling planet, will turn retrograde three times in 2026. Those periods are from February 25 to March 20, June 29 to July 23 and October 24 to November 13. Mercury retrograde periods are especially felt by Virgo because of this rulership. This year it's important to note that all three retrograde periods will entirely occur in water signs. As a result, Mercury will be in the element of water for over half the year (202 days). This matters to Virgo as it indicates 2026 is a more emotional and intuitive year than normal. You'll find that if you take on the challenge of tackling your insecurities and freeing yourself from the fears that haunt you, your intuitive prowess will grow this year in tandem with your confidence.

Jupiter, the planet of expansion and conviction, will enter Leo at the very end of June. Leo is the sign of the zodiac which rules the heart, encouraging you to be intentional about how you care for your heart this year, metaphorically and literally. Virgo is a fine-detail-oriented sign often associated with a heavy self-critical nature. Being ruled by Mercury, Virgo often finds the balance between head and heart strongly tips in favour of logic and reason. This year give your head a break and let your heart shine.

For a quarterly view of the year ahead, the first quarter of 2026 centres on the overarching theme of confronting fears and insecurities. The second quarter introduces a focus on career. The third quarter includes mental health and wellness as a dominant theme, while the final quarter of the year echoes the overarching theme of tackling anxiety while also highlighting patterns of communication and relationship with finances.

Health (1st/6th/12th houses)

(Please note that this is an astrological perspective on health and not a medical one. Any health-related symptoms should be evaluated by a qualified healthcare professional.)

Pluto, the planet of transformation, has been present in your physical health sector for the last 18 months and will continue to occupy the sector this year. However, it won't be there alone this year. For the first time in 18 years, the north node will enter this space. Where the moon's nodes go, so do eclipses! Your first eclipse in the sector for nine years occurs on February 13. As a reminder, eclipses are evolutionary transits which catalyse change through scrutiny and shake-ups. It is strongly recommended to take diet, exercise and physical health routines more seriously this year. The north node may not enter this chart sector until July 27, but the eclipse early in 2026 will reverberate for several months. With Saturn being your physical health planet, discipline and hard work really is the only pathway to create abundance in this area of life.

Just as the north node enters your physical health sector, the south node enters your mental health sector at the same time. The south node brings the innate need to shed with it to the area of life corresponding to the chart sector it is transiting through. As mentioned above, 2026 is the year you're called on to confront the anxieties or insecurities that have haunted you and held you back for some time. The eclipse in your mental health sector occurs on August 12, just two weeks after the south node moves into your mental health sector. It is imperative that if you accept this need to fight your fears, you don't do it alone. Work with an expert in navigating anxiety, grief or fear to shed your stifling patterns of thought and evolve in 2026.

Here are the specific areas of the body to focus on this year:

- Digestive system: this is a perennial area of focus for Virgo as your sign rules this part of the body in medical astrology. With your physical health planet Saturn entering Aries this year, be mindful around the consumption of inflammatory foods this year. Consult your doctor if you feel as though a particular type of food causes this reaction in you.
- Thighs, knees and buttocks: Saturn, your physical health planet, enters the chart sector which correlates to these parts of the body. Proper stretching of muscle groups in these parts of the body prior to weightlifting, athletics or general exertion is strongly recommended.

- Face and head: Saturn enters Aries which is the sign ruling over these parts of the body. Monitoring how tension is stored in the face and head is recommended for Virgo this year. If the storage of excessive stress is felt in these areas, professional craniosacral massage could be a good outlet. Also important to be mindful around grinding your teeth or clenching your jaw when stressed this year.

Love and Social Life (5th/7th/11th houses)

Your partnership planet is Jupiter, which spends the first half of the year in your social life sector. So, the planet which rules your partnership sector transits your social life sector for six months of the year, from January 1 to June 30! If you're single, there's merit in being open to finding romantic connections within or through your social circles. And if you're partnered, this transit could rather indicate there's abundance to be unlocked through immersing yourself in a social group with your partner. Examples are any community centred around a hobby you both enjoy, such as running, sports, arts, culture or gaming. Moreover, Mercury will turn retrograde in your partnership sector early in 2026, from February 25 to March 20. Mercury's retrograde is a time to rethink, re-evaluate and regroup in this realm. For those Virgos already partnered, this is more an audit on the efficacy and health of how you and your partner communicate. If you're single, this is a similar audit centred around how communication either enables or hinders you in dating.

Jupiter exits your social life sector and enters your mental health sector on June 30, where it stays until the end of the year. Given that Jupiter is in Leo during this time, the emphasis will be on listening to your heart for the latter half of 2026. This is easier said than done for Virgo as it is undoubtedly one of the most cerebral signs. Regardless of partnership status, it is vital you tune into what your heart wants/needs in this area of life. If you do encounter relationship turbulence during this time, couples therapy would be a recommended heart-centred strategy to navigate this dynamic. There will be one eclipse in this chart sector, on August 28, promoting evolution in how you approach partnership.

Speaking of eclipses, your social life planet is the Moon, so eclipse seasons are always noteworthy times of year for you in this realm. As a reminder, eclipses are evolutionary transits which stimulate growth through scrutiny. Tread lightly in your social circles during the two eclipse seasons (February/March and August). Eclipses tend to make people extra reactive, so do your best to respond thoughtfully instead of just reacting if you encounter provocation during these times. Eclipses catalyse growth, so these periods can also yield new social circles that support your holistic growth. This is especially the case for the first eclipse season given that Jupiter, the planet of growth and expansion, will be present in this chart sector.

Career and Finances (10th/2nd/8th houses)

This is a noteworthy year for career as Uranus enters and stays in your career sector. Uranus dipped in and out of this chart sector last year when it briefly occupied Gemini, but now it fully shifts into the sign in April and stays there for the next six or seven years. Uranus is the planet of innovation, individuality and instability. Often when Uranus transits an area of the chart related to career, an individual feels the sudden urge to change or reinvent whatever long-term career goals they're chasing. It is important to note that Uranus will spend an extensive time in this area of the chart and astrology is a study of cycles, so 2026 is just the initial foray into conceiving what these changes may look like for you. Even if the career industry doesn't change, the astrology could indicate a new or unexpected change in your role within the industry.

Your finance planet, Venus, will be retrograde this autumn and will actually transit the finance sector for half the year. A Venus retrograde is an opportune time to reflect on and revise your existing budget or spending practices. More specifically, this retrograde centres on reviewing how your wealth may be intertwined or dependent on others. Is this sustainable? This is especially the case as Saturn and Neptune will enter the area of Virgo's chart related to joint finances early in the year.

Home and Domestic Life (4th house)

This is a relatively neutral area of life for Virgo in 2026 as there are no planets transiting this sector, nor are there any eclipses in this area of the chart. Jupiter is your home and domestic life planet and it will spend the first part of 2026 in Cancer. Cancer, the sign of home and family, is strongly influenced by the energy and layout of its living space. This year is a good year to revise or revitalize the energy of your home. Jupiter spends the second part of 2026 in Leo. Your home planet in Leo strongly supports making changes to your living space which brighten it or make it a warmer, more inviting space. The astrology of 2026 asks you to assess how factors such as the amount of light or how you use the surface area of your living space affects your psyche and emotional wellbeing.

Self-improvement (1st/3rd/5th/9th houses)

Since 2025, there have been eclipses in your sign, signalling the call to shed old ways of being and to evolve. Your totem this year is the Exorcist because the astrology of this year signifies you are in the thick of confronting anxieties and outdated patterns of thought and behaviour which keep you stuck. The eclipse in your sign this year occurs on March 3, and will be felt for several months after the fact. August is a noteworthy month for tackling your personal demons as your planetary ruler, Mercury, faces off with Pluto on the 10th. Other important times of year related to this are May 5 and October 2, which are additional dates when these two planets tensely aspect each other. April 18, May 19 and September 12 are days when these two planets harmoniously align.

Your communication planet, Mars, will not turn retrograde this year, clearing the path for you to make substantial strides in using your voice to advocate for your needs. Mars finds harmony with your planetary ruler on April 20, promoting supportive communication with yourself around this date. Mars will be in your sign from November 26 to December 31, giving you a boost of energy to accomplish your 2026 goals at the end of the year. Your spirituality planet is Venus, which rules values, worthiness and pleasure. How do your spiritual routines reinforce your innate worthiness? This is a question that you'll be confronted with this year, especially when Venus is retrograde in October and November. Your spirituality planet will be co-present with Jupiter from May 19 to June 13, promoting expanding upon the routines which root you in your beliefs and convictions.

Month-by-month Forecasts

January

Best Days Overall: 1–6
Most Stressful Days Overall: 21–27
Best Days for Love: 15–19
Best Days for Money: 8–11
Best Days for Career: 19–22
Power Word: Create

Happy New Year, Virgo! The cosmic weather for 2026 starts off with a focus on romance, creativity and socializing. Mercury, the planet of thinking and communication, enters Capricorn on the first day of the year and shifts into Virgo's creativity and romance sector. The Sun and Venus are already present in this sector, so consider this a noteworthy build-up of energy. The first Full Moon in Cancer of the year occurs on the 3rd and illuminates social life for you. What friend groups feel like home to you? This Full Moon highlights how comfortable you are being yourself in the various groups and organizations you're immersed in. This will be a theme in this summer's astrology as well. The Sun meets up with Venus and Mars where all three planets find tension with Jupiter between the 6th and the 10th. This time can feel very kinetic, albeit frenetic, so don't spread yourself too thin.

The New Moon in Capricorn is a great lunation for identifying forms of creative self-expression or recreation which can be used as grounding agents this year when times get tough or overwhelming. Everyone needs time to play, Virgo, even you. New Moons indicate the start of a new emotional cycle, with this lunation highlighting the importance of integrating more pleasure or scheduled recreation into your regime.

Speaking of routines, the Sun moves into Aquarius on the 19th. Aquarius season is your annual spotlight on routines and physical wellness. Aquarius's season starts off very noticeably for the second year in a row with the Sun (and Mercury) conjoining with Pluto. Pluto rules shedding, unearthing and transformation in astrology, so is not known for being particularly cuddly. The first eight days or so of Aquarius's season centre around shedding beliefs or behaviours which may be deleterious to your physical health. On the 26th, after oscillating back and forth between Pisces and Aries all last year, Neptune finally enters Aries where it'll stay until 2039. More information about how this influences your year can be found above in the annual overview of your Horoscope.

February

Best Days Overall: 12–16
Most Stressful Days Overall: 25–28
Best Days for Love: 10–14
Best Days for Money: 4–8
Best Days for Career: 1–5
Power Word: Wellbeing

It's Aquarius season, Virgo! The Full Moon in Leo leads the astrology of this month off on the 1st. This Full Moon centres around emotional wellness for you. Do you allow yourself to feel your feelings and do you have healthy strategies to process emotions? This Full Moon brings to your attention your relationship with mental health and will probably encourage you to take steps to best support yourself. This will be a big theme in August, too, so take note of what comes up this month regarding this area of life. On the 5th, Mercury finds tension with Uranus right before entering Pisces the next day. Uranus brings a destabilizing energy to any planet it aligns with, so plan on carving out time this first week or so of the month for nesting, resting and recharging. Venus finds similar tension with Uranus on the 8th, further reinforcing this message as a necessity.

Venus enters your polar sign, Pisces, on the 10th. Venus in Pisces is heavily partnership-oriented for you. If you're single, this could be an opportune time to put yourself out there, before Mercury's retrograde at the end of the month. If you're partnered, schedule some quality time for you and your special someone before the retrograde at the end of the month. Pisces brings a softer and more cuddly energy to Venus, so lean into that. Just like Neptune, Saturn finally enters Aries after bouncing back and forth all last year, on the 13th. This transit defines your year and is analysed in detail in your annual overview above.

Boom! On the 17th we have our first eclipse of the year! Eclipses stimulate growth through tension or shake-ups. For you, this eclipse centres around physical wellness. The spotlight from the Sun in Aquarius I described last month is much more scrutinizing under this eclipse. This eclipse can also be felt in the physical body, so please be as kind to your body as possible. Pisces's season begins on the 18th, providing your annual spotlight on partnership. Speaking of which, Mercury turns retrograde at the end of the month and centres around existing and past partnerships. Be prepared for people from your past to resurface in some capacity as a means to remind you who you were when you knew them and how much you've grown.

March

Best Days Overall: 22-27
Most Stressful Days Overall: 1-5
Best Days for Love: 27-31
Best Days for Money: 6-10
Best Days for Career: 9-13
Power Word: Attitude

March begins on the heels of a volatile meet up between Mars and Uranus. Mars and Uranus together are figuratively (and potentially literally) explosive, so do your best to filter your words if you feel provoked into conflict during this first week. Also, be extra cautious if handling anything flammable around the first few days of the month. The second eclipse of the year occurs on the 3rd and centres around partnership for you, Virgo. If you're single, this eclipse will have you examining your attitudes towards partnership and will likely prompt you into action if you're actively seeking it. If you're partnered, this eclipse will scrutinize this dynamic by highlighting whether all of your needs are being met.

The Sun harmoniously aligns with Jupiter on the 5th, making it the perfect day to spend quality time with friends. Venus enters Aries the next day and then meets up with Neptune on the 7th and Saturn on the 8th. These transits encourage you to check in on your budgeting behaviour going into the spring. Mercury finds harmony with Jupiter on the 9th which supports reconnecting with friends or loved ones you may have lost touch with.

On the 18th, the New Moon in Pisces ushers in a new emotional cycle around partnership. This lunation occurs as Mercury is in its final days of being retrograde in the same sign. This lunation firstly functions as a final check-in on Mercury's retrograde and the themes that have come up around partnership. Moreover, this New Moon is an ideal time to reminisce with loved ones about experiences which bonded you together. On the 20th, the Sun enters Aries and it's the start of a new astrological year! Mercury also ends its retrograde period on the same day. While Aries is known for being quick and pioneering, the first few days of Aries's season centres around the 'slow and steady wins the race' philosophy. This is especially the case around the 25th when the Sun meets up with Saturn. This is a noteworthy year because throughout 2026 all the slow-moving outer planets will align or find tension with one another. On the 28th, Saturn finds harmony with Pluto. This transit more affects wider society through economic shifts, but it can be productive on the personal level for launching new business ventures.

April

Best Days Overall: 26–30
Most Stressful Days Overall: 18–22
Best Days for Love: 13–16
Best Days for Money: 1–4
Best Days for Career: 9–13
Power Word: Worth

April's astrology kicks off with the Full Moon in Libra on the 1st. This Full Moon further emphasizes the shift in focus to finances that occurs over the spring. If you haven't audited how your money enters and leaves your bank account, now is an opportune time to do so, Virgo. Furthermore, if your money is influenced by or intertwined with others, it's especially important to ensure that you are receiving or earning what you should. On the 9th, Mars enters pioneering Aries. Mars in Aries typically amps up the kinetic energy immediately but given that Mars meets up with Neptune on the 13th, this transit may actually have you feeling unproductive. Remember, Virgo, productivity does not equal worthiness. You are worthy regardless of if you can get your complete to-do list taken care of.

The New Moon in Aries occurs on the 17th. On this date there will be six planetary bodies in the fire sign: the Sun, the Moon, Mercury, Mars, Saturn and Neptune. That's a whole lot of fire! Be mindful that all this energy may evoke large or spicy reactions in others. Also note that the Aries, Libras, Cancers and Capricorns in your life are extra scrutinized by this build-up of cosmic energy, so do what you do best and support them, sweet Virgo. On the 19th, the Sun shifts into grounded Taurus. Taurus season is your annual spotlight on spirituality and higher education. Taurus is known for being rooted in its principles. Take the opportunity over the next few weeks to connect with and deepen your relationship to the values or tenets which guide your life.

Venus and Uranus connect at the final degree of Taurus on the 24th encouraging spontaneity, especially around planning a voyage or adventure. Venus then enters Gemini and begins to shift the cosmic focus towards career and legacy. More to come next month and in June on career. The month ends with Uranus formally entering Gemini after ping-ponging back and forth between Taurus and Gemini last year. Uranus will stay in Gemini until 2032/2033. This transit ushers in a six- to seven-year journey around career, which was discussed earlier in the annual overview.

May

Best Days Overall: 12-17
Most Stressful Days Overall: 26-30
Best Days for Love: 1-4
Best Days for Money: 21-25
Best Days for Career: 17-21
Power Word: Poise

It's May, Virgo! The cosmic weather for May features two Full Moons book-ending the month. On May 1, the Full Moon in Scorpio illuminates patterns of communication for you. This Full Moon is inquisitive and investigative in nature, so if you have questions to ask, don't censor yourself. That being said, read the room first given that Mercury, your planetary ruler and the planet of communication, finds tension with Pluto on the 5th, which can make people feel on edge around vulnerable conversations. Mars finds tension with Jupiter on the same day. The energy around the 5th is very busy, so strive for balance and poise if possible.

Mercury finds harmony with Jupiter on the 13th which supports writing and all other forms of communication. The New Moon in Taurus on the 16th is the opportune time to integrate new spiritual practices into your daily routine which can ground and centre you. It is important to get a jumpstart on these routines because the summer has the busiest energy of the year. Mercury enters chatty Gemini on the 17th and meets up with Uranus. This transit inspires 'word vomit', or people speaking without thinking!

On the 20th, the Sun enters Gemini. Gemini's season is your annual spotlight on career, public perception and legacy. Gemini season starts off a little angsty with Mars finding tension with

Pluto in the first week and making an exact tense alignment on the 26th. Mars and Pluto together often makes us grapple with deep-seated wounds. That being said, it is also a transit associated with perseverance and resilience, so do your best to lean into that component of this complex transit. Be gentle with yourself, given that Venus will also find tension with Saturn on the 28th. The month ends with the Full Moon in Sagittarius. This Full Moon spotlights the energy within your home. If you're feeling like the energy is stale, take it upon yourself to do some much-needed feng shui work. Relationships with family and those within the home are highlighted by this lunation as well.

June

Best Days Overall: 1-5
Most Stressful Days Overall: 18; 27-30
Best Days for Love: 22-25
Best Days for Money: 13-16
Best Days for Career: 7-10
Power Word: Nurture

Gemini season focuses on social life for Virgo at the beginning of this month. On the 1st, Mercury joins Venus and Jupiter by entering the same sign, Cancer. This brings a confluence of energy centred around community. The biggest ask from the astrology of June is that you feel 'at home' in the circles and groups you immerse yourself in. Venus approaches Jupiter at the start of the second week of the month and meets up with the gas giant on the 10th. The weekend before and the days leading up to the 10th are ideal times to intentionally mark time in your calendar to spend with the groups of friends that nurture and care for you. Venus enters Leo on the 13th, beginning a cosmic shift in focus towards emotional wellbeing for Virgo.

On the 14th, the New Moon in Gemini occurs. This lunation ushers in new beginnings in the area of career, legacy and public perception. If you've been seeking to be seen more by others or by the general public, this is one of the best lunar cycles to work with to plant those seeds. The same advice is true if you're seeking to evolve or pivot your current career. Venus then begins a trend which will be recited by many planets this summer where, in the span of a few days, it forms either harmonious or tense alignments with the three slowest-moving planets: Uranus, Neptune and Pluto. On the 16th, Venus finds harmony with Uranus. The next day, it does the same with Neptune. On the 18th, it finds tension with Pluto. All of these transits centre around the increasing importance of prioritizing your peace and emotional wellbeing for the remainder of the year.

On the 21st, the Sun moves into Cancer. Cancer season is your annual spotlight on social life. This summer it is vital that you have reciprocity in your friendships as you'll likely need to lean on and lend support to your community given the noteworthy astrology coming over the next couple of months. Mercury turns retrograde again, this time in Cancer. This retrograde strongly supports reconnecting with friends you may have lost touch with and with whom you'd like to reignite your relationship. This retrograde also invites you to express gratitude to those friends who are there for you through thick and thin. The month ends with Jupiter, the planet of growth and expansion, entering Leo.

July

Best Days Overall: 8-12
Most Stressful Days Overall: 19-23
Best Days for Love: 17-21
Best Days for Money: 27-30
Best Days for Career: 5-9
Power Word: Self-care

It's July, Virgo! The next two months feature some of the most noteworthy astrology of the year, so we have a lot to discuss. Mars starts things off by meeting up with Uranus on the 4th. This transit is volatile, so prepare for people to be extra reactive around this date. Moreover, please take extra precautions if you're handling fireworks or anything flammable around this date. Mars finds harmony with Pluto the next day, which is a supportive transit for launching new endeavours. Venus enters your sign on the 9th reminding you of the importance of self-care this month.

The slowest-moving planets all take a very long time to orbit the zodiac: Uranus takes about 84 years, Neptune about 160 years, and Pluto about 250 years. On the 15th, these three slow-moving bodies all begin to harmoniously align with one another, which is a rare occurrence indeed! These alignments influence societies on a macro-level. Noticeable shifts in the structure and hierarchy within countries and changes in how governments operate occur under the orb of these alignments. It is important to note that while these alignments are exact between the 15th and 18th, they've been active for a while and essentially influence the year as a whole. What's more, Jupiter, the planet of growth and expansion, follows suit on the 20th and 21st by forming aspects with these three planets. Jupiter finds harmony with Uranus and Neptune and tension with Pluto. On the personal level, these transits function as a critical check-in to see how your life has changed since 2020. Jupiter and Pluto met up three times that year and are finally opposing one another this month.

Leo's season begins on the 22nd and kicks off with Mercury ending its retrograde period the following day. The north node enters Aquarius and the south node leaves your sign and enters Leo on the 26th. The 18-month journey of shedding aspects of your identity which don't serve you has come to an end and the focus is now on physical and mental wellness. The Sun copies Jupiter's movements and forms the same aspects with the three slow-moving generational planets on the 27th. Expect emotions to run high as the moon becomes full on the 29th. This Full Moon highlights the importance of you taking care of your physical body. It's a kinetic summer, so take time to nest and rest.

August

Best Days Overall: 5–9
Most Stressful Days Overall: 26–29
Best Days for Love: 28–31
Best Days for Money: 14–18
Best Days for Career: 1–4
Power Word: Somatic

The fast-paced cosmic weather continues as the eclipse seasons roll back around this month. Before the first eclipse mid-month, Venus moves into Libra on the 6th. This is important to note because in a couple of months Venus will turn retrograde and spend part of that period in this sign. Venus will begin to slow down later this month in preparation for that event. Between the 7th and the 10th, the Sun and Venus find harmony with Pluto, supporting productivity. Mars enters Cancer on the 11th, inspiring drive and assertion in friendship groups and professional organizations.

On the 12th, the first eclipse of the month occurs in Leo. This eclipse functions as an audit of the practices and behaviours in your daily/weekly routine which support or detract from your mental health. Moreover, coping mechanisms for stress are also being scrutinized at this time. If you're feeling especially stressed this month, please reach out to those you can lean on or a mental health expert for support. This eclipse reminds you of the importance of balancing social and solo time. Mercury mimics what Jupiter and the Sun did last month and harmonizes with Uranus and Neptune while finding tension with Pluto between the 12th and the 13th. Doing somatic work – getting out of your head and into your body – is the ideal way to ground yourself at this time.

On the 22nd, it's the start of your own season. Happy birthday and happy Virgo season! Virgo season is your annual spotlight on your relationship with yourself, and now it rockets off with the final eclipse of the year, a lunar eclipse in Pisces on the 28th. This eclipse centres around partnership, both with yourself and with a significant other. If you're single, this eclipse could very well catalyse a big change in this partnership status. If you're already partnered, equity and reciprocity in your relationship is the emotional focus of this lunation. In addition to the eclipse, the Sun (and Moon) square off with Pluto between the 28th and 29th. Once again, this is a month where emotions run high: do your best to remain cool, calm and collected.

September

Best Days Overall: 11–15
Most Stressful Days Overall: 27–30
Best Days for Love: 16–20
Best Days for Money: 3–6
Best Days for Career: 7–11
Power Word: Identify

September's astrology begins on the heels of a harmonious alignment between Jupiter and Saturn. On the macro-level, this is another societal transit centring around governments and their economies. On the personal level, this is an incredibly productive transit for personal growth and manifestation. With the Sun being in your sign, this is the opportune time to identify two to three words you seek to embody and integrate them into your journalling or self-empowerment practices.

On the 10th, Venus enters Scorpio, indicating it is really slowing down and getting ready to turn retrograde. This date also features the New Moon in your sign. This lunation brings an emotional focus to new beginnings for you. In line with the prompt around growth and manifestation, work with this lunation to check in on your 2026 goals and plan how to best make use of the last quarter of the year. The Sun finds harmony with Mars and Neptune finds harmony with Pluto, motivating you to check items off your to-do list.

On the 22nd, the Sun moves out of your sign and enters Libra. Libra's season is your annual spotlight on finances, which will be scrutinized over the next couple of months with Venus's retrograde. September ends with a bright Full Moon in Aries on the 26th. This lunation draws your attention to joint ventures and finances that are shared with others. If you're looking to launch a new income stream, do so now before Venus's retrograde at the start of next month. Mars rounds out the month by entering Leo on the 27th. This transit reminds you of the importance of prioritizing your peace and enforcing boundaries. Just like a lion, it is important you stand in your power and advocate for your needs in your relationships this autumn. On the last day of the month, Mercury enters Scorpio and will begin to slow down in preparation for its retrograde next month as well. The autumn is going to be a time of reflection and review, Virgo.

October

Best Days Overall: 6-10
Most Stressful Days Overall: 2-4; 24-26
Best Days for Love: 5-9
Best Days for Money: 25-28
Best Days for Career: 13-17
Power Word: Frugal

October begins with Venus turning retrograde on the 3rd. Venus will be retrograde in both Scorpio and Libra over the next six weeks. Venus's retrogrades are always times to re-evaluate and reflect on interpersonal relationships. For you, Virgo, this Venus retrograde centres around the role communication plays in these relationships and if there are changes or adjustments you need to make or demand around communication in partnerships. This retrograde period is also significantly money-oriented for Virgo. It would be best to adopt a frugal approach over the next six weeks as spending is scrutinized. The 3rd also features Mars and Pluto finding tension with one another. Tussles with power dynamics are likely at this time. The Sun and Saturn add to this energy by finding tension on the 4th. It's best to approach the first week of this month striving for neutrality in all areas of life.

The New Moon in Libra on the 10th brings an emotional focus to finances for you. Typically, this would be the time to plant seeds for new streams of income, but with Venus's retrograde it would be better to review and revise plans for endeavours already in the works. Venus finds tension with Pluto on the 20th. This transit can heighten insecurities or anxieties related to self-esteem. It may be best to limit screen time or behaviours that result in comparison with others. Trust that you are running your own race, Virgo.

Scorpio's season begins on the 23rd and amplifies the spotlight on communication. This is compounded by Mercury turning retrograde in Scorpio the next day. Venus re-enters Libra on the 25th, bringing the Venus-retrograde theme to focus more on spending and budgeting habits. A bright Full Moon in Taurus is live on the 26th. This lunation centres around spirituality and higher education for you. You may feel the pull to get additional qualifications or training to help you in your career. This lunation also emphasizes the importance of immersing yourself in nature as a means to ground yourself.

November

Best Days Overall: 15-19
Most Stressful Days Overall: 4-8
Best Days for Love: 21-25
Best Days for Money: 27-30
Best Days for Career: 24-27
Power Word: Balancing

Both the Mercury and Venus retrograde periods have roughly two weeks left, so November is essentially divided into two halves: the first half with the retrogrades and the second half with the planets having turned direct. The New Moon in Scorpio on the 9th functions as an important check-in on assessing what the major themes of the retrogrades ended up being for you. New Moons are fertile times for planting seeds for new beginnings, so take advantage of this opportunity to enter the final part of the year on the right foot. On the 13th, both planets end their retrograde periods. Yay! Remember though, neither planet will be back to their normal speeds for a couple of weeks, so there still may be some technological, communication or transport wonkiness.

Mars conjoins with Jupiter in Leo on the 16th, which livens up the energy of November. For you, this transit stresses balancing social and solo time going into Sagittarius's season. This transit is helpful for productivity, especially after the two retrogrades. The Sun finds tension with Mars on the 20th, so don't spread yourself too thin.

The Sun enters Sagittarius on the 22nd, bringing your annual spotlight on home and domestic life. Family dynamics will be a focus of the cosmic weather over the next month. On the 24th, the Full Moon in Gemini lights up the night sky and finds harmony with Neptune. This is a visionary lunation inspiring you to dream up your goals for 2027. You spent the last six to eight weeks in reflection mode, so use what you learned to guide what your next steps will be. The Sun finds tension with Uranus on the 26th, reminding you of the importance of owning and taking pride in what makes you unique. The last transit of the month is a harmonious alignment between the Sun in Sagittarius and Saturn in Aries. This transit supports work you are currently doing to conquer deep-seated fears and anxieties which stifle your ability to chase certain goals. With 2027 around the corner, it's time to declare who it is you seek to become.

December

Best Days Overall: 11–15
Most Stressful Days Overall: 8–9; 29–31
Best Days for Love: 23–26
Best Days for Money: 12–15
Best Days for Career: 14–18
Power Word: Cheerleader

Happy December, Virgo! You've made it to the end of the year! Sagittarius's season continues with Venus entering Scorpio on the 4th. Venus is providing one last check-in on interpersonal communication for you this year. That being said, with Mars and Uranus squaring off on the 5th you should know that the cosmic weather is like a powder keg right now, so it's best to think before you speak. Mercury in Sagittarius finds harmony with Neptune on the 7th, which supports carving out time to express gratitude to those you consider family.

The New Moon in Sagittarius on the 9th ushers in a new emotional cycle around home and domestic life. Family dynamics are a big emotional focus at this time. With Venus finding tension with Pluto the next day, it is important to seek external validation at this time. Sagittarius is typically represented by the cheerleader or coach, so this is the time to be your own biggest cheerleader. Mercury finds harmony with Saturn on the 11th, supporting organization and planning out your goals for next year. Remember, Jupiter is currently centring its expansive energy around emotional wellness for you. This would be an ideal time to nest, rest and plan for next year. Venus finds harmony with Mars the next day, supporting hunkering down indoors and building intimacy with a special someone. This could also be applied to spending quality time with your closest friends.

The Sun enters Capricorn on the 21st. Capricorn season is your annual spotlight on creative self-expression and romance. This year's second Full Moon in Cancer occurs on the 23rd. This Full Moon hearkens back to the first one in January and encourages you to reflect on which friends have been there for you from the start of the year to the end. Prioritize those relationships in 2027. The last week of the year is slow, astrologically speaking, and arguably a little frustrating if you're trying to get a lot done. Lean into the universal cues to take it easy and get ready for an exciting 2027!

Libra

THE SCALES

Birthdays from
September 23
to October 22

Personality Profile

LIBRA AT A GLANCE

Element – Air

Ruling Planet – Venus
   Career Planet – Moon
   Love Planet – Mars
   Money Planet – Mars
   Planet of Communications – Jupiter
   Planet of Health and Work – Jupiter
   Planet of Home and Family Life – Saturn
   Planet of Spirituality and Mental Health – Mercury

Totem – the Dancer

Colours – cerulean, jade green

Colours that promote love, romance and social harmony – carmine, red, scarlet

Colours that promote earning power – burgundy, red-violet, violet

Gems – carnelian, chrysolite, coral, emerald, jade, opal, quartz, white marble

Metal – copper

Scents – almond, rose, vanilla, violet

Quality – cardinal (= activity)

Qualities most needed for balance – a sense of self, self-reliance, independence

Strongest virtues – social grace, charm, tact, diplomacy

Deepest needs – love, romance, social harmony

Characteristic to avoid – violating what is right in order to be socially accepted

Signs of greatest overall compatibility – Gemini, Aquarius

Signs of greatest overall incompatibility – Aries, Cancer, Capricorn

Sign most helpful to career – Cancer

Sign most helpful for emotional support – Capricorn

Sign most helpful financially – Scorpio

Sign best for marriage and/or partnerships – Aries

Sign most helpful for creative projects – Aquarius

Best Sign to have fun with – Aquarius

Signs most helpful in spiritual matters – Gemini, Virgo

Best day of the week – Friday

Understanding a Libra

In the sign of Libra the universal mind – the soul – expresses its genius for relationships; that is, its power to harmonize diverse elements in a unified, organic way. Libra is the soul's power to express beauty in all of its forms. And where is beauty if not within relationships? Beauty does not exist in isolation. Beauty arises out of comparison – out of the just relationship between different parts. Without a fair and harmonious relationship there is no beauty, whether it in art, manners, ideas or the social or political forum.

There are two faculties humans have that exalt them above the animal kingdom: their rational faculty (expressed in the signs of Gemini and Aquarius) and their aesthetic faculty, exemplified by Libra. Without an aesthetic sense we would be little more than intelligent barbarians. Libra is the civilizing instinct or urge of the soul.

Beauty is the essence of what Librans are all about. They are here to beautify the world. One could discuss Librans' social grace, their sense of balance and fair play, their ability to see and love another person's point of view – but this would be to miss their central asset: their desire for beauty.

No one – no matter how alone he or she seems to be – exists in isolation. The universe is one vast collaboration of beings. Librans, more than most, understand this and understand the spiritual laws that make relationships bearable and enjoyable.

A Libra is always the unconscious (and in some cases conscious) civilizer, harmonizer and artist. This is a Libra's deepest urge and greatest genius. Librans love instinctively to bring people together, and they are uniquely qualified to do so. They have a knack for seeing what unites people – the things that attract and bind rather than separate individuals.

Finance

In financial matters Librans can seem frivolous and illogical to others. This is because Librans appear to be more concerned with earning money for others than for themselves. But there is a logic to this financial attitude. Librans know that everything and everyone is connected and that it is impossible to help another to prosper without also prospering yourself. Since enhancing their partner's income and position tends to strengthen their relationship, Librans choose to do so. What could be more fun than building a relationship? You will rarely find a Libra enriching him- or herself at someone else's expense.

Scorpio is the ruler of Libra's solar 2nd house of money, giving Libra unusual insight into financial matters – and the power to focus on these matters in a way that disguises a seeming indifference. In fact, many other signs come to Librans for financial advice and guidance.

Given their social grace, Librans often spend great sums of money on entertaining and organizing social events. They also like to help others when they are in need. Librans would go out of their way to help a friend in dire straits, even if they have to borrow from others to do so. However, Librans are also very careful to pay back any debts they owe, and like to make sure they never have to be reminded to do so.

Career and Public Image

Publicly, Librans like to appear as nurturers. Their friends and acquaintances are their family and they wield political power in parental ways. They also like bosses who are paternal or maternal.

The sign of Cancer is on Libra's 10th career house cusp; the Moon is Libra's career planet. The Moon is by far the speediest, most changeable planet in the horoscope. It alone among all the planets travels through the entire zodiac – all twelve signs and houses – every month. This is an important key to the way in which Librans approach their careers, and also to what they need to do to maximize their career potential. The Moon is the planet of moods and feelings – Librans need a career in which their emotions can have free expression. This is why so many Librans are involved in the creative arts. Libra's ambitions wax and wane with the Moon. They tend to wield power according to their mood.

The Moon 'rules' the masses – and that is why Libra's highest goal is to achieve a mass kind of acclaim and popularity. Librans who achieve fame cultivate the public as other people cultivate a lover or friend. Librans can be very flexible – and often fickle – in their career and ambitions. On the other hand, they can achieve their ends in a great variety of ways. They are not stuck in one attitude or with one way of doing things.

Love and Relationships

Librans express their true genius in love. In love you could not find a partner more romantic, more seductive or more fair. If there is one thing that is sure to destroy a relationship – sure to block your love from flowing – it is injustice or imbalance between lover and beloved. If one party is giving too much or taking too much, resentment is sure to surface at some time or other. Librans are careful about this. If anything, Librans might err on the side of giving more, but never giving less.

If you are in love with a Libra, make sure you keep the aura of romance alive. Do all the little things – candle-lit dinners, travel to exotic locales, flowers and small gifts. Give things that are beautiful, not necessarily expensive. Send cards. Ring regularly even if you have nothing in particular to say. The niceties are very important to a Libra. Your relationship is a work of art: make it beautiful and your Libran lover will appreciate it. If you are creative about it, he or she will appreciate it even more; for this is how your Libra will behave towards you.

Librans like their partners to be aggressive and even a bit self-willed. They know that these are qualities they sometimes lack and so they like their partners to have them. In relationships, however, Librans can be very aggressive – but always in a subtle and charming way! Librans are determined in their efforts to charm the object of their desire – and this determination can be very pleasant if you are on the receiving end.

Home and Domestic Life

Since Librans are such social creatures, they do not particularly like mundane domestic duties. They like a well-organized home – clean and neat with everything needful present – but housework is a chore and a burden, one of the unpleasant tasks in life that must be done, the quicker the better. If a Libra has enough money – and sometimes even if not – he or she will prefer to pay someone else to take care of the daily household chores. However, Librans like gardening; they love to have flowers and plants in the home.

A Libra's home is modern, and furnished in excellent taste. You will find many paintings and sculptures there. Since Librans like to be with friends and family, they enjoy entertaining at home and they make great hosts.

Capricorn is on the cusp of Libra's 4th solar house of home and family. Saturn, the planet of law, order, limits and discipline, rules Libra's domestic affairs. If Librans want their home life to be supportive and happy they need to develop some of the virtues of Saturn – order, organization and discipline. Librans, being so creative and so intensely in need of harmony, can tend to be too lax in the home and too permissive with their children. Too much of this is not always good; children need freedom but they also need limits.

Horoscope for 2026

Libra's totem for 2026 is 'the Dancer' because partnership and creativity are two of the most highlighted areas of life for you this year. Saturn, the planet of responsibility, shifts into Aries and enters your partnership sector in February, where it will stay for the next two and a half years. That's not all. Neptune, the planet of dreams and aspirations, also shifts into Aries and enters your partnership sector for the first time in your lifetime. It takes Neptune about 160 years to orbit the zodiac, so the last time it was in Aries was in the 1860s! These two planets co-present in your chart's partnership sector place a heavy emphasis on themes of partnership in 2026, regardless of if you're single or in a relationship. More to be explored below in that section of this Horoscope.

Creativity is another area of focus for Libra as the north node shifts into Aquarius for the first time in 18 years and enters this chart sector. It is important to note that this chart sector also pertains to romance and children, so those themes are fair game too. Where the north node goes it brings increase, and eclipses, to that chart sector. Eclipses are evolutionary transits which stimulate growth through scrutiny and shake-ups. Just as a dancer expresses themselves through this modality of creativity, you are being prompted to amplify how you creatively self-express as well. In times when you're feeling in flux, lean into creativity as a means to ground yourself.

Your planetary ruler is Venus, the planet of values, worthiness and intimacy. Venus will turn retrograde from October 3 to November 13. Venus's retrograde periods are strongly felt by Libras, so anticipate feeling a bit of a slowdown during this period of time. Venus's retrogrades are important because they function as audits and recalibrations of value systems and the ways we demonstrate that we value ourselves. For you, Libra, this Venus retrograde will partially occur in your own sign (from October 25 to November 13). The entire Venus retrograde period, and especially the portion occurring Libra, is heavily relationship-oriented for you. If you're single, you can anticipate shifts and changes to how you feel about or desire partnership. If you're partnered, existing dynamics in the relationship that are outdated or need to evolve will have to be addressed to ensure the sustainability of the partnership.

For a quarterly view of your year ahead, the first quarter of 2026 centres around partnership, creativity and children. The second quarter focuses on your social life and spirituality. The third quarter once again highlights romance and creativity. And the final quarter centres around your relationship with yourself and how you approach partnership.

Health (1st/6th/12th houses)

(Please note that this is an astrological perspective on health and not a medical one. Any health-related symptoms should be evaluated by a qualified healthcare professional.)

Libra's physical health sector has been occupied and busy for several years with Saturn and Neptune both being in Pisces. That all changes in 2026 when both planets shift into Aries and leave this sector within the first two months of the year. Saturn is the planet of restriction and discipline, so this shift might orient you towards overindulgence or being lax with your fitness. Definitely be mindful of a potential spike in such behaviour. Your physical health planet, Jupiter, shifts into heart-centred Leo on April 25. For Libra, Jupiter in Leo promotes turning physical wellness into a community or social gathering. Group fitness classes, cooking classes or meal-prepping with friends are all examples of ways you can work with Jupiter in Leo to stay on top of your physical health. There is a lunar eclipse in this sector on August 28, so bookmark the week leading up to and following this lunation to take it easy as eclipses can be felt in the body.

Libra's mental health sector has had the south node occupying it since the beginning of last year, and where it will stay until July 27. Moreover, there were two eclipses in this sector last year and a third occurring early in 2026, on March 3. Mental health is once again a noteworthy focus area for Libra. The potential for an overactive mind is high with this astrology and practising somatic forms of grounding – whether breathwork, meditation or another somatic technique – is strongly recommended. Your mental health planet, Mercury, will be retrograde in all three water signs this year. This is an important year to not suffer in silence if you're navigating any sort of struggle with mental health. Seek out the support of a licensed expert or lean on your community members you trust to help you through tough periods.

Here are the specific areas of the body to focus on this year:

- Kidneys: this is a perennial area of focus for Libra as your sign rules this part of the body in medical astrology. Be mindful around how your diet impacts the kidneys and consider incorporating supportive food for the kidneys such as fish, red bell peppers and berries.
- Heart: your physical health planet Jupiter enters Leo which rules this part of the body in medical astrology. Take special care to avoid behaviour known to be deleterious to the heart. Similarly to supporting the kidneys, identify and incorporate heart-healthy foods into your diet this year.
- Knees and ankles: your physical health planet, Jupiter, will begin transiting the chart sector ruling these parts of the body in traditional astrology. Being intentional about dynamic stretching prior to exercise and recovery stretching after the fact is strongly recommended. Leg massages and other recovery practices are also sincerely advised this year.

Love and Social Life (5th/7th/11th houses)

It takes two to tango, Libra. Your totem for 2026 is the Dancer, given the emphasis placed on partnership this year. Saturn, the planet of responsibility and hard work, will enter your partnership sector as it shifts into Aries on February 13. The last time Saturn entered Aries on its orbit of the zodiac was 1996! Saturn isn't the only planet entering this chart sector; Neptune, the planet of dreams and rose-tinted glasses, also enters Aries this year, on January 26. Neptune takes about 160 years to orbit the zodiac so this will be the first time this has occurred in your lifetime. What's especially interesting is that generally, these two planets have contradictory energies. Saturn is all about reality and restriction while Neptune is all about fantasy and faith. However, both these planets will be in your polar sign, Aries. Aries's mantra is 'I with myself'. Therefore, a major component for how this energy plays out for you centres around your relationship with yourself as you navigate partnership. Regardless of partnership status, self-effacing thoughts and patterns of behaviour will likely rise to the surface for you to address and push aside. There's great potential for you to carve out a long-lasting sustainable partnership if you're willing to sit in vulnerability and discomfort when prompted. Moreover, your partnership planet, Mars, will not turn retrograde this year, providing you with the kinetic energy you need to make moves in this area of life.

Social life is an area ripe with abundance in 2026 for Libra as Jupiter, the planet of growth and expansion, enters this chart sector for Libra on June 30. Jupiter forms several aspects to all the slow-moving planets in July (see July's monthly forecast, below) and to Saturn in August, meaning this summer is especially a time to grow this area of life. Actively investing in your community will pay dividends down the road. Your social life planet is the Sun, so pay attention to how each new solar season influences the vibe of your social life. The Sun conjoins with Jupiter in July as well, setting this month up for expansion in this area of life.

Career and Finances (10th/2nd/8th houses)

The first half of 2026 is noteworthy for career for Libra as Jupiter will still be occupying this chart sector while it transits the remainder of Cancer. Jupiter is the planet of growth and expansion – traditionally known as 'the Greater Benefic'. However, modern astrologers have come to learn that Jupiter is more an augmenter. This means Jupiter brings 'more is more' to the chart sector's area of life it is transiting. Essentially, if you've been cultivating the seeds for a promotion or some form of career growth, Jupiter is the rain which will water those seeds and allow them to grow. However, if there is already existing turbulence within the office or in your career in general, Jupiter will function as a magnifying glass. Enter 2026 with a refined and well-thought-out plan regarding the steps you want to take in your career, and the planet of abundance will work with you to achieve them.

Aside from Jupiter, the only noteworthy transit in this sector is the Mercury retrograde period occurring from June 29 to July 23. Mercury's retrograde periods are times of reflection and redirection. Utilize this retrograde by reviewing and revising the plan around achieving your career goals you entered into 2026 with. It's also important to note that the Moon is your career planet, so the eclipse seasons (February/March and August) are noteworthy times of scrutiny and evolution in this area of life.

Finances is an area of life that remains relatively neutral for Libra in 2026 (until the end of the year). Your financial planet is Mars, which does not turn retrograde in 2026. The important event regarding finances is Venus, the modern ruler of finances, turning retrograde in the chart sector related to finances on October 3. Venus will occupy this chart sector from October 3 to October 25. October may be your solar return, Libra, but it is a month to embrace a frugal mentality towards money. Retrogrades encourage re-evaluations of the areas the retrograde planet rules. Re-evaluating your relationship towards money and how you grow your money are two themes for Libra with this Venus retrograde. During Venus's retrograde period, Mercury will also turn retrograde in this chart sector, from October 24 to November 13. While Venus rules relationships and values, Mercury rules thinking and communication. The Mercury retrograde period centres around analysing how your money is either intertwined with, dependent upon or influenced by other people.

Home and Domestic Life (4th house)

Your home and domestic life sector does not have any major transits occurring within it, but your home planet, Saturn, will form several noteworthy aspects this year. Saturn conjoins with Neptune on February 20, inspiring an early 'spring cleaning'. Mars and Saturn conjoin on April 19, bringing potential fireworks into the home or supporting physical modifications to the home like a renovation. Jupiter and Saturn harmoniously align on August 31, providing supportive energy around a move (if you've been planning on one) or making your home more inviting for guests.

It is also important to note that Saturn will be transiting your partnership sector for the majority of the year, meaning there's an inherent link between these two areas of life. If you've been meaning to make moves to share a living space with an existing partner, this transit would support this after February 13. If you've already been living with a partner, Saturn linking these two chart sectors functions as a litmus test analysing the structure and foundation of the relationship. For more on how Saturn in Aries functions in this dynamic, check out the 'Love and Social Life' section above.

Self-improvement (1st/3rd/5th/9th houses)

As mentioned in the overview of this Horoscope, creative self-expression is a major theme in 2026 for Libra. This is because the north node finally re-enters the creativity sector for Libra for the first time in about 18 years. The north node shifts into Aquarius on July 27. Prior to this, there will be a solar eclipse in this chart sector on February 17th Using creative self-expression as a means to ground yourself amid the turbulence of an eclipse season is strongly recommended. Moreover, 2026 reinforces intentionally carving out time for play as a means to offset the hustle and grind of this year. The modern ruler of your creativity sector, Uranus, enters Gemini on April 25. Finding a way to utilize technology to enhance your unique forms of creative self-expression is very much supported by Uranus's shift into Gemini.

Month-by-month Forecasts

January

Best Days Overall: 3-8
Most Stressful Days Overall: 17-22
Best Days for Love: 10-14
Best Days for Money: 20-24
Best Days for Career: 15-18
Power Word: Order

Happy New Year, Libra! The astrology of 2026 kicks off with emotional energy surrounding your career, as the night sky is lit up by the first Full Moon of the year, in Cancer, on the 3rd. This lunation encourages goal-setting for the year ahead, and is co-present in Cancer with Jupiter, the planet of growth and expansion. Honour this rich lunar energy by putting pen to paper and writing out what you seek to achieve this year or how you seek to grow. The Sun in Capricorn meets up with your planetary ruler, Venus, on the 6th. This is joyous energy encouraging socializing and prioritizing pleasure. Pleasure in moderation though – Venus and Jupiter find tension three days later, which is a transit notoriously correlated with overindulging.

This energy is further compounded by the Sun following suit on the 10th, as does Mars. Both planets finding tension with Jupiter can lead more to knee-jerk reactions and confrontation. You're represented by the scales for a reason, so strive for balance around this date. The week of the 11th is relatively neutral, so work with that and get productive with strategizing your year ahead. The New Moon in Capricorn is live on the 18th. This lunation reminds you of the importance of making sure your home is in order before venturing out to conquer the various goals you've set forward. Be open to purging excess junk or items in your home which no longer serve a useful purpose.

The next day, the Sun moves into Aquarius. Aquarius's season is your annual spotlight on creative self-expression and romance. This Aquarius season starts off a little rockily with the Sun and Venus both meeting up with transformative Pluto. Pluto rules what we bury and what needs to be unearthed, so anticipate confronting some anxieties, insecurities or behaviours which may be stifling you from wholeheartedly chasing the goals you desire to achieve. Mars follows suit a few days later and meets up with Pluto on the 27th. The energy of the end of the month centres around power dynamics in your life, and in society, which may be unequal or need to be addressed.

February

Best Days Overall: 19–23
Most Stressful Days Overall: 4–8
Best Days for Love: 1–3
Best Days for Money: 21–24
Best Days for Career: 10–14
Power Word: Outlook

It's February, Libra! February's cosmic weather begins with the Full Moon in Leo on the 1st. This lunation spotlights the communities and groups of friends you immerse yourself in. More specifically, this lunation asks the question, 'In which of these circles can you truly be 100 per cent authentically yourself?' Take it upon yourself to express gratitude to those friends who not only embrace your individuality but uplift you for it. On the 6th and the 10th, Mercury and Venus enter Pisces respectively. The astrological focus of the next month or so is shifting towards awareness of and possible alterations to your physical wellness routine. Before Mercury's retrograde at the end of this month, it would be helpful for you to make your healthy routines more concrete.

After spending all last year bouncing between Pisces and Aries, Saturn finally enters your polar sign, Aries, on the 13th. Saturn, the planet of discipline and hard work, will stay in Aries for about two and a half years. This places a broader emphasis on partnership for you for the year. More specifics are described in the annual overview, above. The first eclipse of the year occurs on the 17th and is a solar eclipse in Aquarius. This eclipse motivates you to more readily integrate creative self-expression and recreation into your routines, and also to use them as a means to emotionally regulate yourself.

The next day, the Sun moves into Pisces. Pisces's season brings your annual spotlight on health and wellness. This is especially the case because come early next month, all three personal planets – Mercury, Venus and Mars – will be in the sign, in addition to the Sun. Moreover, this Pisces season features Mercury turning retrograde and spending its entire retrograde period in the sign.

Mercury's retrogrades always centre around reflecting on patterns of thought and communication. Outlooks related to your physical body are especially up for review and revision during this transit. The month concludes with a volatile alignment between Mars and Uranus. This transit brings a frenetic or erratic energy, so double down on the poise Libras are known for at this time.

March

Best Days Overall: 22–27
Most Stressful Days Overall: 1–4; 7–8
Best Days for Love: 5–7; 20–21
Best Days for Money: 29–31
Best Days for Career: 4–7; 9–10
Power Word: Link

The astrology of March begins with Mars joining the Sun, Mercury (still retrograde) and Venus in Pisces. The next day, there's the second eclipse of the year, a lunar eclipse in Virgo. This eclipse will likely be felt mentally/emotionally for you, Libra, so make sure you're prioritizing rest and recovery for the next couple of weeks. The eclipse highlights the link between physical health and emotional wellbeing. The Sun forms a harmonious aspect with buoyant Jupiter on the 5th. This transit is great for checking items off your to-do list or for putting yourself out there if you're seeking any sort of public recognition. On the 6th, your planetary ruler Venus enters fiery Aries. Venus in Aries is a partnership-oriented aspect for you. If you're single, this is a recitation of similar themes from the day before and supportive energy for putting yourself out there (this time for the attention of prospective partners). If you're not single, this transit encourages carving out additional time for pleasure with your significant other over the next two to three weeks. Venus does bump into Saturn on the 8th, which can be a bit sobering but only further supports intentionally making time for good vibes with your special someone.

The week of the 9th kicks off with Mercury finding harmony with Jupiter. This transit supports all forms of communication, especially at work or in your career. Pisces's season concludes on the 18th with the New Moon in that sign. This lunation functions as a check-in on the themes you were confronted with around routines, diet and exercise over the last month. New Moons are ideal times for new beginnings, so take what you've learned and adjust your regime accordingly.

On the 20th, Pisces's season ends as the Sun moves into Aries and your annual spotlight on partnership. This Aries season begins with a gift – Mercury's retrograde ending on the same day. Mercury will not be moving forwards at full speed for a couple of weeks, though, so anticipate a little bit of communication, transport and technological wonkiness over the next week or so. Venus rounds out the month by entering its other favourite sign (other than yours) – Taurus. Venus in Taurus is financial in nature for Libra. This is an ideal time to survey your budget or identify new streams of income you can create.

April

Best Days Overall: 26–30
Most Stressful Days Overall: 15–19
Best Days for Love: 13–17
Best Days for Money: 1–4
Best Days for Career: 5–8
Power Word: Needs

Aries season continues with the Full Moon in your sign on the 1st. What a way to start the month, Libra! Full Moons are emotional culminations and this lunation centres around your relationship to yourself and how you've been treating yourself. Have you been your own biggest ally? This lunation encourages emotional regulation through partnering with and supporting yourself. On the 9th, Mars, the planet of drive and assertion, enters your polar sign, Aries. Mars in Aries typically brings considerable kinetic energy to all things to do with partnership and collaboration. However, given Saturn has now also moved into the fire sign, this transit initially functions as an audit around existing partnerships. If you're partnered, this is more around ensuring you get your needs met. If you're single, this is more around your drive to date and put yourself out there. Mars will meet up with Saturn on the 19th but this is the general vibe for the first two weeks of this lunation (from the 9th when Mars enters the sign).

Before the two planets officially meet, there is a New Moon in the fire sign on the 17th. It is important to note that on this date the Sun, Moon, Mercury, Mars, Saturn and Neptune are *all* in Aries. Wow! This New Moon encourages an entrepreneurial and pioneering spirit. With all the planets currently in direct motion (nothing is retrograde), this is the ideal time to launch new endeavours or to try your hand at new trades or hobbies.

The Sun enters Taurus on the 19th and given it's the day Mars and Saturn meet up, Taurus season begins slowly, which is fitting for the fixed earth sign. Taurus's season spotlights how your finances are influenced by and intertwined with others. Moreover, Taurus season encourages you to tackle long-standing fears and anxieties which keep you small or prevent you from living authentically. After spending all last year oscillating between Taurus and Gemini, Uranus finally moves into Gemini on the 25th. This transit will revolutionize the way society learns and communicates. Uranus will be in Gemini until 2032/2033, so more specifics behind how it shapes your year can be found above, in your annual Horoscope overview.

May

Best Days Overall: 12–19
Most Stressful Days Overall: 21–28
Best Days for Love: 2–5
Best Days for Money: 16–19
Best Days for Career: 10–13
Power Word: Joint

May begins on the heels of a harmonious alignment between your planetary ruler, Venus, and transformative Pluto. The astrological weather from now on through the summer is going to be pushing you to grow, shift and shed. Speaking of which, this month there's not just one but two Full Moons! The first occurs on the 1st of the month and is the annual Full Moon in Scorpio. This lunation brings your emotional focus towards finances and warns you against extravagant spending. This is because Mars, Scorpio's traditional ruler, squares off with Jupiter, the planet of growth and expansion, a few days later on the 5th. The 5th is an edgy day with this transit, plus Mercury finds tension with Pluto. Though this energy can be channelled into investigation and getting to the bottom of lingering matters, it can easily go overboard into paranoia or hypervigilance. Be gentle with yourself around this date.

The New Moon in Taurus on the 16th encourages collaborating with others, especially those you seek to become business partners with or joint creators of some new initiative. Taurus is the sign associated with the five senses, so this lunation also encourages prioritizing pleasure associated with the five senses. Carve out time to make your taste buds, sense of smell or one of the other senses happy. May's focus on spending habits is only amplified by Mars entering Taurus on the 18th. If you are in the process of co-creating new streams of income with a business partner, this transit reminds you of the importance of clear communication and contracts.

On the 20th, the Sun enters Gemini, bringing your annual spotlight on spirituality and higher education. Venus squares off with Neptune on this date, making it more likely for you to be looking through rose-tinted glasses when meeting new people or when being pitched new business proposals. If you're presented with a contract around this date, have a trusted ally review it before signing. The last week of the month leading into the second Full Moon is edgy with Mars and Pluto finding tension. Prioritize your peace, Libra. The Full (Blue) Moon in Sagittarius on the 31st brings an emotional focus to your patterns of communication. Be open to what is brought to your attention within this area of life.

June

Best Days Overall: 6-10
Most Stressful Days Overall: 15-19
Best Days for Love: 13-16
Best Days for Money: 21-24
Best Days for Career: 1-4
Power Word: Contemplate

The cosmic weather is starting to shift towards career and legacy for you, Libra. On the 1st, Mercury enters Cancer where Venus, your planetary ruler, and Jupiter are already present. Venus and Jupiter meet up in harmony on the 10th, which supports career pursuits and entrepreneurship for you. Venus and Jupiter together is also an indulgent transit so lean in and prioritize some pleasure around this date. On the 13th, Venus enters Leo. Venus in Leo supports intentionally scheduling quality time with the communities and circles of friends you most enjoy immersing yourself in.

The New Moon in Gemini on the 14th strongly encourages you to utilize journalling or some other sort of communication medium as a means to ground yourself or help you regulate your emotions. Moreover, this New Moon invites you to plan a voyage or trip which will help you gain a much-needed new perspective, or which supports spiritual contemplation. Your planetary ruler Venus finds harmony with Uranus on the 16th, with Neptune on the 17th, and tension with Pluto on the 18th. Bookmark the week of 15th to be a busy, albeit chaotic, one. Venus opposing Pluto can also stir up some deep-seated insecurities or spike self-esteem issues. Place extra emphasis on self-compassion at this time, Libra.

On the 21st, the Sun enters Cancer. Cancer's season is your annual spotlight on career and legacy. Venus finds harmony with Saturn on the 25th, supporting checking items off your to-do list. This is important as another Mercury retrograde period is imminent. On the 29th, Mercury turns retrograde in Cancer where it'll stay for the entirety of its retrograde. This retrograde centres around you reflecting on and revising career goals and aspirations. Your relationship to public perception is also under review at this time. The last day of the month features Jupiter, the planet of growth and expansion, entering Leo for the first time in 12 years. The next year is all about growing and expanding your networks, communities and circles of friends. Get ready to get social, Libra! Jupiter will stay in Leo for the next 12 months, so don't think this growth needs to be accomplished overnight.

July

Best Days Overall: 6-10
Most Stressful Days Overall: 13-15; 28-30
Best Days for Love: 19-22
Best Days for Money: 17-20
Best Days for Career: 15-18
Power Word: Hustle/Bustle

July features the most eventful cosmic weather of the year, Libra! The first week of the month features a volatile meeting between Mars and Uranus. This transit is figuratively (and literally) explosive. Do your best to think before you speak if provoked. Also, if you are handling anything flammable or explosive around the 4th, please take extra care. Mars also finds harmony with Neptune and Pluto on the 5th, supporting energetic hustle and bustle. On the 9th, your planetary ruler Venus enters caring Virgo. This transit reminds you that amid the kinetic and frenetic energy of the next seven or eight weeks, it is important to prioritize your emotional wellbeing. Striking a balance between social and solo time is pivotal this summer.

As mentioned in earlier months and in your annual Horoscope, this year featured Uranus and Neptune moving into new signs. On the 15th, the two slow-moving generational bodies associated with collective shifts harmoniously align. Moreover, Uranus also harmoniously aligns with Pluto, the slowest of the generational planets, which changed signs a couple of years ago but has now moved past the first few degrees in Aquarius. This harmonious alignment occurs on the 18th. These transits are important to note as they affect you since you are a part of the collective. Monitor shifts in how countries govern themselves and how economies change this summer. The noteworthy astrology doesn't end there though! On the 20th, Jupiter, the planet of growth and expansion, finds harmony with Neptune and tension with Pluto, followed by finding harmony with Uranus the next day. The tense transit with Pluto is actually a cosmic check-in on the ways you've grown and transformed since 2020 (the year when these planets met three times).

Leo's season kicks off on the 22nd, and when the Sun follows Jupiter's lead and forms the same aspects with Uranus, Neptune and Pluto. Embracing your uniqueness is vital at this time. The next day, Mercury ends its retrograde period. As with the Mercury retrograde in March, remember that it will take the planet a couple of weeks to be back to functioning at full speed. The Full Moon in Aquarius finds tension with expansive Jupiter on the 29th making this an extra-angsty lunation. Utilize recreation and creative self-expression to ground yourself or emotionally regulate at this time.

August

Best Days Overall: 2–6
Most Stressful Days Overall: 24–28
Best Days for Love: 3–7
Best Days for Money: 13–17
Best Days for Career: 29–31
Power Word: Pace

It's eclipse season (again), Libra! After an eventful July, the cosmic weather for this month features both of the remaining eclipses of 2026. As a reminder, eclipses are evolutionary transits which stimulate growth through scrutiny and shake-ups. Before the first eclipse occurs, your planetary ruler, Venus, enters your sign on the 6th. Venus in your sign reminds you of the importance of scheduling in pleasure amid a chaotic summer. Venus will begin to slow down later this month as it prepares to enter its own retrograde period in eight weeks' time. On the 7th, the Sun in Leo finds harmony with Saturn in Aries. This is a supportive transit for partnership, dating and outings with friends. Venus finds harmony with Pluto on the 10th, which softly supports creative endeavours you're currently undertaking.

The first eclipse of August occurs on the 12th and is a solar eclipse in Leo. On the same day, Mercury finds tension with Pluto (and harmony with Uranus and Neptune). Overall this eclipse brings noticeably fiery energy to the middle of the month. This eclipse brings an emotional focus to circles of friends and professional organizations. You may feel the push to seek out new circles or to assume additional responsibility in professional organizations you're already a part of.

On the 22nd, the Sun enters Virgo. Virgo's season provides your annual spotlight on emotional wellness and mental health. It is also the ideal time to hide away, nest and rest, Libra. The second eclipse of the month (and the final one for the year) occurs on the 28th and is a lunar eclipse in Pisces. This lunation harks back to the focus on physical health and wellness at the beginning of the year. It may very well function as an audit for how you've been treating your body this year. This eclipse can be felt in the physical body so it is very important not to overload your schedule too much at the end of this month. August ends with Jupiter and Saturn harmoniously aligning. This is a financial transit for the macroenvironment and a supportive personal transit for checking items off your to-do list.

September

Best Days Overall: 8-12
Most Stressful Days Overall: 15-20
Best Days for Love: 26-29
Best Days for Money: 27-30
Best Days for Career: 2-6
Power Word: Prepare

The energy from last month's eclipse permeates the beginning of September. Remember, Virgo season is all about balancing solo and social time for Libra. On the 10th, your planetary ruler, Venus, enters Scorpio. This is important to note because Venus is getting ready to turn retrograde in four weeks' time and is now slowing down. The 10th also features Mercury entering your sign and the New Moon in Virgo. This New Moon supports nesting, resting and rejuvenating. In medical astrology, Virgo rules the digestive system. This New Moon also supports resetting your diet or ensuring you're supporting this part of the body with what you consume.

On the 14th, the Sun finds harmony with Mars. This transit softly supports career pursuits and entrepreneurial efforts. If you plan on launching any new endeavours, do so now before Venus's retrograde period begins at the start of next month. Speaking of Venus, the love planet finds tension with Pluto for the first of three times as it prepares to go retrograde. This transit is associated with bringing to the surface insecurities which affect self-esteem and feelings of worthiness. A major part of next month's retrograde centres around your values system which anchors your sense of self.

On the 22nd, the Sun moves into your sign. Happy birthday! Next month's planetary retrogrades prompt significant reflection for you. With a new trip around the Sun imminent, identify two or three words you seek to embody and integrate them into your journalling or spiritual practices. The Full Moon in Aries spotlights partnership for you on the 26th. If you're single, be careful about rose-tinted views if you're dating at this time. If you're partnered, this lunation encourages future planning with your significant other. On the 27th, Mars enters fiery Leo. Mars in Leo emboldens you to emerge from your period of nesting and resting and chase after your remaining 2026 goals. The month ends with Mercury entering Scorpio, the sign it will turn retrograde in next month. Mercury in Scorpio right now draws your focus to finances and budgeting practices. Take note.

October

Best Days Overall: 10-14
Most Stressful Days Overall: 18-22
Best Days for Love: 7-10
Best Days for Money: 25-28
Best Days for Career: 27-30
Power Word: Prioritize

It's October, Libra! October's astrology begins with a very eventful first week. Mercury and Mars find tension with one another on the 2nd and then the two of them both find tension with Pluto on the 3rd. These transits are commonly associated with heightening the inner critic, so be gentle with yourself. October 3 is a very important date for you to note because your planetary ruler, Venus, turns retrograde. Venus will be retrograde in Scorpio and will also move back into your sign. Venus's retrogrades always function as values – and relationship – audits. That being said, for Libra, this retrograde also centres around finances. Take this month to really get an understanding of all the ways your money enters and leaves your bank account. This retrograde period also highlights relationships in your life you may need to enforce boundaries with, or to reset their power dynamics. On the 4th, the Sun finds tension with Saturn. This transit can have you feeling unproductive or like you're working really hard but it's getting you nowhere. Trust that this feeling shall pass and that your worthiness is not tied to your productivity.

The New Moon in your sign occurs on the 10th. This is an important time to prioritize your emotional needs. If that means cancelling plans or planning a big party for yourself, do what you need to do for *you*. Venus continues to frustrate this month by finding tension with Mars on the 11th. This transit may have you feeling like you're stretched in multiple directions, which highlights why it's paramount you prioritize your own needs this month. Venus then finds tension with Pluto for the second time, on the 20th.

The Sun exits your sign and enters Scorpio on the 23rd. Scorpio's season brings your annual spotlight on finances. The next day, Mercury joins Venus by turning retrograde. This Mercury retrograde functions like a financial audit. It is best to adopt a frugal mindset for the next three weeks. On the 25th, Venus re-enters Libra, amplifying the effects of this retrograde. The next day, the Full Moon in Taurus lights up the night sky. This lunation highlights joint finances and urges you to ensure you're getting your fair share from any business collaborations or partnerships.

November

Best Days Overall: 27–30
Most Stressful Days Overall: 11–14
Best Days for Love: 14–17
Best Days for Money: 9–12
Best Days for Career: 26–29
Power Word: Stories

Mercury and Venus continue their retrogrades as November begins. These retrogrades encourage revisiting or revising existing ideas, goals or endeavours, rather than launching or creating new ones. The New Moon in Scorpio leads the astrology of this month off on the 9th. This lunation supports reviewing and revising your current budget as you go into the end of the year. Thankfully, both Mercury and Venus end their retrograde periods on the 13th. (It will take a few weeks for them to be functioning at their normal speeds once again, though.) Mars in Leo meets up with Jupiter on the 16th. This transit strongly encourages getting rid of any angst by spending quality time with your favourite people. There is a spontaneity associated with this transit. Go on an adventure, Libra!

The Sun enters Sagittarius on the 22nd. Sagittarius's season is your annual spotlight on patterns of communication. Sagittarius is typically represented by one or more of three archetypes: the preacher, the teacher and the cheerleader. For the next four weeks, lean into embodying one or more of these archetypes as a means to support yourself or others as they try to check off the remaining items on their 2026 to-do list. Sagittarius season is the ideal time for you to use exercise or movement as a means to regulate your emotions.

On the 24th, the Moon is full again, this time in the sign of Gemini. With the Moon in the sign of the storyteller, this Full Moon begs the question, 'What stories do you seek to tell in 2027?' Sagittarius is a visionary sign, so this lunation encourages you to get an early start on goal-setting. Mars enters Virgo on the 25th, prompting you to be of service to others or those in need. The month rounds out with the Sun finding tension with Uranus on the 26th and harmony with Saturn on the 29th. These transits could very well inspire a change in aesthetics or the desire to express yourself in a different way.

December

Best Days Overall: 9-13
Most Stressful Days Overall: 2-6
Best Days for Love: 17-20
Best Days for Money: 12-16
Best Days for Career: 22-25
Power Word: Nurture

Happy end of the year, Libra! Sagittarius's season rolls on with Venus re-entering Scorpio now that it is no longer retrograde; Venus will soon be back to full speed. The next day, Mars finds tension with Uranus. As mentioned in your July Horoscope, Mars and Uranus together is an inflammatory transit. This transit can have those around you (or yourself) flying off the handle more readily than typical. Moreover, if you're handling anything flammable around this date, take extra precautions. Mercury enters

Sagittarius on the 6th and finds harmony with dreamy Neptune on the 7th. The New Moon on the 9th in Sagittarius encourages carving out quality time with a significant other or treating yourself to a self-date.

The New Moon in Sagittarius is a visionary lunation encouraging you to dream about what you seek to accomplish next year. Don't only dream though: this lunation strongly supports writing or speaking out loud these goals as a means to ground the intention in reality. Venus finds tension with Pluto for the last time this year. This transit is often associated with insecurities spiking, so make sure you are being very mindful of the messaging you're telling yourself. If necessary, create some distance from the narrator in your head if you're grappling with your self-esteem. Venus and Mars find harmony on the 12th, supporting one last stab at your 2026 to-do list.

On the 21st, the Sun enters Capricorn. Capricorn season is your annual spotlight on home and domestic life. Doing some reorganization of your living space as a means to revitalize the energy of the space is recommended at this time. On the 23rd, the Full Moon in Cancer occurs (the second of the year). This lunation supports nurturing your inner child. This could be through play, recreation or simply by adjusting your internal dialogue to support this version of yourself. The last week of the year is slow as Mercury finds tension with Saturn which is exact on the last day of the year. Remember, Libra, your productivity does not equal your worth. Overall, 2026 has been an eventful year, so take this time to recharge.

Scorpio

♏

THE SCORPION

Birthdays from
October 23
to November 22

Personality Profile

SCORPIO AT A GLANCE

Element – Water

Ruling Planet – Mars
 Career Planet – Sun
 Love Planet – Venus
 Money Planet – Jupiter
 Planet of Health and Work – Mars
 Planet of Home and Family Life – Saturn

Totem – the Mountaineer

Colour – cyan

Colour that promotes love, romance and social harmony – green

Colour that promotes earning power – blue

Gems – bloodstone, malachite, topaz

Metals – iron, radium, steel

Scents – cherry blossom, coconut, sandalwood, watermelon

Quality – fixed (= stability)

Quality most needed for balance – a wider view of things

Strongest virtues – loyalty, concentration, determination, courage, depth

Deepest needs – to penetrate and transform

Characteristics to avoid – jealousy, vindictiveness, fanaticism

Signs of greatest overall compatibility – Cancer, Pisces

Signs of greatest overall incompatibility – Taurus, Leo, Aquarius

Sign most helpful to career – Leo

Sign most helpful for emotional support – Aquarius

Sign most helpful financially – Sagittarius

Sign best for marriage and/or partnerships – Taurus

Sign most helpful for creative projects – Pisces

Best Sign to have fun with – Pisces

Signs most helpful in spiritual matters – Cancer, Libra

Best day of the week – Tuesday

Understanding a Scorpio

One symbol of the sign of Scorpio is the phoenix. If you meditate upon the legend of the phoenix you will begin to understand the Scorpio character – his or her powers and abilities, interests and deepest urges.

The phoenix of mythology was a bird that could re-create and reproduce itself. It did so in a most intriguing way: it would seek a fire – usually in a religious temple – fly into it, consume itself in the flames and then emerge a new bird. If this is not the ultimate, most profound transformation, then what is?

Transformation is what Scorpios are all about – in their minds, bodies, affairs and relationships (Scorpios are also society's transformers). To change something in a natural, not an artificial way, involves a transformation from within. This type of change is radical change as opposed to a mere cosmetic make-over. Some people think that change means altering just their appearance, but this is not the kind of thing that interests a Scorpio. Scorpios seek deep, fundamental change. Since real change always proceeds from within, a Scorpio is very interested in – and usually accustomed to – the inner, intimate and philosophical side of life.

Scorpios are people of depth and intellect. If you want to interest them you must present them with more than just a superficial image. You and your interests, projects or business deals must have real substance to them in order to stimulate a Scorpio. If they haven't, he or she will find you out – and that will be the end of the story.

If we observe life – the processes of growth and decay – we see the transformational powers of Scorpio at work all the time. The caterpillar changes itself into a butterfly; the infant grows into a child and then an adult. To Scorpios this definite and perpetual transformation is not something to be feared. They see it as a normal part of life. This acceptance of transformation gives Scorpios the key to understanding the true meaning of life.

Scorpios' understanding of life (including life's weaknesses) makes them powerful warriors – in all senses of the word. Add to this their depth, patience and endurance and you have a powerful personality. Scorpios have good, long memories and can at times be quite vindictive – they can wait years to get their revenge. As a friend, though, there is no one more loyal and true than a Scorpio. Few are willing to make the sacrifices that a Scorpio will make for a true friend.

The results of a transformation are quite obvious, although the process of transformation is invisible and secret. This is why Scorpios are considered secretive in nature. A seed will not grow properly if you keep digging it up and exposing it to the light of day. It must stay buried – invisible – until it starts to grow. In the same manner, Scorpios fear revealing too much about themselves or their hopes to other people. However, they will be more than happy to let you see the finished product – but only when it is completely unwrapped. On the other hand, Scorpios like knowing everyone else's secrets as much as they dislike anyone knowing theirs.

Finance

Love, birth, life as well as death are Nature's most potent transformations; Scorpios are interested in all of these. In our society, money is a transforming power, too, and a Scorpio is interested in money for that reason. To a Scorpio money is power, money causes change, money controls. It is the power of money that fascinates them. But Scorpios can be too materialistic if they are not careful. They can be overly awed by the power of money, to a point where they think that money rules the world.

Even the term 'plutocrat' comes from Pluto, the modern planetary ruler of the sign of Scorpio. Scorpios will – in one way or another – achieve the financial status they strive for. When they do so they are careful in the way they handle their wealth. Part of this financial carefulness is really a kind of honesty, for Scorpios are usually involved with other people's money – as accountants, lawyers, stockbrokers or corporate managers – and when you handle other people's money you have to be more cautious than when you handle your own.

In order to fulfil their financial goals, Scorpios have important lessons to learn. They need to develop qualities that do not come naturally to them, such as breadth of vision, optimism, faith, trust and, above all, generosity. They need to see the wealth in Nature and in life, as well as in its more obvious forms of money and power. When they develop generosity their financial potential reaches great heights, for Jupiter, the Lord of Opulence and Good Fortune, is Scorpio's money planet.

Career and Public Image

Scorpio's greatest aspiration in life is to be considered by society as a source of light and life. They want to be leaders, to be stars. But they follow a very different road than do Leos, the other stars of the zodiac. A Scorpio arrives at the goal secretly, without ostentation; a Leo pursues it openly. Scorpios seek the glamour and fun of the rich and famous in a restrained, discreet way.

Scorpios are by nature introverted and tend to avoid the limelight. But if they want to attain their highest career goals they need to open up a bit and to express themselves more. They need to stop hiding their light under a bushel and let it shine. Above all, they need to let go of any vindictiveness and small-mindedness. All their gifts and insights were given to them for one important reason – to serve life and to increase the joy of living for others.

Love and Relationships

Scorpio is another zodiac sign that likes committed clearly defined, structured relationships. They are cautious about marriage, but when they do commit to a relationship they tend to be faithful – and heaven help the mate caught or even suspected of infidelity! The jealousy of the Scorpio is legendary. They can be so intense in their jealousy that even the thought or intention of infidelity will be detected and is likely to cause as much of a storm as if the deed had actually been done.

Scorpios tend to settle down with those who are wealthier than they are. They usually have enough intensity for two, so in their partners they seek someone pleasant, hard-working, amiable, stable and easy-going. They want someone they can lean on, someone loyal behind them as they fight the battles of life. To a Scorpio a partner, be it a lover or a friend, is a real partner – not an adversary. Most of all a Scorpio is looking for an ally, not a competitor.

If you are in love with a Scorpio you will need a lot of patience. It takes a long time to get to know Scorpios, because they do not reveal themselves readily. But if you persist and your motives are honourable, you will gradually be allowed into a Scorpio's inner chambers of the mind and heart.

Home and Domestic Life

Uranus is the modern planetary ruler of Scorpio's 4th solar house of home and family. Uranus is the planet of science, technology, changes and democracy. This tells us a lot about a Scorpio's conduct in the home and what he or she needs in order to have a happy, harmonious home life.

Scorpios can sometimes bring their passion, intensity and wilfulness into the home and family, which is not always the place for these qualities. These traits are good for the warrior and the transformer, but not so good for the nurturer and family member. Because of this (and also because of their need for change and transformation) the Scorpio may be prone to sudden changes of residence. If not carefully constrained, the sometimes inflexible Scorpio can produce turmoil and sudden upheavals within the family.

Scorpios need to develop some of the virtues of Aquarius in order to cope better with domestic matters. There is a need to build a team spirit at home, to treat family activities as truly group activities – family members should all have a say in what does and does not get done. For at times a Scorpio can be most dictatorial. When a Scorpio gets dictatorial it is much worse than if a Leo or Capricorn (the two other power signs in the zodiac) does. For the dictatorship of a Scorpio is applied with more zeal, passion, intensity and concentration than is true of either a Leo or Capricorn. Obviously this can be unbearable to family members – especially if they are sensitive types.

In order for a Scorpio to get the full benefit of the emotional support that a family can give, he or she needs to let go of conservatism and be a bit more experimental, to explore new techniques in childrearing, be more democratic with family members and to try to manage things by consensus rather than by autocratic edict.

Horoscope for 2026

Having a disciplined regime is the name of the game in 2026 for you, Scorpio. This year your totem, 'the Mountaineer', reflects that hard work and diligence will pay off for you. This is a noteworthy year with several planets shifting into (and staying in) new signs. Saturn, the planet of discipline, will enter Aries for the first time since 1996 and, in doing so, moves into Scorpio's chart sector ruling routines. Saturn also rules consequences, so it's extra important those routines are right and tight this year. Saturn is joined in this chart sector by Neptune who will move into and stay in Aries in January for the first time since the 1860s! Neptune rules dreams and idealism, so it's important you set metrics and benchmarks to track your progress as you climb your personal mountains.

Another reason why your totem this year is the Mountaineer is because Jupiter, the planet of growth and expansion, enters your career sector when it moves into Leo mid-year. Jupiter amplifies the themes of the chart sector it's transiting. So 2026 is a year to really make moves in your career and/or with crafting the legacy you want to leave. Because Jupiter is all about augmentation, it's equally important you don't spread yourself too thin. Identify which summit is the most important to reach this year and focus on that goal.

There's also going to be a noteworthy shift as the north node enters Aquarius and brings with it eclipses. For Scorpio, 2026 is the year there will start to be eclipses in the home and career sectors of their chart. Eclipses are evolutionary transits which catalyse growth through shake-ups and scrutiny. The eclipses, plus the south node entering your career sector, has major implications for these areas of life. Essentially, these transits indicate that, just like a mountaineer may discover that a path to the top of a mountain is no longer viable, you may decide to go another way in the pursuit of new or updated career goals. More on this in the career section of this Horoscope, below.

Saturn, Uranus, Neptune, and the north and south nodes all shift signs this year. From a societal standpoint, this indicates that major shifts and changes are under way that will define the next generation. Embodying the Mountaineer means persevering through pressure and altitude changes in the environment around you. Scorpio's ruling planet, Mars, will not turn retrograde this year, clearing the route for you to tackle important feats.

For a quarterly view of the year ahead, the first quarter features a focus on routines and physical health. The second quarter continues these themes and centres around finances as well. Career is a major theme of the third quarter in 2026, while the final quarter is once again financially oriented, and also centred around the values which define your relationships.

Health (1st/6th/12th houses)

(Please note that this is an astrological perspective on health and not a medical one. Any health-related symptoms should be evaluated by a qualified healthcare professional.)

Physical health is a major area of focus for Scorpio in 2026 as Saturn and Neptune both enter the chart sector associated with it. Saturn rules reality, restriction and consequences. Saturn transiting this sector functions as an audit of your physical wellness routines and the way you take care of – or neglect – the needs of your physical body. Becoming regimented with diet and exercise is strongly advised with Saturn transiting this chart sector. Moreover, if you've been avoiding getting your yearly physical check-up or getting any nagging issue checked out, please do so. Neptune will also be present in this sector and has associations with medications and substances. You should definitely only take medications or supplements under supervision of a licensed professional. Your physical health planet, Mars, will be direct the entire year, supporting efforts you put into adopting and keeping sustainable healthy routines.

Mental health is a relatively neutral area this year, astrologically speaking, as there are no more eclipses in the mental health or physical health sectors, as there have been from 2023 to 2025. That being said, your mental health planet, Venus, will be retrograde in this chart sector from October 25 to November 13. This retrograde asks the question, 'Have you been able to strike a healthy balance between social and solo time?' Moreover, 'How has this balance or lack thereof impacted your mental health?' These questions will be important to investigate during this retrograde as Mercury will also be retrograde in your sign, further focusing the cosmic energy on re-evaluation and recalibration.

Here are the specific areas of the body to focus on this year:

- Reproductive organs: these are a perennial area of focus for Scorpio as it rules this part of the body. Checking in with a medical professional on how to ensure your physical health routines support these parts of the body is recommended, given Saturn's transition into Scorpio's physical health sector.
- Digestive system and liver: Saturn will be moving into the chart sector which rules these parts of the body. This means 2026 is a year to be responsible with your diet and how you imbibe. Saturn will be in Aries, a sign associated with inflammation, so be especially mindful around consuming inflammatory foods.
- Bones and joints: Saturn is the planet which rules these parts of the body and will be transiting your physical health sector. In addition to diet, take special care to support these parts of the body through movement.

Love and Social Life (5th/7th/11th houses)

These areas of life were more scrutinized by the astrology of 2025; in 2026 there's a lessening of the activity in these chart sectors. That being said, there's still some important transits to cover for Scorpio's partnership, romance and social life sectors. With regards to partnership and romance, the first half of 2026 features

Uranus still occupying your relationship sector until April 25 and the north node in the romance sector until July 27. Uranus rules innovation, instability and individuality. During its eight-year stint in your partnership sector, there've been breakdowns and/or breakthroughs in this area of life. Uranus brings a frenetic and kinetic energy to the chart sector it's transiting. For Scorpio, 2026 is a year you're prompted to strive for calmness and stability in this area of life. If you're single, Uranus occupying your partnership sector for the first four or so months of the year reinforces the importance of maintaining your authenticity as you date and meet people. Arguably, this advice also applies to those Scorpios who are partnered, except instead of maintaining your authenticity while dating, it is more of a case of staying true to yourself even as your partnership adopts/maintains an identity of its own.

The second half of 2026 features a lunar eclipse in your romance sector on August 28. Eclipses are evolutionary transits, so how you approach romance is subject to change towards the end of 2026. Your partnership planet, Venus, turns retrograde in your sign on October 3 and will stay retrograde until November 13. Venus's retrograde periods inspire reviews and reflections on your current relationship status and the values you embody. If you're single and want to date, identify what values you seek to embody in order to be open to the right relationship. If you're partnered, this retro-grade period could be a time to slow down and make sure there's still the necessary values alignment between you and your partner. Venus's retrograde periods invite slowing down to prioritize inti-macy and connection in your partnership.

Social life in 2026 is another area of life that starts to settle after being scrutinized by the astrology of 2025. There's a lunar eclipse in Virgo on March 3rd which lights up this chart sector for Scorpio. This eclipse reminds you of the importance of ensuring reciprocity in your friendships and that the communities you support also bring you much-needed comfort. Your social life planet, Mercury, will be retrograde in only water signs this year. While Scorpio isn't necessarily known for being forthright with its emotions, this is a year to identify members of your community you can lean on for emotional support.

Career and Finances (10th/2nd/8th houses)

As mentioned in the introduction above, career is an area of life which is a major focus for Scorpio this year. Jupiter, the great augmenter, enters Scorpio's career sector on June 30. Jupiter brings growth to the chart sector it transits, so plan for this expansion before this transit happens to best set yourself up for success. It would behove you to enter 2026 with an action plan on what career goals you seek to accomplish this year. Given the emphasis placed on maintaining routines for Scorpio, using this plan as a guide will be very helpful once Jupiter moves into your career sector. Jupiter spends roughly 12 months in a chart sector, so don't assume that just because it begins its transit at the end of June, all of a sudden you'll see growth and expansion. Jupiter functions like a watering can nourishing seeds which have already been planted in fertile soil. Given that your career planet is the Sun, the two eclipse seasons are also integral times for career progression this year. The first eclipse season occurs from February to March and the second is primarily in August. Eclipses bring shake-ups, so be open to unexpected changes to existing career goals as well.

Finances are an area of life even more linked to your career than typical, as your finance planet, Jupiter, enters your career sector mid-year. While this is a year to be intentional with your time and not to spread yourself too thin, Jupiter moving into your career sector opens up the potential to create a new, secondary stream of income, if this is something you've been considering. Tied to this, it is important you're mindful about how you approach joint ventures or mixing your finances with other people this year. This is because Uranus will move into the chart sector related to joint ventures mid-year. Uranus in this sector opens the potential to adopt new and innovative forms of making money with others. That being said, Uranus's is a frenetic energy, so it's important you don't rush into any sort of joint arrangement, and that you have proper legal documents in place to afford protection should you need it.

Home and Domestic Life (4th house)

Pluto, the planet of transformation, began its roughly 20-year transit in this chart sector last year. This year, the north node will join Pluto on July 27. The north node brings increase and eclipses with it where it transits. The first eclipse of the year, a solar eclipse in Aquarius, occurs in this chart sector on February 17. Your ability to be authentically yourself around family or within your home is one prominent theme under review with this eclipse. Your home planet is Saturn, which shifts into Aries on February 13. Saturn conjoins with dreamy Neptune on February 20 and frames the importance of ensuring that your living situation supports you maintaining the routines you need to keep to achieve your big goals this year. Whether that means having exercise equipment in the home, the proper ingredients to prepare healthy food, a minimalist office space to prevent distractions or something else – it's important your home is designed to enhance your ability to succeed in 2026.

Self-improvement (1st/3rd/5th/9th houses)

Assessing which values you hold dear and live your life by is a necessary practice for Scorpio in 2026, given that Venus, the planet of values, turns retrograde on October 3 in your sign. This year your totem is the Mountaineer. In order to be willing to climb your proverbial mountains, you need to identify what your 'why?' is. What values will sustain you and imbue you with the perseverance required to tackle the challenge of achieving the goals you set out for yourself in 2026? Saturn is your communications planet and, by shifting into Aries this year, it indicates the importance of being able to assert yourself. Moreover, one mantra of Aries is 'I with myself'. Paying close attention to how you speak to yourself is also important. Be especially mindful to quash negative self-talk. In order to climb your personal mountains this year, you have to be your biggest cheerleader, dear Scorpio.

Month-by-month Forecasts

January

Best Days Overall: 5–9
Most Stressful Days Overall: 26–30
Best Days for Love: 8–11
Best Days for Money: 20–24
Best Days for Career: 1–4
Power Word: Mountain

Happy New Year, Scorpio! The astrology of 2026 kicks off on the first day of the year with Mercury entering earthy Capricorn. Mercury joins the Sun, Venus and Mars already in this sign creating a build-up of earth energy. Capricorn is represented by the seagoat, which looks to the top of a mountain or to the bottom of the ocean and knows that, while it will take substantial time to get there, if it works little by little it will achieve its goal. Take a cue from Capricorn and apply that philosophy to the goals you set for yourself this year. On the 3rd, the Full Moon in Cancer shines bright. This Full Moon brings an emotional focus to play, pleasure and creativity. You have a lot to accomplish this year, but that doesn't mean it needs to be all work and no play. The Sun and Venus meeting up on the 6th is the ideal day to carve out some time for recreation.

Emotions run high around the 10th when the Sun and Mars meet up and then find tension with Jupiter, the planet of growth and expansion. On the 18th, the New Moon in Capricorn ushers in a new emotional cycle around your patterns of communication. If you have identified any way you hold yourself back by a pattern of communication that's become ingrained, this lunation invites you to develop a new outlook or approach to how you speak. Remember, little by little you can achieve your goals, sweet Scorpion. The next day, the Sun enters Aquarius. Aquarius's season is your annual spotlight on home and domestic life. The start of the year is the time for you to get your home in order. Things start off a bit rockily, however, as the Sun and Venus conjoin with Pluto between the 20th and the 22nd.

Mars enters Aquarius on the 23rd, meaning that the Sun, Mercury, Venus and Mars are now all in Aquarius. Aquarius is the only other sign apart from yours which is associated with really asking thoughtful, provoking questions. Now is the time to direct this energy inwards and identify what you truly seek to attain or accomplish this year. After oscillating back and forth between Pisces and Aries, Neptune enters Aries on the 26th and will stay in the fire sign until 2039. This transit more affects your year as a whole and more info is provided in your annual Horoscope. The month ends with Mars and Pluto meeting up which makes the vibes edgy. Mars and Pluto together do support feats of perseverance, which is one way to lean into this typically harsh energy.

February

Best Days Overall: 2-6
Most Stressful Days Overall: 16-19
Best Days for Love: 19-23
Best Days for Money: 14-17
Best Days for Career: 3-7
Power Word: Temple

It's February, Scorpio! February's cosmic weather kicks off with the Full Moon in Leo. After directing all that Aquarian energy inwards to ask yourself what you truly want, this lunation brings an emotional focus to career and legacy. What do you want to be remembered for, Scorpio? This year features major energy shifts which influence the collective. With the times definitely a changing, who do you want to be on the other side? Mercury enters your fellow water sign Pisces on the 6th, which supports grounding the answer to the Full Moon question in a philosophical system or your spiritual values. Venus further reinforces the importance of spirituality in your life as it also enters Pisces on the 10th.

Just like Neptune, Saturn had also spent all last year bouncing between Pisces and Aries. On the 13th, the planet of discipline and hard work enters Aries to stay, for the next two and a half years. Saturn in Aries directs its proverbial magnifying glass to physical

health and daily/weekly routines. Does your current regime actually support you in achieving the goals you've set for yourself this
year? Place greater emphasis on treating your body like the temple
it is.

Boom! The first eclipse of the year occurs on the 17th. Eclipses
scrutinize as a means to precipitate evolution. For you, Scorpio,
this eclipse centres around home and domestic life. This pertains
to either/both the physical layout/organization of your home or
relationships within the home itself. Moreover, this eclipse could
very well trigger a move – or the desire for one at least. The next
day, the Sun leaves Aquarius and enters Pisces. Pisces's season is
your annual spotlight on how spirituality or your values system
informs your creative self-expression and how much you value/
prioritize recreation. Eclipse season is a hectic time of year, so
make sure you are carving out a helpful amount of downtime.
Venus finds harmony with Jupiter on the 22nd, which makes it the
ideal weekend to prioritize the most important interpersonal relationships in your life. This could be going on a date with a significant other or spending quality time with a best friend. Mercury
turns retrograde on the 26th in Pisces. This transit lasts about
three weeks and has you reflecting on your patterns of
communication.

March

Best Days Overall: 28–31
Most Stressful Days Overall: 1–3
Best Days for Love: 18–21
Best Days for Money: 3–6
Best Days for Career: 20–23
Power Word: Pioneer

Don't fear the retrograde, Scorpio! March begins just as Mercury
has turned retrograde in Pisces. Mercury's retrograde is a time to
slow down and re-evaluate which patterns of thought and communication may need to be addressed in order to best support you in
achieving your goals or maintaining healthy relationships. This is

hard and vulnerable work, so be gentle with yourself. The second eclipse of the year occurs on the 3rd in Virgo. This eclipse brings an emotional focus to your friend groups, professional organizations and the general company you keep. You only have so much bandwidth and this eclipse demands you only prioritize relationships predicated on reciprocity. The Sun finds harmony with Jupiter on the 5th and Mercury does so on the 9th. These transits create the ideal window for you to reconnect with old friends you still hold in high esteem.

The New Moon in Pisces ushers in a new emotional cycle around how you utilize creative self-expression as a means to emotionally regulate yourself. This lunation also pertains to your relationship with children and the younger generation. On the 20th, the Sun exits Pisces and enters Aries – your annual spotlight on physical health and routines. Moreover, the 20th is also the day Mercury ends its retrograde period. Yay! Aries is the first sign of the zodiac and is often associated with pioneering. Lean into the Aries energy that will build over the next four weeks and challenge yourself to explore new horizons. This especially applies in the realm of fitness, diet and overarching physical wellness. If you've been avoiding getting an annual check-up or seeing any sort of medical specialist, this is the season to do so.

Aries season's astrology begins with the Sun meeting up with Neptune on the 22nd and with Saturn on the 25th. This first week of Aries's season is complex as Neptune and Saturn are antithetical in nature. Neptune rules dreams, fantasy and compassion while Saturn rules reality, discipline and restriction. As a result, you'll likely feel a touch more discombobulated this week than normal. Doing somatic work or getting out of your head and into your body is ideal at this time. The month concludes with Venus entering Taurus, beginning an astrological focus on partnership for you.

April

Best Days Overall: 9–13
Most Stressful Days Overall: 18–22
Best Days for Love: 20–24
Best Days for Money: 1–4
Best Days for Career: 4–8
Power Word: Regulate

Aries season continues with the Full Moon in Libra. This lunation centres around emotional wellbeing and regulation for you. Libra is the sign represented by the scales. This Full Moon reminds you about the inherent link between physical wellness and emotional wellbeing. If you can support one, the other is in turn supported as well. The fiery Aries energy continues to build as Mars, your planetary ruler, enters the fire sign on the 9th. Mars in Aries provides productive go-getter energy for the most part. The only time there's a slowdown with this transit is when Mars meets up with Neptune on the 13th and with Saturn on the 19th.

On the 17th, there's a New Moon in Aries as well. This means that on this date, there are *six* planets in the fire sign: the Sun, the Moon, Mercury, Mars, Saturn and Neptune. That's a *lot* of energy. Prioritizing physical health and wellness is paramount at this time. This lunation supports trying new forms of fitness or healthy ways of eating as a means to support your physical body. On the 19th, the Sun enters Taurus. Taurus is the fixed earth sign associated with sensuality and security. Taurus is your polar sign and reminds you of the importance of finding intrinsic security in the values you live your life by. Taurus also reminds you of the importance of pausing to enjoy life with your five senses.

On the 24th, Venus in Taurus meets up with Uranus at the very last degree of the sign. This transit supports spontaneity within partnership. If you're partnered, a spontaneous adventure with your special someone is exactly how to maximize the energy of this transit. If you're single, this transit would support putting yourself out there or finding ways to be seen by prospective partners. Venus moves into Gemini on the 24th, bringing a soft focus to joint ventures or the way your money is wrapped up with other people. After spending all last year oscillating between Taurus and Gemini, Uranus finally moves into Gemini on the 25th, where it will stay until 2032/2033. This transit influences your year as a whole and is described in detail in your annual Horoscope's overview, above.

May

Best Days Overall: 21-25
Most Stressful Days Overall: 5; 26-29
Best Days for Love: 16-19
Best Days for Money: 18-21
Best Days for Career: 29-31
Power Word: Emotions

It's May, Scorpio! This month there's double the number of Full Moons as normal so expect emotions to run a little higher this month. May's astrology begins with a Full Moon in your sign. Full Moons in our own sign tend to be ones of heightened emotions as Full Moons represent emotional culminations. This lunation centres around your relationship with yourself. Are you partnering with yourself and being your own biggest ally? Scorpio is known for asking questions, so spend some time investigating this. Mercury enters your polar sign, Taurus, on the 2nd, drawing your attention more so towards partnership. The 5th is a tense day with two disharmonious transits: Mercury and Pluto square off just as Mars and Jupiter do the same. These transits can spark your inner critic, so be gentle with yourself, Scorpio.

Mercury and Jupiter find harmony on the 13th, supporting recreation and play for Scorpio. Give yourself permission to integrate a little more fun into your life around this date. The New Moon in Taurus on the 16th centres around partnership. If you're partnered, this New Moon is the ideal time to progress the relationship to new heights if you so desire. If you're single, this lunation supports planting seeds in this area of life. This could mean utilizing dating apps or joining hobby organizations to meet new people.

On the 20th, the Sun leaves Taurus and enters Gemini. Gemini season represents the transition from spring to summer. This is noteworthy because the summer this year is the season of the year with the most noteworthy astrology. Gemini is the narrator and storyteller of the zodiac. For you, Gemini season poses the question, 'What stories or narratives have you told yourself which drive your overarching fears and insecurities?' You are presented with the opportunity to tackle these anxieties this solar season. This question is especially pertinent at the end of this month, given that Mars and Pluto square off on the 26th and Venus and Saturn do the same on the 28th. The month ends with a Blue Moon, a second Full Moon, this time in Sagittarius. This lunation centres around budgeting and finances for you. Are you aware of all the ways your money exits and enters your bank account?

June

Best Days Overall: 6–10
Most Stressful Days Overall: 18–22
Best Days for Love: 2–5
Best Days for Money: 28–30
Best Days for Career: 13–16
Power Word: Perspective

Hi, Scorpio! Gemini's season continues with Mercury entering your fellow water sign Cancer on the 1st. Mercury is the planet of thinking and communication. In watery Cancer, Mercury inspires you to feel your feelings and express your gratitude for those who nurture you. The first week of June is pretty neutral, astrologically, which is great because from the second week through into August, the kinetic energy really picks up! On the 10th, Venus in Cancer meets up with Jupiter in Cancer. This transit strongly supports immersing yourself in nature to ground yourself or gain a shift in perspective. Venus enters Leo on the 13th, bringing a bit of the astrological focus to career, public perception and legacy for you.

On the 14th, the New Moon in Gemini occurs. This lunation ushers in a new emotional cycle around your relationship with fear and anxiety. If you've been contemplating working with a mental health professional, this lunation presents the opportune time to do so. Moreover, this lunation would support processing your emotions with those you trust. You don't need to keep everything hidden and bottled up, Scorpio. Venus then gets busy finding harmony with Uranus on the 16th, harmony with Neptune on the 17th and tension with Pluto on the 18th. This summer is key for figuring out how to balance career and home life, your public and private life. Chiron, the minor planet associated with turning wounds into purpose, enters Taurus briefly, having you address deep-seated wounds which affect interpersonal relationships and partnership.

On the 21st, summer begins as the Sun enters Cancer, bringing your annual spotlight on spirituality and higher education. Venus and Saturn find harmony on the 25th, which is an ideal time to check items off your to-do list before Mercury begins its retrograde three days later. On the 28th, Mercury turns retrograde in Cancer. This retrograde centres around the ways you support the inner child within you. Moreover, this retrograde is especially prone to communication being indirect. Always clarify with others what they actually said to you at this time, instead of just assuming you've understood. Jupiter moves into Leo for the first time in 12 years on the 30th. This transit affects your year as a whole and is discussed in your Horoscope's overview, above.

July

Best Days Overall: 13-17
Most Stressful Days Overall: 1-4; 28-29
Best Days for Love: 9-13
Best Days for Money: 27-30
Best Days for Career: 23-27
Power Word: Legacy

It's July, Scorpio! This month is a *big deal* astrologically and we have a lot to discuss. On the 4th, your planetary ruler Mars meets up with volatile Uranus. Mars and Uranus together function like a cosmic powder keg, so be mindful that people may more readily lose their cool. Also, this transit is literally associated with explosions. If you're handling fireworks or anything flammable around this date, take extra care. Mars then finds harmony with both Neptune and Pluto on the 5th. Mars in harmony with these two slow-moving influential planets provides much needed productive energy, even amid the Mercury retrograde. Venus enters Virgo on the 9th, encouraging immersing yourself in the communities that uplift you.

As mentioned in earlier months' forecasts, Uranus and Neptune both switched into new signs for the first time in a long time. It takes Uranus about 84 years to orbit the zodiac and it takes Neptune about 160 years to do the same. And with Pluto having moved into a new sign a couple of years ago, this month sees the rare occurrence of Uranus harmoniously aligning to both other slow-moving planets in the span of a few days. Uranus finds harmony with Neptune on the 15th and harmony with Pluto on the 18th. These transits influence the collective and signify that the societal shifts observed last year are really starting to take root. Even more noteworthy astrology takes place just a few days later as Jupiter, the planet of growth and expansion, finds harmony with Uranus and Neptune, but tension with Pluto, between the 20th and the 21st. On the personal level, this transit functions as an important check-in on how much you've transformed since 2020. Jupiter and Pluto met up three times during that year, so this is the mid-way point in that cycle.

On the 22nd, the Sun leaves Cancer and enters Leo. Leo's season is your annual spotlight on career, public perception and legacy, but this year it starts off a bit rockily with the Sun forming the same aspects with the slow-moving trio that Jupiter just did. Be mindful that Pluto rules what we bury and what needs to be unearthed, so don't be surprised if there are revelations or important realizations during this Leo season. Mercury ends its retrograde on the 23rd and will be functioning at its normal speed in a couple of weeks. The month ends with the Full Moon in Aquarius spotlighting home and domestic life.

August

Best Days Overall: 14-19
Most Stressful Days Overall: 25-28
Best Days for Love: 22-25
Best Days for Money: 29-31
Best Days for Career: 7-11
Power Word: Prioritize

It's eclipse season again, Scorpio! The fast-paced astrology of the summer continues into August with two eclipses occurring this month. Before the first eclipse occurs, Venus moves into Libra on the 6th. This is important to note because Venus will turn retrograde in your sign in a couple of months and will move back into Libra. Venus will begin to slow down shortly to prepare for this retrograde. The Sun finds harmony with Saturn, which supports the steps you're taking to get better regimented. Venus finds harmony with Pluto, which supports prioritizing rejuvenation or emotional wellbeing. Your planetary ruler, Mars, enters Cancer on the 11th and will be there for six weeks. If possible, consider planning or taking some sort of trip or voyage over this period. This transit supports utilizing travel as a means to gain enlightenment, do some important emotional processing, or to connect with the universe.

The first eclipse of the month occurs on the 12th and is a solar eclipse in Leo. This eclipse's energy centres around career, public perception and legacy for Scorpio. This eclipse also functions as a check-in on the career goals you've been pursuing all year. Are you on track, Scorpio, or do you need to pivot or change course? The 12th also features a harsh alignment between Mercury and Pluto. This transit can spark your inner critic. Do your best to accept your flaws and give yourself unconditional love.

On the 22nd, the Sun exits Leo and enters Virgo. Virgo's season is your annual spotlight on social life and the groups/communities you immerse yourself in. Virgo is known as the sign of service, which is why this season especially emphasizes the importance of reciprocity in relationships for Scorpio. The final eclipse of the year is a lunar eclipse in Pisces. This eclipse scrutinizes your relationship to creativity, recreation and romance. What is the balance between work and play in your life? The month ends with a harmonious alignment between Jupiter and Saturn. If you were planning on launching any new endeavours, over the next couple of weeks is an opportune time to do so.

September

Best Days Overall: 12–16
Most Stressful Days Overall: 23–27
Best Days for Love: 10–14
Best Days for Money: 1–4
Best Days for Career: 18–22
Power Word: Self-care

Virgo season rolls on into September. On the 10th, Venus enters your sign. Remember, Venus will turn retrograde next month in your sign, so start to pay attention to themes within your interpersonal relationships this month as they'll be front and centre next month. The New Moon in Virgo also occurs on the 10th. This lunation ushers in a new cycle around the concept of community for you. If you've been tempted to immerse yourself in any new communities or professional organizations, this is an opportune time to do so. This New Moon also supports creating your own group or community as well.

Mercury in Libra finds tension with Neptune and harmony with Pluto on the 12th. These transits support making an extra effort over the next week or so to quieten your mind. On the 14th, the Sun finds harmony with your planetary ruler, Mars. This transit encourages asserting yourself and moving your body. Even if it means just taking a five-minute walk, find some way to work with this energy and get kinaesthetic this week. On the 16th, Venus and Pluto square off for the first of three times over the next few months. Venus and Pluto finding tension is typically associated with having to confront insecurities or narratives you've told yourself around worthiness. It is very important to look after yourself and take steps to empower yourself over the next few months.

Venus turning retrograde means this transit will be a focal point of the rest of the year.

On the 22nd, the Sun exits Virgo and enters Libra, bringing your annual spotlight on mental health and emotional regulation. Venus's retrograde will partially centre around emotional wellness as well. On the 26th, the Full Moon in Aries functions as a check-in on physical wellness and any steps you took in the spring and summer to improve your health. This Full Moon can have you on edge as it functions as an emotional culmination of sorts as well. With this lunation being conjoined with Neptune, it is very possible to feel a little more disconnected from your body at this time. Leaning into meditation, mindfulness or other somatic practices as a source of grounding is recommended at this time.

October

Best Days Overall: 10–14
Most Stressful Days Overall: 2–6
Best Days for Love: 26–28
Best Days for Money: 12–15
Best Days for Career: 7–10
Power Word: Audit

Libra season continues with Venus turning retrograde in your sign on the 3rd. Venus's retrograde periods typically function as audits of interpersonal relationships and value systems. For you, this retrograde firstly centres around how you partner with yourself. Venus turning retrograde in your sign encourages you to slow down and imagine what you'd be able to achieve if you championed yourself in a more explicit and confident way. When Venus re-enters Libra later this month, the focus of the retrograde will be on finding a balance between social and solo time. The 3rd also features Mercury finding tension with Pluto. This transit can embolden your inner critic, only further reinforcing the importance of championing yourself. The Sun finds tension with Saturn on the 4th, which can make you feel like you're working tirelessly with no payoff. Trust that good things take time, Scorpio.

The New Moon in Libra on the 10th centres around your routine behaviours that either support or detract from your mental health. This also includes analysing your coping mechanisms when stressed. Libra is represented by the scales and as such the primary theme to be striving for in all aspects of life right now is balance. Venus squares off with Pluto again on the 20th. This transit can be sobering, so it's important you are actively surrounding yourself with those who lift your spirits.

Happy birthday! On the 23rd, the Sun exits Libra and enters Scorpio. This Scorpio season is an especially reflective one as Venus is retrograde and Mercury turns retrograde on the 24th. As such, given you are embarking on a new trip around the Sun, identify two or three words you seek to embody and integrate them into your reflective or spiritual practices. This Mercury retrograde period occurs entirely in your sign. With all the Scorpio and retrograde energy, it is important you are carving out time for self-care. Venus re-enters Libra on the 25th and then the Full Moon in Taurus is bright on the 26th. This lunation brings an emotional focus to partnership. With Venus being retrograde in addition to the Full Moon, there's a lot of energy centred around this area of life. This Full Moon encourages you to shed aspects of your identity or narratives you've told yourself which inhibit your ability to grow or evolve in partnership.

November

Best Days Overall: 27-30
Most Stressful Days Overall: 9-13
Best Days for Love: 21-24
Best Days for Money: 23-26
Best Days for Career: 4-8
Power Word: Themes

Scorpio season continues into November with the first week of the month being fairly neutral – apart from being defined by the two existing retrograde periods. On the 9th, there's a New Moon in your sign. This New Moon functions as a check-in on what themes have presented themselves during these two retrogrades. What have you learned about your interpersonal relationships and your patterns of communication? Mercury and Venus both end their retrograde periods on the 13th. While they technically aren't retrograde, it will take the two planets a couple of weeks to be moving at full speed, so anticipate that the retrograde energy will feel more like it's gradually dissipating rather than completely disappearing all at once.

On the 16th, your planetary ruler Mars meets up with Jupiter in Leo. This transit strongly supports career, public perception and work you're doing in cementing your legacy. Leo is a sign associated with being seen and heard. Be open to opportunities which afford you the ability to deliver a message or create these moments yourself. Now that the retrograde periods are over, you may be feeling restless to check off lingering items on your to-do list. This unease is likely around the 20th when the Sun squares off with Mars. Just remember, haste makes waste, Scorpio, so don't succumb to the restlessness.

On the 22nd, the Sun exits your sign and enters Sagittarius. Sagittarius's season is your annual spotlight on budgeting and finances. Sagittarius is a fire sign commonly associated with coaching, mentorship and wisdom. This solar season is the ideal time to work with a financial expert to maximize the way you save and/or accrue money. The Full Moon in Gemini occurs on the 24th. This Full Moon is angsty as it pushes you to shed insecurities which keep you stuck. This lunation is also ideal for identifying potential business partners or collaborators if you're looking to launch a new endeavour. Your planetary ruler, Mars, enters Virgo on the 26th, reminding you of the importance of service and helping those in need. The month concludes with a harmonious alignment between the Sun and Saturn which supports cementing your routine amid the winter holidays.

December

Best Days Overall: 13–17
Most Stressful Days Overall: 6–10
Best Days for Love: 5–9
Best Days for Money: 19–23
Best Days for Career: 12–16
Power Word: Heartfelt

Happy December, Scorpio! As the last month of the year begins, Venus prepares to move back into your sign, which it does on the 4th. This time, this transit centres around prioritizing pleasure and heartfelt connections. Your planetary ruler Mars finds tension with Uranus on the 5th. This makes the first week of the month feel a little volatile or explosive. People may be especially reactive seeing that Mercury, the planet of communication, also finds tension with Uranus three days later, on the 8th. The importance of prioritizing pleasure is ever more present as Venus finds tension with Pluto one last time. As a reminder, this transit tends to rile up anxieties or self-deprecating thoughts. It is vital you take care of yourself at this time. Thankfully, Mercury finds harmony with Saturn, which is a good palate-cleanser to the chaotic astrology of the first week.

Venus and Mars find harmony on the 12th, which makes this weekend the ideal time to cosy up to a significant other, someone special or with close friends. Venus and Mars finding harmony really supports cultivating intimacy and connecting with others. Sagittarius typically embodies the archetypes of the preacher, teacher and cheerleader. Be mindful about getting on your soapbox during this solar season. That being said, embodying the role of mentor or coach is a great way to lean into Sagittarius season.

On the 21st, the Sun exits Sagittarius and enters Capricorn, spotlighting your patterns of communication. Given the retrograde periods you've just been through, what reflections do you currently have around how you communicate to yourself and/or others? The Full Moon in Cancer is exact on the 23rd. This is an emotional Full Moon which encourages nurturing yourself and your loved ones. With Capricorn's focus on communication, work with this energy by verbally expressing how much those who support you mean to you. Mercury, the planet of communication, enters Capricorn on the 25th. Mercury in Capricorn is actually relatively sobering in nature and very focused on facts. Mercury in Capricorn supports planning out the next steps for how you want to walk into 2027. The year ends with Mercury finding tension with Saturn, essentially slowing productivity down. Take a break at the end of this year, Scorpio.

Sagittarius

THE ARCHER

Birthdays from
November 23
to December 20

Personality Profile

SAGITTARIUS AT A GLANCE

Element – Fire

Ruling Planet – Jupiter
  Career Planet – Mercury
  Love Planet – Mercury
  Money Planet – Saturn
  Planet of Health and Work – Venus
  Planet of Home and Family Life – Jupiter
  Planet of Spirituality and Mental Health – Mars

Totem – the Progenitor

Colours – blue, dark blue

Colours that promote love, romance and social harmony – yellow, yellow-orange

Colours that promote earning power – black, indigo

Gems – garnet, citrine, turquoise

Metal – tin

Scents – carnation, jasmine, myrrh

Quality – mutable (= flexibility)

Qualities most needed for balance – attention to detail, administrative and organizational skills

Strongest virtues – generosity, honesty, broad-mindedness, tremendous vision

Deepest need – to expand mentally

Characteristics to avoid – over-optimism, exaggeration, being too generous with other people's money

Signs of greatest overall compatibility – Aries, Leo

Signs of greatest overall incompatibility – Gemini, Virgo, Pisces

Sign most helpful to career – Virgo

Sign most helpful for emotional support – Pisces

Sign most helpful financially – Capricorn

Sign best for marriage and/or partnerships – Gemini

Sign most helpful for creative projects – Aries

Best Sign to have fun with – Aries

Signs most helpful in spiritual matters – Leo, Scorpio

Best day of the week – Thursday

Understanding a Sagittarius

If you look at the symbol of the archer you will gain a good, intuitive understanding of a person born under this astrological sign. The development of archery was humanity's first refinement of the power to hunt and wage war. The ability to shoot an arrow far beyond the ordinary range of a spear extended humanity's horizons, wealth, personal will and power.

Today, instead of using bows and arrows we project our power with fuels and mighty engines, but the essential reason for using these new powers remains the same. These powers represent our ability to extend our personal sphere of influence – and this is what Sagittarius is all about. Sagittarians are always seeking to expand their horizons, to cover more territory and increase their range and scope. This applies to all aspects of their lives: economic, social and intellectual.

Sagittarians are noted for the development of the mind – the higher intellect – which understands philosophical and spiritual concepts. This mind represents the higher part of the psychic nature and is motivated not by self-centred considerations but by the light and grace of a Higher Power. Thus, Sagittarians love higher education of all kinds. They might be bored with formal schooling but they love to study on their own and in their own way. A love of foreign travel and interest in places far away from home are also noteworthy characteristics of the Sagittarian type.

If you give some thought to all these Sagittarian attributes you will see that they spring from the inner Sagittarian desire to develop. To travel more is to know more, to know more is to be more, to cultivate the higher mind is to grow and to reach more. All these traits tend to broaden the intellectual – and indirectly, the economic and material – horizons of the Sagittarian.

The generosity of the Sagittarian is legendary. There are many reasons for this. One is that Sagittarians seem to have an inborn consciousness of wealth. They feel that they are rich, that they are lucky, that they can attain any financial goal – and so they feel that they can afford to be generous. Sagittarians do not carry the burdens of want and limitation which stop most other people from giving generously. Another reason for their generosity is their religious and philosophical idealism, derived from the higher mind. This higher mind is by nature generous because it is unaffected by material circumstances. Still another reason is that the act of giving tends to enhance their emotional nature. Every act of giving seems to be enriching, and this is reward enough for the Sagittarian.

Finance

Sagittarians generally entice wealth. They either attract it or create it. They have the ideas, energy and talent to make their vision of paradise on Earth a reality. However, mere wealth is not enough. Sagittarians want luxury – earning a comfortable living seems small and insignificant to them.

In order for Sagittarians to attain their true earning potential they must develop better managerial and organizational skills. They must learn to set limits, to arrive at their goals through a series of attainable sub-goals or objectives. It is very rare that a person goes from rags to riches overnight. But a long, drawn-out process is difficult for Sagittarians. Like Leos, they want to achieve wealth and success quickly and impressively. They must be aware, however, that this over-optimism can lead to unrealistic financial ventures and disappointing losses. Of course, no zodiac sign can bounce back as quickly as Sagittarius, but only needless heartache will be caused by this attitude. Sagittarians need to maintain their vision – never letting it go – but they must also work towards it in practical and efficient ways.

Career and Public Image

Sagittarians are big thinkers. They want it all: money, fame, glamour, prestige, public acclaim and a place in history. They often go after all these goals. Some attain them, some do not – much depends on each individual's personal horoscope. But if Sagittarians want to attain public and professional status they must understand that these things are not conferred to enhance one's ego but as rewards for the amount of service that one does for the whole of humanity. If and when they figure out ways to serve more, Sagittarians can rise to the top.

The ego of the Sagittarian is gigantic – and perhaps rightly so. They have much to be proud of. If they want public acclaim, however, they will have to learn to tone down the ego a bit, to become more humble and self-effacing, without falling into the trap of self-denial and self-abasement. They must also learn to master the details of life, which can sometimes elude them.

At their jobs Sagittarians are hard workers who like to please their bosses and co-workers. They are dependable, trustworthy and enjoy a challenge. Sagittarians are friendly to work with and helpful to their colleagues. They usually contribute intelligent ideas or new methods that improve the work environment for everyone. Sagittarians always look for challenging positions and careers that develop their intellect, even if they have to work very hard in order to succeed. They also work well under the supervision of others, although by nature they would rather be the supervisors and increase their sphere of influence. Sagittarians excel at professions that allow them to be in contact with many different people and to travel to new and exciting locations.

Love and Relationships

Sagittarians love freedom for themselves and will readily grant it to their partners. They like their relationships to be fluid and ever-changing. Sagittarians tend to be fickle in love and to change their minds about their partners quite frequently.

Sagittarians feel threatened by a clearly defined, well-structured relationship, as they feel this limits their freedom. The Sagittarian tends to marry more than once in life.

Sagittarians in love are passionate, generous, open, benevolent and very active. They demonstrate their affections very openly. However, just like an Aries they tend to be egocentric in the way they relate to their partners. Sagittarians should develop the ability to see others' points of view, not just their own. They need to develop some objectivity and cool intellectual clarity in their relationships so that they can develop better two-way communication with their partners. Sagittarians tend to be overly idealistic about their partners and about love in general. A cool and rational attitude will help them to perceive reality more clearly and enable them to avoid disappointment.

Home and Domestic Life

Sagittarians tend to grant a lot of freedom to their family. They like big homes and many children and are one of the most fertile signs of the zodiac. However, when it comes to their children Sagittarians generally err on the side of allowing them too much freedom. Sometimes their children get the idea that there are no limits. However, allowing freedom in the home is basically a positive thing – so long as some measure of balance is maintained – for it enables all family members to develop as they should.

Horoscope for 2026

Last year was a year of shifts, with planets oscillating back and forth between the past and future; 2026 solidifies the societal changes which have been brewing. Sagittarius, your totem for 2026 is 'the Progenitor'. The dictionary defines a progenitor as one of two things: 'a person or thing from which a person, animal, or plant is descended or originates; an ancestor or parent' or 'a person who originates an artistic, political, or intellectual movement'. Creativity, children/your lineage and communication are three areas of life strongly highlighted by this year's astrology.

One of the most noteworthy astrological events of 2026 happens early in the year when Saturn and Neptune both finally settle into Aries, a sign they dipped in and out of last year. Saturn rules discipline, responsibility and hard work. Neptune rules dreams and compassion. The two planets will be co-present in your creativity and children chart sector. This is a year when your unique form of creative self-expression should be used as a means to cement your legacy. Moreover, these two planets strongly support your efforts to better support the next generation, especially those in your lineage.

This year will also feature the north node and the south node shifting out of Pisces/Virgo and into Aquarius/Leo. For the collective, the concept of monarchy vs democracy will be widely discussed and an area of major policy debate. For Sagittarius, this shift indicates the importance of you speaking your truth in your personal life and even on a broader scale. The north node brings with it eclipses which will stimulate evolution, through scrutiny and shake-ups, in how you communicate.

Your role as a teacher or a student is another aspect of your identity strongly impacted by this shift and another very important planetary change. Your planetary ruler, Jupiter, moves into radiant Leo for the first time in 12 years. Jupiter moves into your higher education and spirituality sector where it will be co-present with the south node. Shedding spiritual practices or belief systems which no longer serve your highest good is a noteworthy by-product of this change. Moreover, stepping into your role as an authority or a teacher (possible through first becoming a student) is another likely path in 2026.

For a quarterly view of the year ahead, the first quarter of 2026 features a strong focus on creative self-expression and children/your lineage. The second quarter centres on higher education, spirituality and partnership. The third quarter of the year emphasizes communication, in addition to reiterating the importance of creativity and children, while the final quarter of the year features noteworthy astrological transits influencing mental health and your social life.

Health (1st/6th/12th houses)

(Please note that this is an astrological perspective on health and not a medical one. Any health-related symptoms should be evaluated by a qualified healthcare professional.)

The cosmic weather for the majority of 2026 is relatively neutral around health. Uranus, the planet of instability and innovation, exits Sagittarius's physical health sector after roughly eight years of transiting it. There are no other outer planets transiting through this sector, but your physical health planet, Venus, will turn retrograde in the final quarter of 2026. Venus will be retrograde from October 3 until November 13, and will spend half of its retrograde period transiting Sagittarius's mental health sector. This means that a major focus of this retrograde period for you will be on mind–body connections and how stress is uniquely stored or expressed through your physical body.

Though Sagittarius is known for its kinetic spirit, it is strongly recommended you slow down during the autumn and allow yourself to take stock of how your physical health is uniquely impacted by stress or anxiety. If your natal chart possesses a significant amount of Sagittarius placements, it's highly likely you actually keep busy and keep moving as a means to avoid deep-rooted stress or anxiety. Slowing down isn't meant to inhibit productivity, but rather is a way to unlock long-lasting endurance through lessening outstanding internal pressures. Your mental health planet, Mars, will not turn retrograde in 2026, affording you the leeway to make significant strides in your relationship to stress and/or anxiety.

Here are the specific areas of the body to focus on this year:

- Hips and thighs: this is a perennial area of focus for Sagittarius as your sign rules these parts of the body in medical astrology. Ensuring proper mobility of these areas through appropriate stretching and movement exercise is strongly recommended. Maintenance through massage, physical therapy or chiropractic care is also recommended.
- Groin and reproductive organs: your physical health planet, Venus, will be retrograde in Scorpio which rules over these parts of the body in medical astrology. Similar recommendations for supporting the hips and thighs are offered for the groin. Be mindful of how diet impacts reproductive organs this year.
- Skin: Venus will also transit part of Libra during its retrograde period, which rules this part of the body. Venus first enters Libra at the beginning of August, strongly reinforcing incorporating a sunscreen regime into your daily routines.

When out in the sun, remember to cover all exposed areas with sunscreen and not just the face and arms. Moreover, if you have any concerns regarding your skin, please seek the support of a licensed medical professional.

Love and Social Life (5th/7th/11th houses)

Both Sagittarius's romance and partnership sectors see an increase in astrological activity this year. Arguably the most noteworthy astrological event of 2026 is the joint transition and settling into Aries by Saturn and Neptune. Saturn, the planet of discipline, reality and hard work, enters Aries and shifts into Sagittarius's romance sector on February 13. Saturn will stay in Aries for about two and a half years. You are called to mature in the themes of the chart sector Saturn transits. For those Sagittarians who have often grappled with the weight of commitment, Saturn will press you to identify and address the root causes of this. Moreover, for Sagittarians who are single or newly partnered, Saturn in your romance sector bodes well for adding structure around romance and pleasure. Instead of approaching romance entirely spontaneously, being more intentional about planning romantic endeavours into your schedule will support the growth of budding relationships. With Neptune co-present in this chart sector, being extra mindful about seeing things through rose-tinted glasses is strongly recommended. Optimism is healthy, as long as it is grounded in reality.

For Sagittarians who have been partnered for a while, the energy surrounding your partnership sector actually promotes almost the opposite behaviour. Uranus, the planet of sudden shifts, moves into this chart sector and supports spontaneity and breaking down of the mundane same old day-to-day dynamic. Lean into Sagittarius's desire for adventure and prioritize exploring new uncharted waters with your partner. Mercury, your partnership planet, will turn retrograde in water signs this year, supporting the need to emotionally reconnect and align with your significant other.

Social life is a more neutral area of life this year, seeing that no outer planet transits in this chart sector in 2026 and only one personal planet, transiting retrograde. Venus, the planet of values and intimacy, will be retrograde in this chart sector from October 25 to November 13. Venus retrograde in the sign of Libra typically centres around equity, fairness and mutual respect. Given this planet will be retrograde in your social life chart sector, an audit or review of these themes in your social circles is the primary focus of this retrograde for you.

Career and Finances (10th/2nd/8th houses)

Career was an area of life heavily scrutinized by the astrology of 2025 and it is still a focus of the cosmic weather this year. The major cause for last year's substantial focus on career was the south node occupying this chart sector and the two eclipses it brought with it to this area of life for Sagittarius. In 2026, the south node gets ready to make its exit and does so on July 27. In the lead up to this exit, the south node does invite one final eclipse in this chart sector, which occurs on March 3. The south node itself is associated with shedding what no longer serves us. Consider this eclipse to be one of the concluding events in a chapter of transition related to career or cementing your legacy. The nodal axis takes 18 years to orbit the zodiac and nine years to reverse signs (the south node occupying the sign the north node is in and vice versa), so you are starting on a new 18-year cycle related to career (with a note-worthy checkpoint in nine years). Your career planet, Mercury, will occupy water signs for over half the year and turn retrograde in all three water signs over the course of the year. Water being the element of emotion and intuition strongly supports prioritizing emotional fulfilment in your career over other factors such as prestige or money.

Speaking of money, finances this year is a relatively neutral area of life, with one explicit theme being very apparent. While there are no outer planets transiting through this chart sector for Sagittarius, your finance planet is Saturn. Saturn moves into Aries on February 13, where it will stay for approximately two and a half years. Aries is the sign of the pioneer, and its primary focus is itself. While Saturn always supports frugality and practicality related to finances,

Saturn in Aries would also promote entrepreneurship and/or investing in new streams of income. If you are someone who is not fully informed on all your assets or finances, this is a top priority before making any other decisions related to finances. August 31 features a beautiful alignment between Jupiter and Saturn, which is ideal for investing.

Home and Domestic Life (4th house)

The north node has been transiting your home sector since January 2025 and will do so until July 27. Where the north node transits it brings increase to that area of the chart, and eclipses. The final eclipse in this chart sector for the next nine years or so will occur on August 28. As a reminder, eclipses stimulate evolution. For you Sagittarius, there's been a strong emphasis on changing family dynamics which have long needed to be addressed. Moreover, the astrology of 2026 centres around the importance of turning your home into a warm environment. Your home planet (and overall planetary ruler), Jupiter, enters Leo on June 30. Jupiter in Leo promotes taking steps to making your home feel more inviting and expansive. Addressing the physical layout and amount of lighting in your living space is strongly recommended. The summer is a significant season in the realms of home and family life this year.

Self-improvement (1st/3rd/5th/9th houses)

Your totem for 2026 is the Progenitor because of the emphasis the astrology of this year places on creativity and children/your lineage. With Saturn and Neptune both entering Aries early in 2026, Sagittarians are tasked with leveraging how they uniquely creatively self-express to inspire others or create something new. Creative self-expression can take numerous forms, whether it's through a visual arts medium, a technological creative medium or any form of storytelling. This is supported with the north node shifting into Sagittarius's communication sector when it enters Aquarius in July.

Moreover, Saturn and Neptune work with Jupiter in Leo to highlight the importance children and your family lineage play in your life this year. For those Sagittarians who have children, this applies to the interpersonal relationships you have with them. For those Sagittarians who do not have children themselves, this applies to the members of the younger generations both in your life and who are impacted by the work you do. Saturn and Neptune emphasize that there is a responsibility to maintain and strengthen these relationships this year.

Overall, the astrology of 2026 for Sagittarius is creative in nature because it supports expanding how you contribute in the world, both on a personal level and on the collective level. Jupiter moving into Leo supports Sagittarians trusting their hearts with important life decisions. Taking extra-special care to nurture the inner child within you is another important role for you this year.

Month-by-month Forecasts

January

Best Days Overall: 15–19
Most Stressful Days Overall: 6–10
Best Days for Love: 20–23
Best Days for Money: 1–4
Best Days for Career: 28–31
Power Word: Budget

Happy New Year, Sagittarius! The cosmic weather of 2026 kicks off with a financial focus for you as Mercury, the planet of thinking and communication, enters Capricorn on the 1st. Capricorn is a pragmatic earth sign known for strategy. The astrology of January strongly encourages you to adopt a strategy around finances if you don't already have one. Even if you do, this first week of January is the time to check in on it and cement your game plan for how you're going to be successful financially this year. On the 3rd, the Full Moon in Cancer is bright in the night sky. This lunation highlights how your money is intertwined and influenced by others.

Joint ventures are especially under review with the astrology of this lunation. Dot your i's, cross your t's and review your contracts, Centaur.

The Sun and Venus joyously meet up on the 6th, which is an excellent day to do any sort of investing or to take steps towards growing your finances. That being said, the astrology of the next four days can drive you to go overboard, so there's no need to be hypervigilant around finances at this time. This is because on the 9th, Venus and Jupiter, the planet of growth and expansion, find tension. The next day, the Sun and Mars follow suit and also find the same tension with Jupiter. Mars and Jupiter finding tension is also associated with tempers flaring. Do your best to ground yourself at this time, fire sign. The week of the 11th allows for the expansive energy of the previous week to linger and dissipate a bit before the New Moon on the 18th.

The New Moon in Capricorn is also a fertile time around finances for you. If you didn't take it upon yourself to do any investing or identify new streams of income on the 6th, this is another astrological opportunity to do so. This New Moon also represents a new cycle around how you approach spending and budgeting as well. The next day, the Sun exits Capricorn and enters Aquarius. Aquarius's season is your annual spotlight on communication and speaking your truth. The Sun, Mercury, Venus and Mars all meet up with edgy, yet transformative Pluto between the 20th and 27th. This week is one where many people, including yourself, are really going to feel the pull to get their ducks in a row from the coming year. Lots of people will be shedding habits, views or goals from 2025 which no longer serve them.

February

Best Days Overall: 19-23
Most Stressful Days Overall: 25-28
Best Days for Love: 8-11
Best Days for Money: 16-19
Best Days for Career: 2-5
Power Word: Domestic

February begins on the heels of a noteworthy transit which influences your year as a whole. After spending all of 2025 bouncing to and from Aries, Neptune, the planet of dreams and spirituality, entered the pioneering fire sign at the end of last month. A detailed analysis of how this influences your year can be found in your annual Horoscope overview. Saturn, the planet of responsibility and hard work, will be following suit in the middle of this month. The astrology of February kicks off with the Full Moon in your fellow fire sign, Leo. This Full Moon strongly encourages utilizing spirituality and philosophical systems as a means to ground yourself and wholeheartedly embrace all the ways you consider yourself unique. Owning your authenticity is the name of the game, Sagittarius.

Mercury and Venus both enter Pisces this month, on the 6th and 10th respectively. The build-up of Piscean energy brings a cosmic focus to home and domestic life for you. On the 13th, Saturn enters Aries, where it stays for the next two and a half years. On the 16th, Mercury in Pisces finds harmony with your planetary ruler, Jupiter, which is currently in Cancer. Mercury and Jupiter finding harmony supports efforts around making or keeping your home in order. Projects related to remodelling or reorganization are supported by this quick transit.

On the 17th, the first eclipse of 2026 occurs in Aquarius. As a reminder, eclipses stimulate evolution through scrutiny. The week of and after this eclipse is likely to feel heavier or have more people on edge. Many people feel eclipses in their bodies as well, so don't spread yourself too thin, Centaur. This eclipse stimulates growth around how you communicate to yourself and in your closest interpersonal relationships. Whether it's by adopting a much-needed filter or speaking up when you too often censor yourself, be open to what themes in this area of life present themselves. Pisces's season begins on the 18th and is your annual spotlight on the home and family dynamics. Lastly, Mercury turns retrograde in Pisces on the 26th, forcing you to reflect on existing family dynamics and feelings related to the physical home. More cosmic weather around these themes occur in March as well.

March

Best Days Overall: 10-14
Most Stressful Days Overall: 2-6
Best Days for Love: 6-9
Best Days for Money: 28-30
Best Days for Career: 4-7
Power Word: Endeavour

Not only is it still eclipse season, which gets people on edge: February ended with Mars and Uranus finding tension – a transit which sets the stage for the beginning of March. Mars and Uranus at odds tend to produce volatile energy. Mars rules assertion and conflict while Uranus rules breakthroughs and breakdowns. This energy, combined with the second eclipse of the year on March 3, means it's paramount you prioritize your peace during the first couple of weeks of the month. The lunar eclipse in Virgo spotlights themes around career, public perception and the legacy you'll leave. It is likely that some goals you set for yourself in January will already be shifting and changing as a result of the astrology of this week and month.

Thankfully, on the 5th, the Sun and Jupiter, your planetary ruler, find harmony with one another. This is the ideal energy for nesting, resting and recharging amid some frenetic astrology. Venus enters your fellow fire sign Aries on the 6th, and then immediately meets up with Neptune on the 7th and Saturn on the 8th. Venus in Aries invites you to integrate more recreation, play or your favourite hobbies into your weekly routines. On the 9th, Mercury also finds harmony with Jupiter, further supporting the need for more play and pleasure.

The New Moon in Aries on the 18th is a beautiful lunation for supporting long-term goals around creative self-expression or romance. If you've been looking to take one of your hobbies to the next level, or possibly even transform it into a source of income, this lunation supports doing so. That being said, wait until Mercury's retrograde is over before you launch a new endeavour. The New Moon also supports your relationship with children or the younger generation. For those Sagittarians with children or who work with/have strong ties to the younger generations, this lunation presents fertile energy to build on those relationships. Aries's season begins on the 20th, bringing your annual spotlight on creative self-expression and romance. The start of the astrological year also heralds the end of Mercury's retrograde on the 20th. March ends with Venus entering one of its favourite signs, Taurus, on the 30th.

April

Best Days Overall: 1–4
Most Stressful Days Overall: 15–19
Best Days for Love: 25–28
Best Days for Money: 7–11
Best Days for Career: 9–13
Power Word: Company

April's cosmic weather kicks off with a focus on the company you keep, Sagittarius. The Full Moon in Libra is live on the 1st. This Full Moon spotlights the balance of power and reciprocity between you and your friends and in the groups/circles you immerse yourself in. Libra is represented by the scales and centres around themes of equity, fairness and collaboration. Take this opportunity to express your gratitude to those members of your community who support you through thick and thin. On the 9th, Mars enters Aries. The Aries energy is going to build to a fever pitch by mid-month. All the fire energy brewing puts wind in your sails and encourages you to get productive. However, haste makes waste, Sagittarius, and the first three weeks of Mars in Aries reminds you that planning is necessary for execution.

The New Moon in Aries on the 17th is the day when the Aries energy reaches its peak. The Sun, the Moon, Mercury, Mars, Saturn and Neptune are all in Aries on this date. With six planets in the fire sign, you can expect the kinetic and creative energy to be palpable at this time. This New Moon also encourages dreaming up what's possible with how you work with hobbies or creative endeavours. If you have a vision board or like to journal, this is a great lunation for any form of intention work.

On the 19th, the Sun exits Aries and enters principled Taurus. Taurus is the fixed earth sign of the zodiac with the reputation for stubbornness, but in reality Taureans are just rooted in their principles. Taurus season is the time for you to get in touch with the principles which guide your life and use them as a means to conquer fears and anxieties which stifle you. On the 24th, Venus, in the last degree of Taurus, meets up with Uranus. This could present some surprises for you in the realm of finances or any forms of business collaboration. If you have to sign a contract around this date, have a third party you trust review it as well. The month concludes with Uranus, the planet of innovation and instability, leaving Taurus and entering Gemini, where it will stay until 2032/2033. More information on how this influences your year can be found in your annual Horoscope overview.

May

> Best Days Overall: 17–21
> Most Stressful Days Overall: 27–31
> Best Days for Love: 6–10
> Best Days for Money: 16–20
> Best Days for Career: 21–24
> Power Word: Vitality

Happy May, Sagittarius! This month there's double number of Full Moons and I wish I could say that means there's double the fun (but I can't). This month's astrology kicks off with the Full Moon in Scorpio. This emotional Full Moon spotlights mental wellness for Sagittarius. Your ability to emotionally regulate yourself, and your existing coping mechanisms for stress, are all under review at this time. A major audit of these themes occurs later in the year, so if you know you exhibit some self-destructive behaviour in this department, you should jump on addressing that now rather than when there's a cosmic judge and jury later in the year. Speaking of which, on the 5th Mercury finds tension with Pluto. This transit can spark your inner saboteur, the critic in your head which belittles you. Adopting or utilizing practices of self-compassion and self-love is vital. Get out into nature or do whatever you can to support yourself at this time.

Thankfully, Mercury finds harmony with your planetary ruler, Jupiter, on the 13th. Mercury and Jupiter harmoniously aligned support spring cleaning efforts, general organization efforts, or important conversations you may have with others close to this date. The New Moon in Taurus ushers in a new emotional cycle around physical health and wellness routines on the 16th. You're beginning a six-month journey centred around your physical health or virility. Identify a couple of small additions to your routine or small changes in behaviour you can make a habit.

On the 20th, the Sun exits Taurus and enters your polar sign, Gemini. Gemini's season is your annual spotlight on partnership. Gemini is the storyteller and narrator in astrology. What stories do you tell yourself or what internal narratives do you have which influence partnership or dating for you? Given the fact that Venus and Neptune find tension on this date, be mindful around seeing things through rose-tinted glasses this Gemini season, especially if you're single and ready to mingle. The last week of the month is both frustrating and sombre as Mars and Pluto find tension on the 26th, and Venus and Saturn do the same on the 28th. The (second) Full Moon, in Sagittarius, is live on the 31st. This lunation centres around your relationship to yourself. Sagittarius is known for embodying the coach and cheerleader archetypes. It is integral you display that level of support for yourself instead of just for other people.

June

Best Days Overall: 6–10
Most Stressful Days Overall: 18–22
Best Days for Love: 14–17
Best Days for Money: 27–30
Best Days for Career: 1–4
Power Word: Network

It's June, Sagittarius! June's cosmic weather kicks off on the 1st with Mercury, the planet of thinking and communication, entering watery Cancer. Anticipate the energy to support people thinking with their emotions a little more than normal. Thankfully, the first week of June offers fairly neutral astrology – considering the remainder of the summer is chock-full of transits. On the 10th, Venus in Cancer meets up with your planetary ruler, Jupiter. This transit is financial in nature for Sagittarius and supports invest-ments or joint ventures. You may feel the push to splurge on purchases as well around this date. Do so in moderation, Centaur. On the 13th, Venus enters Leo. Venus in Leo supports loving wholeheartedly and carving out time for recreation that would make your inner child happy.

On the 14th, the New Moon in Gemini ushers in a new emotional cycle around partnership. If you're single, this is the ideal time to put yourself out there and meet new people. Gemini is known as the marketeer and networker of the zodiac, so if you're actively seeking a partner, let your friends and community know and ask if they can connect you with prospective partners. If you're not single, this lunation supports communication within the relationship. Whether it's serious, must-need conversations or light-hearted banter, or even asking each other a series of questions to get to know each other, this New Moon encourages you to communicate.

Venus in Leo then finds harmony with Uranus on the 16th, harmony with Neptune on the 17th, and tension with Pluto on the 18th. Pay attention to themes which come up now, because multiple planets entering Leo over the next two months will form the same three alignments. The collective energy around partnership and interpersonal relationships runs high during the week of the 15th. On the 21st, the Sun exits Gemini and enters Cancer. Cancer season provides your annual spotlight on joint finances and the way your money is interwoven or influenced by others. Mercury turns retrograde again on the 29th. This Mercury retrograde will likely force you to confront lingering anxieties, insecurities or fears which prevent you from living the life you want to live or from pursuing the dreams you have for yourself. Be open to what rises to the surface over the next three or so weeks. The Full Moon in Capricorn on the 29th spotlights finances for you and is the ideal time for you to do an audit of your accounts to truly understand where all your money enters and exits from.

July

Best Days Overall: 26–29
Most Stressful Days Overall: 18–22
Best Days for Love: 24–27
Best Days for Money: 16–19
Best Days for Career: 9–13
Power Word: Expansion

Happy July, Centaur! This month features the most noteworthy astrology of the year and is very important for you, as your planetary ruler, Jupiter, is super-involved. Jupiter rules growth, expansion, beliefs and conviction. On the last day of last month, Jupiter left Cancer and entered Leo for the first time in 12 years. The way it influences your year overall has been described earlier, but Jupiter will be forming several important aspects this month that are going to be discussed here. Firstly though, the month begins with Mars forming multiple aspects to the slow-moving outer planets. Mars actually meets up with Uranus on the 4th and then harmoniously aligns to both Neptune and Pluto on the 5th. Mars and Uranus conjoined creates a spontaneous, albeit frenetic energy. This energy is – figuratively and literally – associated with explosions, so if you're handling fireworks or anything flammable around this date please be extra careful.

Venus enters Virgo on the 9th, drawing some cosmic focus towards career, public perception and legacy. Remember how in earlier months' forecasts Uranus and Neptune both entered into new signs? That doesn't happen too often, especially in the same year. As a result, both these planets harmoniously align this month on the 15th. What's more is that Uranus also finds harmony with Pluto, the slowest-moving influential planet, on the 18th. This is a rare occurrence and influences the collective by reinforcing the shifts which took place as these planets were oscillating back and forth between signs last year. What's more is that your planetary ruler Jupiter then finds harmony with Uranus and tension with Pluto on the 20th, and then harmony with Neptune on the 21st. These transits are integral to the structure of your year. Given that

Jupiter and Pluto met up three times in 2020, this astrology also functions as a major checkpoint in how much you've transformed since then. Amid all the kinetic energy, take a moment to pause and reflect on this.

On the 22nd, it's the start of Leo's season. The Sun entering Leo reinforces for Sagittarius the importance of navigating life with some guiding philosophical or spiritual system in place. Thankfully Mercury turns direct the next day. It will take a couple of weeks for it to be functioning at a normal speed, though. The month ends with a big Full Moon in Aquarius, which is augmented by your planetary ruler Jupiter on the 29th. The importance of speaking your truth and not censoring yourself is highlighted at this time. That being said, Sagittarius is *notorious* for not having a filter, so try to think before you speak, Centaur.

August

Best Days Overall: 18–22
Most Stressful Days Overall: 8–12
Best Days for Love: 25–28
Best Days for Money: 6–9
Best Days for Career: 28–31
Power Word: Catalyse

After a busy July, I have to report that August is – in fact – also busy. August functions as the second eclipse season of the year. As a reminder, eclipses are evolutionary transits which catalyse growth through scrutiny and shake-ups. Before the first eclipse of the month occurs, however, Venus enters Libra. Venus will soon slow down as it prepares to turn retrograde in a couple of months. The Sun in Leo finds harmony with Saturn in Aries. This harmonious alignment occurring in your two fellow fire signs supports productivity, especially in relation to creative endeavours. On the 10th, Venus in Libra finds harmony with Pluto in Aquarius. This transit strongly encourages you to spend time with friends who embrace your uniqueness and see it as one of your personal strengths.

On the 12th, the solar eclipse in Leo occurs. This solar eclipse occurs on the same day that Mercury forms the same three aspects that Jupiter and the Sun did last month. This eclipse functions in a couple of ways for Sagittarius. The first is the push to travel, for adventure, or for a spiritual voyage to gain enlightenment of some sort. The second is through shifting your perspective around higher education and the role it plays in achieving year-end or overarching goals. Would some sort of certification or an additional degree support you in achieving the goals you set for yourself in January? Would this type of higher education support the new goals you've formed this year in light of all the astrology you've experienced thus far? These questions linger as August rolls on.

On the 22nd, the Sun exits Leo and enters Virgo. Virgo season is your annual spotlight on career, public perception and the legacy you leave. This is very relevant given the eclipse themes. The second eclipse of the month (and final eclipse of the year) occurs on the 28th. The lunar eclipse in Pisces draws your attention to home and domestic life. This eclipse could inspire a move or some sort of renovation to the physical home. The eclipse could also scrutinize interpersonal dynamics within the home or family to lead to some evolution in those relationships.

September

Best Days Overall: 8–12
Most Stressful Days Overall: 22–26
Best Days for Love: 27–29
Best Days for Money: 3–6
Best Days for Career: 5–8
Power Word: Friendship

The energy of August's eclipse season lingers into the first week of this month, giving you a lot to ponder and navigate. Virgo is the sign of service, and if you're feeling lost right now, lean into this energy and help those in need. Sagittarius often embodies the role of teacher, coach or cheerleader. Those innate strengths should be tapped into at this time. The astrology of September really kicks off with the New Moon in Virgo on the 10th. This New Moon affords fertile energy for new beginnings in relation to existing or new career pursuits. Venus enters Scorpio on this day, highlighting the importance of emotional regulation at this time. Venus is also four weeks away from turning retrograde and officially in its 'pre-shadow' preparation phase for this retrograde period.

On the 14th, the Sun finds harmony with Mars, which provides constructive energy to get back on track with systems and routines which may have fallen by the wayside this summer. Venus forms the first of multiple tense aspects with Pluto over the next few months. To really capitalize on the evolutionary energy of this year, the next few months will require you partnering with yourself like never before. Being your biggest ally and really leaning into self-compassion is vital for you to achieve the goals you've set for the year.

On the 22nd, the Sun exits Virgo and enters Libra. Libra's season provides your annual spotlight on friendship and the communities you immerse yourself in. The Full Moon in Aries on the 26th supports carving out some much-needed time for recreation and play, especially with others. This lunation finds tension with Neptune, which could lead to seeing things through rose-tinted glasses if you're dating around this date. That being said, the Sun harmoniously aligns to both Uranus and Pluto between the 26th and 28th, supporting efforts around any form of communication. The month ends with Mercury entering Scorpio and preparing to slow down before it also turns retrograde next month.

October

Best Days Overall: 5–10
Most Stressful Days Overall: 26–31
Best Days for Love: 13–16
Best Days for Money: 7–9
Best Days for Career: 12–15
Power Word: Reconfigure

October begins pretty loudly with a complex and tense alignment between Mercury, Mars and Pluto occurring between the 2nd and 3rd. These transits feature all three planets finding tension with each other. Given Mercury's emphasis on communication and Mars's on conflict, just plan for people to generally be more reactive around this date. What's more, after slowing down over the last few weeks, Venus turns retrograde in Scorpio on the 3rd as well. Venus's retrograde periods always function as an audit of interpersonal relationships and value systems. For you, the first theme which is being analysed is how successfully you balance social and solo time. Venus turns retrograde in Scorpio which, for Sagittarius, pertains to your emotional wellbeing and your ease (or not) with prioritizing rest above work. Another theme of this retrograde, which will be more apparent later in the month, is around the company you keep. How do you feel before, during and after you spend time with the people in your life? The Sun finds tension with Saturn, compounding any exasperation around work. Prioritizing rest is necessary during this first week of the month.

On the 10th, the New Moon in Libra ushers in a new emotional cycle around friendship and community for you. This lunation also applies to involvement within professional organizations. If you're seeking a community aligned with your career, this is an opportune time to join a professional organization. If you're already immersed in one, this could be the opportunity to seek more responsibility or prestige within the group. Be open to what is shown to you about all the various kinds of interpersonal relationships in your life, Sagittarius. On the 20th, Venus once again finds tension with

Pluto. As mentioned before, this transit is associated with riling up your inner saboteur or the voice in your head which puts you down. Actively carve out time for self-care this month, Centaur.

On the 23rd, Scorpio season begins with a bang, with Mercury in Scorpio turning retrograde the following day. All three of the Mercury retrograde periods this year occur 100 per cent in water signs. As a result, they're a little more emotionally driven than in previous years. Mercury retrograde in Scorpio strongly supports Sagittarians to step away from the limelight for a bit and focus on private matters or rejuvenation. The Full Moon of the 26th in Taurus lights up the physical health and wellness sector of Sagittarius's chart. Regulate the mind through regulating the body, Centaur.

November

Best Days Overall: 15-19
Most Stressful Days Overall: 1-5
Best Days for Love: 21-24
Best Days for Money: 28-30
Best Days for Career: 22-25
Power Word: Functional

It's almost your season, Centaur! The dominant astrological themes of the first week or so of November centre around the two retrograde periods that commenced last month. Reflect, reconfigure and reconnect during the early part of this month. The first half of November is not a good time to start or launch anything new. It would be better to tinker with or circle back to things in the works or that you put down for a while that were in motion at some point. The New Moon in Scorpio on the 9th centres around emotional regulation and how you approach mental health. This lunation lays out fertile energy to address and support your mental wellbeing in new and innovative ways once the retrogrades are over (which will be in a few days). If you've never worked with a mental health expert, this would be an opportune time to do so if you're feeling overwhelmed.

I'm happy to report that both Mercury and Venus end their retrograde periods on the same day – November 13! Remember though, it will take a couple of weeks for the two planets to be back at their fully functional speeds once again. Be aware that communication, transport or technological glitches are still likely for the first week or two after the 13th. Mars joins up with Jupiter in Leo and brings some much-needed kinetic energy to you to capitalize on. Dust off your 2026 to-do list and use this energy.

On the 22nd, the Sun exits Scorpio and enters Sagittarius. Happy birthday! After such a reflective six weeks, identify two or three characteristics you seek to embody in this next trip around the Sun. If you journal or do any self-reflective work, integrate these words into those practices. Mars enters Virgo on the 25th, jump starting any slowdowns you experience in the realms of career or public perception. Mars in Virgo also encourages you to serve the less fortunate or help those in need. The month ends with the Sun finding harmony with Saturn on the 30th. The last couple of days of this month and the first couple of days of December are ideal for planning or organizing how you seek to approach 2027.

December

Best Days Overall: 12-16
Most Stressful Days Overall: 27-31
Best Days for Love: 1-3
Best Days for Money: 9-12
Best Days for Career: 23-26
Power Word: Truth

Happy December, Sagittarius! Your season rolls on into December with the first bit of astrology being Venus's re-entry into Scorpio on the 4th. The cosmic weather focusing on emotional regulation is still present for the remainder of this month. Mars and Uranus find tension one more time this year on the 5th. As a reminder, this transit is figuratively and literally associated with explosiveness, so be mindful around any confrontation at this time and be extra cautious if handling things that are particularly flammable. The next day, Mercury enters your sign. Mercury in Sagittarius is associated with speaking without a filter. Speak your truth, Centaur, but please think through what you have to say first.

The New Moon in Sagittarius occurs on the 8th and ushers in a new emotional cycle around how you relate to and treat yourself. Sagittarius is known for being able to cheer everyone else up. Do you direct this energy inwards towards yourself too? Venus finds tension one final time with Pluto, reminding you of the importance of being kind to yourself. Intentionally carve out time for self-care during your solar season. Thankfully, the 11th and 12th feature two harmonious transits. Firstly, Mercury and Saturn align on the 11th. This is a softer transit supporting last-ditch efforts to check off items on your to-do list. It also supports leaning into creative self-expression. Sing, dance, paint, etc. On the 12th, Venus and Mars find harmony. This transit supports heartfelt interpersonal connection.

On the 21st, the Sun exits your sign and enters pragmatic Capricorn. Capricorn's season is your annual spotlight on finances and budgeting. The Full Moon in Cancer illuminates joint ventures and business collaborations. This lunation also encourages tackling fears or insecurities which may have held you back this year. On the 25th, Mercury, the planet of thinking and communication, enters practical Capricorn. Mercury in the cardinal earth sign is ideal for getting a plan together for next year. Spend the last week of 2026 doing what Sagittarius is known to do best – looking at and chasing the horizon.

Capricorn

♑

THE GOAT

Birthdays from
December 21
to January 19

Personality Profile

CAPRICORN AT A GLANCE

Element – Earth

Ruling Planet – Saturn
   Career Planet – Venus
   Love Planet – Moon
   Money Planet – Saturn
   Planet of Communications – Jupiter
   Planet of Health and Work – Mercury
   Planet of Home and Family Life – Mars
   Planet of Spirituality and Mental Health – Jupiter

Totem – the Pioneer

Colours – black, indigo

Colours that promote love, romance and social harmony – puce, silver

Colour that promotes earning power – ultramarine blue

Gem – black onyx

Metal – lead

Scents – magnolia, pine, sweet pea, wintergreen

Quality – cardinal (= activity)

Qualities most needed for balance – warmth, spontaneity, a sense of fun

Strongest virtues – sense of duty, organization, perseverance, patience, ability to take the long-term view

Deepest needs – to manage, take charge and administrate

Characteristics to avoid – pessimism, depression, undue materialism and undue conservatism

Signs of greatest overall compatibility – Taurus, Virgo

Signs of greatest overall incompatibility – Aries, Cancer, Libra

Sign most helpful to career – Libra

Sign most helpful for emotional support – Aries

Sign most helpful financially – Aquarius

Sign best for marriage and/or partnerships – Cancer

Sign most helpful for creative projects – Taurus

Best Sign to have fun with – Taurus

Signs most helpful in spiritual matters – Virgo, Sagittarius

Best day of the week – Saturday

Understanding a Capricorn

The virtues of Capricorns are such that there will always be people for and against them. Many admire them, many dislike them. Why? It seems to be because of Capricorn's power urges. A well-developed Capricorn has his or her eyes set on the heights of power, prestige and authority. In the sign of Capricorn, ambition is not a fatal flaw, but rather the highest virtue.

Capricorns are not frightened by the resentment their authority may sometimes breed. In Capricorn's cool, calculated, organized mind all the dangers are already factored into the equation – the unpopularity, the animosity, the misunderstandings, even the outright slander – and a plan is always in place for dealing with these things in the most efficient way. To the Capricorn, situations that would terrify an ordinary mind are merely problems to be managed, bumps on the road to ever-growing power, effectiveness and prestige.

Some people attribute pessimism to the Capricorn sign, but this is a bit deceptive. It is true that Capricorns like to take into account the negative side of things. It is also true that they love to imagine the worst possible scenario in every undertaking. Other people might find such analyses depressing, but Capricorns only do these things so that they can formulate a way out – an escape route.

Capricorns will argue with success. They will show you that you are not doing as well as you think you are. Capricorns do this to themselves as well as to others. They do not mean to discourage you but rather to root out any impediments to your greater success. A Capricorn boss or supervisor feels that no matter how good the performance there is always room for improvement. This explains why Capricorn supervisors are difficult to handle and even infuriating at times. Their actions are, however, quite often effective – they can get their subordinates to improve and become better at their jobs.

Capricorn is a born manager and administrator. Leo is better at being king or queen, but Capricorn is better at being prime minister – the person actually wielding power.

Capricorn is interested in the virtues that last, in the things that will stand the test of time and trials of circumstance. Temporary fads and fashions mean little to a Capricorn – except as things to be used for profit or power. Capricorns apply this attitude to business, love, to their thinking and even to their philosophy and religion.

Finance

Capricorns generally attain wealth and they usually earn it. They are willing to work long and hard for what they want. They are quite amenable to forgoing a short-term gain in favour of long-term benefits. Financially, they come into their own later in life.

However, if Capricorns are to attain their financial goals they must shed some of their strong conservatism. Perhaps this is the least desirable trait of the Capricorn. They can resist anything new merely because it is new and untried. They are afraid of experimentation. Capricorns need to be willing to take a few risks. They should be more eager to market new products or explore different managerial techniques. Otherwise, progress will leave them behind. If necessary, Capricorns must be ready to change with the times, to discard old methods that no longer work.

Very often this experimentation will mean that Capricorns have to break with existing authority. They might even consider changing their present position or starting their own ventures. If so, they should be willing to accept all the risks and just get on with it. Only then will a Capricorn be on the road to highest financial gains.

Career and Public Image

A Capricorn's ambition and quest for power are evident. It is perhaps the most ambitious sign of the zodiac – and usually the most successful in a worldly sense. However, there are lessons Capricorns need to learn in order to fulfil their highest aspirations.

Intelligence, hard work, cool efficiency and organization will take them a certain distance, but will not carry them to the very top.

Capricorns need to cultivate their social graces, to develop a social style, along with charm and an ability to get along with people. They need to bring beauty into their lives and to cultivate the right social contacts. They must learn to wield power gracefully, so that people love them for it – a very delicate art. They also need to learn how to bring people together in order to fulfil certain objectives. In short, Capricorns require some of the gifts – the social graces – of Libra to get to the top.

Once they have learned this, Capricorns will be successful in their careers. They are ambitious hard workers who are not afraid of putting in the required time and effort. Capricorns take their time in getting the job done – in order to do it well – and they like moving up the corporate ladder slowly but surely. Being so driven by success, Capricorns are generally liked by their bosses, who respect and trust them.

Love and Relationships

Like Scorpio and Pisces, Capricorn is a difficult sign to get to know. They are deep, introverted and like to keep their own counsel. Capricorns do not like to reveal their innermost thoughts. If you are in love with a Capricorn, be patient and take your time. Little by little you will get to understand him or her.

Capricorns have a deep romantic nature, but they do not show it straightaway. They are cool, matter of fact and not especially emotional. They will often show their love in practical ways.

It takes time for a Capricorn – male or female – to fall in love. They are not the love-at-first-sight kind. If a Capricorn is involved with a Leo or Aries, these Fire types will be totally mystified – to them the Capricorn will seem cold, unfeeling, unaffectionate and not very spontaneous. Of course none of this is true; it is just that Capricorn likes to take things slowly. They like to be sure of their ground before making any demonstrations of love or commitment.

Even in love affairs Capricorns are deliberate. They need more time to make decisions than is true of the other signs of the zodiac, but given this time they become just as passionate. Capricorns like a relationship to be structured, committed, well regulated, well defined, predictable and even routine. They prefer partners who are nurturers, and they in turn like to nurture their partners. This is their basic psychology. Whether such a relationship is good for them is another issue altogether. Capricorns have enough routine in their lives as it is. They might be better off in relationships that are a bit more stimulating, changeable and fluctuating.

Home and Domestic Life

The home of a Capricorn – as with a Virgo – is going to be tidy and well organized. Capricorns tend to manage their families in the same way they manage their businesses. Capricorns are often so career-driven that they find little time for the home and family. They should try to get more actively involved in their family and domestic life. Capricorns do, however, take their children very seriously and are very proud parents – particularly should their children grow up to become respected members of society.

Horoscope for 2026

Capricorn's 2026 totem is 'the Pioneer' because the astrology of this year points to breaking the mould and blazing new trails for yourself. Your planetary ruler, Saturn, spent 2025 oscillating between Pisces and Aries, setting last year up as a year of transition. This year, Saturn settles into Aries early in the year (February 13). Aries is the first sign of the zodiac and associated with swift, decisive action – similar to your sign; although Aries is more associated with being the first at doing something while Capricorn is associated with maintaining longevity when endeavouring to start something new. Saturn in the sign of Aries empowers Capricorn to take a risk on carving out a new path for itself. Though often focused on career, given that this is your planetary ruler undergoing this shift, it applies to all areas of life.

Saturn isn't the only noteworthy planet entering a new sign after spending last year in transition. Neptune, the planet of dreams, compassion and the collective, enters Aries on January 26 and will be present in the sign with Saturn from February onwards. Though Capricorn is known for its realistic, pragmatic views, Neptune conjoining with your planetary ruler inspires you to dream big this year. The most interesting thing about the combination of Saturn and Neptune is that Saturn rules reality and pragmatism while Neptune rules fantasy and optimism. Given your innate Saturnian nature, there will always be some element of pragmatism as you navigate a new year. But Neptune joining Saturn allows for you to consider possibilities you may have ruled out due to their grandiose nature or because of their lack of practicality.

While this year is about pioneering new paths, another major focus for the year, especially the latter half of 2026, is finances. The north and south nodes will be switching signs from Pisces/Virgo to Aquarius/Leo respectively. While this change occurs later into the year, on July 27, the shift affects both eclipse cycles and, as a result, there will be eclipses with financial implications for Capricorn as early as February 13. Eclipses are evolutionary transits which catalyse change through scrutiny and shake-ups. It's very possible that how you uniquely embody the pioneer relates to how the cosmic weather centres around finances this year.

Jupiter, the planet of growth and expansion, will shift into Leo mid-year after spending about 12 months in Cancer. Jupiter in Leo promotes childlike wonder in the face of new challenges. Embodying a 'glass half full' mindset in the face of apparent setbacks will only support Capricorn's call to blaze new trails in 2026. Jupiter in Leo specifically calls on Capricorn to conquer fears and anxieties which have kept you stifled for some time. More will be explored in the self-improvement section of this Horoscope.

For a quarterly view of the year ahead, the first quarter features a focus on self-improvement and home/domestic life. The second quarter of the year centres around conquering anxiety and understanding your budget better. The third quarter of 2026 is also financially focused and also has a bent towards spirituality, while the final quarter of the year continues the themes of self-improvement and finances.

Health (1st/6th/12th houses)

(Please note that this is an astrological perspective on health and not a medical one. Any health-related symptoms should be evaluated by a qualified healthcare professional.)

Your physical health planet, Mercury, will spend over half the year in water signs, and turns retrograde in all three water signs too over the course of 2026. Those retrograde periods are February 25 to March 20, June 29 to July 23 and October 24 to November 13. Mercury's retrograde periods are not meant to be feared but are structured times to review and re-evaluate. Because Mercury is a health planet for Capricorn, these are important periods within which to revise and reimplement your physical health routines. Water is the element of emotion, so it's especially important to monitor how your mood influences your adherence to healthy behaviours. Moreover, there's the possibility coping behaviours will spike with your health planet spending over half the year in water signs. Having your physical health routines in place is especially important because Uranus, a planet that brings inspiration and a frenetic energy, will enter Capricorn's health sector in April. This transit could bring with it ingenuity and innovation in how you approach diet or fitness. However, it can also bring disorganization if you don't have existing routines in place.

Your mental health planet, Jupiter, will stay in Cancer for the first half of the year and then shift into Leo on June 30. Given there are two even halves to Jupiter's transits this year, it's important to distinguish how this influences mental health for Capricorn. Jupiter in Cancer is a very partnership-focused planetary transit for you, Seagoat. As a result, there's an even stronger link between your mental wellness and partnership. This applies regardless of partnership status. When Jupiter moves into Leo, the focus moves to general anxiety exploration and management, plus being open to conquering fears which may keep you stuck. Of course, it is important to work on your mental health under the guidance of an expert, which both of Jupiter's transits fully support.

Here are the specific areas of the body to focus on this year:

- Bones and joints: this is a perennial area of focus for Capricorn as the sign rules this part of the body. Monitoring bone health with a medical professional and maintaining a diet which nourishes these parts of the body are strongly recommended.
- Feet: your physical health planet, Mercury, will turn retrograde in Pisces, the sign which rules this part of the body, from the end of February through most of March. (Mercury will actually occupy the sign of Pisces from February 7 to April 15.) Reflexology and other remedies to reduce tension in the feet are strongly recommended. It may also be beneficial to identify if you need to modify the soles of your shoes.
- Lungs and breasts/pecs: Mercury, your physical health planet, will also turn retrograde in Cancer, the sign which rules these parts of the body. Mercury will be occupying the sign of Cancer from June 2 to August 10. Monitoring the health of these body parts in the care of a medical expert is recommended. Being mindful to avoid behaviours deleterious to these parts of the body (like smoking) is also recommended.

Love and Social Life (5th/7th/11th houses)

Jupiter, the planet of growth and convictions, will be continuing its transit through Capricorn's partnership sector for the first half of 2026 as it remains in the sign of Cancer. In traditional astrology, Jupiter is regarded as the 'Greater Benefic' because of its association with expansion. However, modern astrologers have a more balanced view of Jupiter transits and recognize that Jupiter tends to augment existing conditions (good or bad). For you, love and partnership in the first half of 2026 will be an area of life that feels like it has a magnifying glass on it. For those Capricorns that are single, it is recommended to work with this energy by intentionally putting yourself out there if you're looking for a partner. Jupiter in Cancer also supports ensuring your physical home is welcoming and inviting to potential partners (more information on this in that section of this horoscope, below). The summer is a noteworthy time of year in regard to partnership for Capricorn as Mercury will be retrograde in Capricorn's partnership sector. This retrograde is a time when ghosts from your past may revisit to remind you of important lessons to carry with you in existing or future relationships. Mercury will be retrograde from June 29 to July 23, but will be in its shadow period (not operating at full speed) for a couple of weeks before and after those dates.

Social life is noteworthy in 2026 as Venus, the planet of values and worthiness, will be retrograde in Capricorn's social life sector from October 3 to October 25. Venus retrograde is a time when you're forced to reassess your values systems and the company you keep. Given Venus will be retrograde in investigative Scorpio just as Mercury slows to turn retrograde in the same sign, it is especially important you are exploring whether your networks and communities are engaging with you in the ways you need them to as you embody the Pioneer this year. Your social life planet, Mars, will not turn retrograde this year, supporting you in immersing yourself in new communities or social circles.

Career and Finances (10th/2nd/8th houses)

As mentioned in the previous section, Venus will turn retrograde in the autumn of 2026, and will spend half of its retrograde period transiting your social life sector and the other half transiting your career sector. Furthermore, in modern astrology, Venus is the planet related to personal finances. Essentially, this means that the autumn is a season where you'll be confronted with assessing whether you feel as though you are earning what you should be, given where you're at in this moment of your career journey. Venus will be retrograde in Capricorn's career sector from October 25 to November 13.

Finances are going to be an ongoing focus this year as the first eclipse of the year, on February 13, occurs in your finance sector. It is strongly advised to be conscious of how your money does or does not grow on its own, considering the north node will enter your finances sector on July 27. The north node initiates an 18-month period of scrutiny and growth in the area of life related to the chart sector it's transiting. Jupiter moves into the sector of Capricorn's chart related to joint ventures on June 30, supporting collaborative endeavours to build new streams of income. However, remember that Mercury will be retrograde over the summer, so it's advised to wait until after Mercury finishes its retrograde period (July 23) to launch something new.

Home and Domestic Life (4th house)

Saturn and Neptune entering Aries early this year means both planets transit Capricorn's home and domestic life sector for almost all of 2026. Saturn in this chart sector signifies the need to take responsibility for your physical home and your existing family relationships. Saturn can function as an auditor, so both these areas are up for audit this year. For your home, if there has been the need for any sort of repairs, it is strongly recommended you address those concerns this year, given that Saturn rules consequences. Moreover, if any of these physical or structural concerns involve water, then especially address those given that Neptune is co-present with Saturn in this chart sector. Saturn and Neptune in this sector present you with the opportunity to make structural changes to your home which promote long-lasting sustainability. For family relationships, if it is necessary to do so, it is important you address any long-standing concerns you've had in a methodical way, as Saturn and Neptune will be in fiery Aries. There is also strong potential for significantly building on existing relationships in a sustainable, rewarding fashion.

Self-improvement (1st/3rd/5th/9th houses)

One focus of self-improvement for this year centres around communication and not censoring yourself. The north node will still be transiting Capricorn's communication sector for the first half of the year (until July 27) and then there will be the final eclipse of the year in this chart sector (on August 28). If you find yourself constantly stifling how you actually wish to express yourself, one way to embody your totem of the Pioneer is to push yourself to speak up. Moreover, given these transits are occurring in the sign of Pisces, another area of self-improvement this year centres around developing a self-compassion practice with your words. One way to do this is to adopt a mantra you say to yourself on a routine basis. Another way to do this would be through journalling.

In addition to communication, spirituality and higher education are two other areas highlighted by the astrology of 2026. There will be an eclipse in the chart sector related to these two on March 3, setting up the spring as a season where these two aspects of life are especially of focus. If you've found yourself feeling particularly ungrounded, adopting a routine spiritual practice is strongly recommended. This should be some way you connect with nature or the universe, be it through meditation, prayer or simply going for a daily walk with no distractions.

Month-by-month Forecasts

January

Best Days Overall: 18–22
Most Stressful Days Overall: 25–28
Best Days for Love: 1–4
Best Days for Money: 3–6
Best Days for Career: 7–10
Power Word: Goals

Happy New Year, Capricorn! The new year begins in the middle of your season. The cosmic weather of 2026 kicks off on the 1st with Mercury joining the Sun, Venus and Mars in your sign. The year begins with a major build-up of Capricorn energy! You're known for your ability to strategize. Lean into all this Capricorn energy and do what you do best – plan. This will be a super-noteworthy year astrologically, so it's important you get your goals, and the plans to achieve those goals, in order. The Full Moon in Cancer, your polar sign, lights up the night sky on the 3rd. This lunation brings an emotional focus to partnership for you. If you're single, this lunation will have you thinking about what your goals around partnership status are for this year. If you're partnered, the focus is similar;

it's just directed towards how you're feeling about your existing partnership dynamic and what you'd like to see shift or change.

The Sun in Capricorn meets up with Venus in Capricorn which provides splendorous energy to take a break from planning world domination to have some fun. Don't go overboard though, because the Sun, Venus and Mars all find tension with expansive Jupiter between the 9th and the 10th, which can coax some people into going overboard with indulgence. The New Moon in your sign occurs on the 18th and is the ideal lunation to start to take action around the goals you set at the start of the year.

The next day, the Sun exits your sign and enters fellow Saturn-ruled Aquarius. Aquarius's season is your annual spotlight on personal finances and material possessions. Mercury, Venus and Mars follow suit and all enter Aquarius as well between the 18th and the 24th. Prioritizing budgeting: gaining a full picture around what your finances look like is vital right now. All these planets meet up with edgy, transformative Pluto between the 20th and the 27th. These meet-ups will have everyone on edge. For you, they pertain to your relationship with finances, budgeting and possible anxieties you have going into this year. Brushing up on financial literacy or seeking counsel with a finance expert is recommended at the end of this month.

February

Best Days Overall: 16–20
Most Stressful Days Overall: 2–6
Best Days for Love: 20–24
Best Days for Money: 13–16
Best Days for Career: 5–8
Power Word: Frugal

It's February, Capricorn! The astrology of this month begins on the 1st with the Full Moon in Leo. This lunation is also financial in nature but highlights the ways your money is influenced, affected or entwined with others. If you're currently involved in any joint ventures, reviewing the contract and balance of power is also a focal point of this lunation. Mercury finds tension on the 5th with Uranus, just before entering Pisces on the 6th. Venus also finds tension with Uranus a few days later, on the 8th, before entering Pisces on the 10th. Bookmark the first week or so of this month to be one where many people around you (and possibly yourself) could lack a filter. Uranus is the planet of instability, breakthroughs and breakdowns. It typically imbues frenetic energy when forming a tense aspect with another planet. Stick to your plans and maintain your routines at this time, Seagoat.

After spending all of 2025 oscillating between Pisces and Aries, Saturn, the planet of discipline and hard work, joins Neptune, which just entered Aries at the end of last month on January 13. Both Saturn and Neptune entering the fire sign influence your year more so than just this month. A detailed description on how both planets affect your year is provided in the overview of your annual Horoscope, earlier. Mercury in Pisces finds harmony with Jupiter in Cancer on the 16th, making it an ideal time to communicate with prospective or existing partners. This could be serious necessary conversation or communication to bring you closer.

The first solar eclipse of the year occurs on the 17th in Aquarius. This eclipse strongly supports adopting a frugal approach over the next four weeks or so. Eclipses stimulate growth through scrutiny, so anticipate you may be feeling a bit of a squeeze in your purse or wallet. Whether or not you are, the astrology of February speaks to avoiding flagrant purchases or being reckless with money at this time. The next day, the Sun exits Aquarius and enters Pisces. Pisces's season is your annual spotlight on patterns of communication. The month ends with the first Mercury retrograde period of the year, starting on the 26th. Reflections around how you communicate with yourself and in your interpersonal relationships is the focus of this transit.

March

Best Days Overall: 27-31
Most Stressful Days Overall: 6-10
Best Days for Love: 28-30
Best Days for Money: 18-21
Best Days for Career: 10-13
Power Word: Talk

Happy March, Seagoat! March begins with Mercury still very much retrograde for the next three weeks. Be mindful that technology and transport glitches abound. Double-check your phone is charging, leave for that appointment 10 minutes early, and ask people to clarify if you don't fully understand what they've said. The cosmic weather of March begins with the second eclipse of the year, a lunar eclipse in Virgo. Virgo is a Mercury-ruled sign, so this eclipse reinforces the scrutiny around communication for Capricorn. If you engage in arguments or have any type of serious conversation around this date, think before you speak and be very intentional with every word you use. The Sun finds beautiful harmony with Jupiter on the 5th, making it an ideal day to spend quality time with a special someone or to take yourself on a self-date.

Between the 6th and the 8th, Venus enters your fellow cardinal sign, Aries, and meets up with Saturn and Neptune. Venus in Aries encourages you to cultivate warmth and abundance within the home. These meet-ups strongly encourage revitalizing the energy of your space through reorganization or, if necessary, repair. Mercury finds harmony with Jupiter on the 9th, supporting interpersonal communication or revisiting conversations that may need readdressing.

On the 18th, the New Moon in Pisces also centres around communication. This New Moon provides fertile energy to turn over a new leaf in how you talk to yourself. Capricorn is a sign known for being especially self-critical or hard on itself. This lunation encourages turning a new leaf where you routinely cut yourself some slack or don't demand perfection from yourself. On the 20th, Aries's season begins and brings the gift of Mercury ending its retrograde period. Aries season is your annual spotlight on home and family dynamics. This is a major year for this area of life for you Capricorn, so definitely make sure you read that section in your annual Horoscope, above. The Sun meets up with Saturn on the 25th, encouraging you to slow down, pause and check in on the progress you're making in achieving your 2026 goals. The month's astrology concludes on the 30th with Venus entering Taurus, encouraging you to carve out time for play and recreation this spring.

April

Best Days Overall: 5-9
Most Stressful Days Overall: 17-21
Best Days for Love: 20-23
Best Days for Money: 28-30
Best Days for Career: 1-4
Power Word: Portray

It's April, Capricorn! Aries season rolls on with the Full Moon in Libra happening on the 1st of the month. This lunation brings an emotional focus to career, public perception and issues of legacy for you. What do you want to be remembered for, Capricorn? Libra is a sign often associated with aesthetics. This lunation motivates you to spend time thinking about the image you portray to the world and if that provides you with emotional fulfilment. This lunation also encourages you to analyse if you feel like you have struck a balance between work and play. You're beginning a six-month journey of striving to achieve this balance. On the 9th, Mars, the planet of action and assertion, enters fiery Aries. However, over its first 10 days in the sign, it meets up with Neptune and Saturn, slowing it down. Adopting the mentality of 'slow and steady wins the race' this month is advised.

On the 17th, the New Moon in Taurus encourages you to ensure your house really feels like a home. What change in dynamics or details would ensure you feel more comfortable in your living space? If there are answers to this question within your control, focus on addressing those deliverables first. On the 19th, the Sun exits Aries and enters Taurus, bringing your annual spotlight on creative self-expression, play and romance. Taurus is the fixed earth sign of the zodiac associated with sensuality and security. Prioritize pleasure involving the five senses this Taurus season.

The slowest, albeit the most restless, part of the month occurs around the 19th as Mars and Saturn officially meet up. This transit reminds you that your productivity does not define your worth. It also highlights that longevity in any activity depends on there being periods of rest or recovery. It's OK to take a breather, Capricorn. On the 24th, Venus enters chatty Gemini, beginning the astrological shift in focus towards physical wellness and routines. The month ends with Uranus, the planet of innovation and instability, shifting in Gemini on the 25th. This is a major shift in energy described in detail in your annual Horoscope.

May

Best Days Overall: 8–11
Most Stressful Days Overall: 27–31
Best Days for Love: 16–19
Best Days for Money: 13–16
Best Days for Career: 2–5
Power Word: Emotions

Hi, Capricorn! As a reminder, the Moon rules all things emotional in astrology. This month, there's not one but two Full Moons occurring, so anticipate emotions to run high this May. The first Full Moon of the month starts things off on the 1st. The Full Moon in Scorpio centres around your friends, networks and the company you keep. Scorpio is the sign associated with investigation, so this lunation could very well have you asking important questions about this area of life. Scorpio is also a sign that is often associated with intense loyalty. This lunation stresses the importance of prioritizing those friendships and relationships which are based in mutual loyalty for one another. On the 2nd, Mercury enters Taurus where it finds tension with Pluto on the 5th. The cosmic weather of May's first week definitely riles up your inner critic, so do your best to treat yourself with kindness. The 5th also features Mars and Jupiter finding tension, making tempers more likely to flare.

Thankfully, Mercury and Jupiter find harmony on the 13th, which supports romantic or creative endeavours for the few days around this happening. On the 16th, the New Moon in Taurus is a lunation which pushes you to not only prioritize time to play but to make it a routine part of your week, to counteract all the ways you work hard. Mercury joins Uranus in Gemini the next day, making it a day where speaking without thinking is more likely.

On the 20th, the Sun exits Taurus and enters Gemini, the season which spotlights physical wellness and routines for you. A build-up of Gemini energy for Capricorn would also highlight the narratives or stories you tell yourself which drive how you regard your physical body. The last week of the month features a fair amount of astrological tension as Mars and Pluto square off with each other on the 26th and Venus and Saturn do the same on the 28th. Mars and Pluto finding tension is associated with illuminating unequal power dynamics in your life, and also centres around conflict style. Trying to remain as cool, calm and collected around this date is vital. Venus and Saturn finding tension with one another tends to spike feelings of doubt you've been grappling with. You never know what you're made of until you take your first step on the road, Seagoat. May's astrology concludes with the second Full Moon of the month. The Full Moon in Sagittarius encourages nesting, resting and prioritizing emotional regulation above all else.

June

Best Days Overall: 20-24
Most Stressful Days Overall: 26-30
Best Days for Love: 7-10
Best Days for Money: 3-6
Best Days for Career: 14-17
Power Word: Ghosts

The first week of June is heavily influenced by the bright Full Moon in Sagittarius on the last day of last month. Remember, this lunation centred around the importance of emotional regulation. Tied to this is the notion of taking time to remove yourself from social spaces to recharge. It would be beneficial to start this month off by limiting social media time, and screen time in general if possible. On the 1st Mercury enters Cancer, bringing a focus to prioritizing one-on-one connections which provide you with a feeling of emotional security. It is recommended that, given there aren't many new transits occurring in the first week of this month, you capitalize on this by maintaining the regular routines that centre, ground and keep you healthy.

On the 10th, Venus in Cancer joyously meets up with Jupiter. If you're single, this is a great day to put yourself out there or take yourself out on a date. If you're partnered, this is the ideal transit for wholehearted connection with your significant other. Venus then enters fiery Leo on the 13th. This transit supports joint ventures and business collaborations if you're seeking to launch any new endeavours. The New Moon in Gemini strongly encourages you to turn over a new leaf in either tackling behaviours which are deleterious to your health or identifying small tweaks to your existing routines which would further support your physical wellness. Venus finds tension with Pluto on the 18th, so it is vital you are not hypervigilant around doing this as this transit is associated with being very critical of your self-image.

On the 21st, the Sun exits Gemini and enters Cancer. Cancer season spotlights partnership for Capricorn. This Cancer season will have you reflecting on past relationships as a way to inform your present, given that Mercury turns retrograde in Cancer on the 29th. It is also likely that 'ghosts' from your past will resurface during this retrograde as a way to highlight how much you've grown since you knew them, or to remind you of patterns of thoughts/behaviours you want to avoid in the present. The Full Moon in your sign occurs on the 29th and spotlights your relationship to yourself. As mentioned during Capricorn season, your sign is known for being very self-critical, so take this as a cue to cut yourself some slack.

July

Best Days Overall: 15–19
Most Stressful Days Overall: 4–8
Best Days for Love: 13–16
Best Days for Money: 24–27
Best Days for Career: 26–29
Power Word: Halfway

It's July, Capricorn! July is the most profound month of 2026 astrologically, so there's lots to talk about. To start things off, Mars meets up with Uranus on the 4th. Mars and Uranus together are associated with volatility and inflammation. Be mindful that people are likely to be a lot quicker to anger around this date. Also, given the fact that Mars and Uranus together have an association with figurative and literal explosions, please take extra precautions if you're handling fireworks or anything flammable around this date. Mars then finds harmony with Neptune and Pluto the next day, providing a jump start of much-needed kinetic energy. On the 9th, Venus enters Virgo, which supports immersing yourself in nature and getting more in touch with your spirituality.

This year is a special year because some of the slowest-moving planets officially entered new signs. Uranus takes about 84 years to orbit the zodiac and Neptune takes about 160 years. It's not a common occurrence for them both to enter new signs in the same year. What's rarer is the fact that Uranus forms harmonious aspects to both Neptune and Pluto within the span of a mere few days. Uranus finds harmony with Neptune on July 15 and with Pluto on the 18th. These alignments influence the collective more so than the personal level. However, a few days later, between the 20th and the 21st, Jupiter finds harmony with Uranus and Neptune, but tension with Pluto. Jupiter finding tension with Pluto functions as a critical juncture in the transformation you've undergone since 2020. Jupiter and Pluto met up three times during that year, and this transit functions as a halfway point in the cycle that was ushered in that year.

Leo's season begins on the 22nd and Mercury ends its retrograde period on the 23rd. Leo's season starts off with some harsher energy as the Sun also finds tension with Pluto. The astrology of this week beseeches you to embrace your quirks and uniqueness. The Full Moon in Aquarius shines brightly on the 29th. This Full Moon finds tension with Jupiter, the planet of growth and expansion, only amplifying the emotions of the day. This Full Moon is yet another transit which centres around finances for Capricorn. With Jupiter's association to growth, it is best to adopt a frugal mindset at this time and avoid flagrant spending.

August

Best Days Overall: 2–6
Most Stressful Days Overall: 11–15
Best Days for Love: 22–25
Best Days for Money: 14–17
Best Days for Career: 9–12
Power Word: Heart

The business of the cosmic weather of last month persists into August as this month features both the remaining two eclipses of the year. Before the eclipses, Venus enters Libra, which is noteworthy because the planet will be retrograde in a few months partially in this sign. On the 7th, the Sun in Leo finds harmony with Saturn in Aries. This transit, in conjunction with Venus and Pluto finding harmony a few days later, supports negotiation or investments. Mars enters Cancer bringing some kinetic energy to the realm of partnership for you. If you're single, you'll feel the call to put yourself out there more. If you're partnered, this is the ideal transit for building up the existing relationship.

The solar eclipse in Leo occurs on the 12th. This transit spotlights fears, insecurities or anxieties which are preventing you from growing, evolving or chasing dreams you haven't allowed yourself to explore. It is important you are extra gentle with yourself around this date as Mercury and Pluto find tension on the same day. This is not the month to overload your schedule either, Capricorn. Given the fact that Leo rules the heart in medical astrology, it's paramount that you nurture and listen to your heart around this date.

On the 22nd, the Sun exits Leo and enters Virgo, ushering in your annual spotlight on spirituality and higher education. Virgo's season starts off busily with the lunar eclipse in Pisces occurring on the 28th. This eclipse calls into question how spirituality influences your sense of self and ability to regulate emotionally. Moreover, there is also a communications association with eclipses occurring in the Virgo/Pisces axis for Capricorn. Have your patterns of how you talk to yourself changed in the wake of such a hectic summer? This is the time to partner with yourself, Seagoat. This eclipse is further amplified by the fact that it finds tension with Uranus. As a result, anticipate this last week of August (and the following week) to feel frenetic. The goal of this eclipse is for you to be able to anchor yourself without needing external validation.

September

Best Days Overall: 10-14
Most Stressful Days Overall: 25-29
Best Days for Love: 17-20
Best Days for Money: 7-11
Best Days for Career: 22-26
Power Word: Perception

After a kinetic summer, September starts off relatively neutrally. The lunar eclipse in Pisces that occurred at the end of last month will be felt through the first week of September. Virgo season centres around your relationship to spirituality and the philosophies which guide your life. On the 10th, Venus enters Scorpio and is only a few weeks away from turning retrograde. Moreover, Mercury enters Libra, directing your focus towards career and public perception. The 10th also features the New Moon in Virgo. If you've been considering getting any sort of qualification or some additional higher education, this New Moon is an opportune time to explore the possibilities. This lunation also supports planning a trip that is either spiritual in nature or will just help you get out of a rut if you're feeling like you're in one.

On the 12th, Mercury finds harmony with Pluto and on the 14th the Sun finds harmony with Mars. These are softer transits which support keeping up with the hustle and bustle. On the 16th, the first of multiple Venus and Pluto tense alignments is exact. This transit is associated with a spike in negative self-talk around self-esteem or self-image. This is an important time to be your own biggest ally.

On the 22nd, the Sun exits Virgo and enters Libra. The Sun joining Mercury in Libra continues the trend of the present astrology focusing more on career, public perception and legacy. The Full Moon in Aries occurs on the 26th. This lunation centres around whether your needs are being met in your closest one-to-one relationships. This applies to partnership as well, if you're partnered. The end of September is an ideal time to prioritize your peace as multiple planets prepare to turn retrograde. The chart of this lunation also features a grand air trine between the Sun, Uranus and Pluto. This is a harmonious alignment supporting all forms of communication. If you're a writer, this is the ideal time to put pen to paper.

October

Best Days Overall: 7-10; 15-16
Most Stressful Days Overall: 3-4; 25-28
Best Days for Love: 26-28
Best Days for Money: 5-8
Best Days for Career: 10-14
Power Word: Reconnect

Are you ready for the retrogrades, Capricorn? October commences with Venus turning retrograde in Scorpio on the 3rd. Venus will spend half of its retrograde in Scorpio and the other half back in Libra. Venus's retrograde periods always centre around reviewing, reflecting and revisiting interpersonal relationships. For Capricorn this retrograde first functions as an audit of the company you keep. Do your friend groups and the communities you immerse yourself in uplift you as much as you do them? This Venus retrograde encourages you to reflect on this. Moreover, if there are important relationships you may have lost touch with for whatever reason, this Venus retrograde period invites you to reach back out and reconnect. The 3rd also features an edgy alignment between Mars and Pluto. Mars and Pluto at odds with one another can absolutely result in people grappling with their relationship to anger and conflict.

The next day, the Sun and Saturn find each other at odds as well. This transit can have you feeling either doubt or that you're working tirelessly with no payoff. Trust the process, Seagoat. The New Moon in Libra is a hopeful lunation centred around career and legacy. What do you want to be remembered for, Capricorn? This lunation encourages taking actionable steps towards the answer to that question. Venus's retrograde creates tension between the 11th and the 20th as the planet finds tension with Mars on the 11th and

Pluto on the 20th. Staying focused on grounding yourself and not being reactive is a must at this time.

On the 23rd, the Sun moves into Scorpio. Scorpio's season always functions as a spotlight on your circles of friends and the organizations you're a part of, and especially this year with Venus's retrograde period. Venus isn't the only planet turning retrograde this month though: Mercury turns retrograde in Scorpio on the 24th. Your patterns of communication are up for review at this time, too. Pay attention to ways you may limit yourself through how you either speak or listen. The Full Moon in Taurus spotlights partnership for you. This Full Moon is especially felt given that the planet of love is retrograde. Carving out quality time to spend with your significant other if you're partnered is highly recommended. If you're single, your overarching views about partnership and your partnership status is the focus of this lunation.

November

Best Days Overall: 26–30
Most Stressful Days Overall: 3–7
Best Days for Love: 15–19
Best Days for Money: 24–27
Best Days for Career: 13–16
Power Word: To-do

November begins with the dominating cosmic weather being both Venus's and Mercury's retrogrades. This is the ideal time to circle back to endeavours or initiatives you were working on before that may have fallen by the wayside. It is recommended not to launch anything new until the retrograde periods are over. The New Moon in Scorpio is live on the 9th. This lunation encourages you to spend time with friends with whom you can let your guard down and be vulnerable with if need be. On the 13th, both Mercury and Venus end their retrograde periods. It will, however, take two or three weeks for the planets to be back functioning at a normal speed, so anticipate some communication, transport or technological glitches for the remainder of the month.

Mars meets up with Jupiter in Leo on the 16th, providing you with the boost you need if you're seeking to put time, effort or energy into creating something new. Nonetheless, now that the retrogrades are over, this is the time to get your to-do list out and really start taking care of deliverables. Scorpio season concludes with the Sun and Mars being at odds with one another on the 20th. Be mindful not to be in so much of a hurry to get things done that the quality of your work suffers as a result.

On the 22nd the Sun exits Scorpio and enters Sagittarius. Sagittarius's season is your annual spotlight on emotional regulation. Sagittarius is represented by the archetypes of the preacher, the teacher and the cheerleader. This Sagittarius season it is important that you practise what you preach, are open to learning and are your own biggest cheerleader. The Full Moon in Gemini functions as an audit of your physical wellness. This is the time to make sure you're not slacking on movement and fitness. Moreover, be mindful about what you put in your body. The month ends with a harmonious alignment between the Sun and Saturn. This transit supports planning and organizing around your goals for 2027.

December

Best Days Overall: 21–25
Most Stressful Days Overall: 6–10
Best Days for Love: 24–27
Best Days for Money: 8–11
Best Days for Career: 10–14
Power Word: Peace

It's almost your season again, Capricorn! December's cosmic weather kicks off with Venus entering Scorpio. This transit functions as a check-in on your lessons learned from Venus's retrograde period from October to mid-November. The next day, Mars and Uranus find tension, making the energy more volatile. Remember, Sagittarius's season is all about prioritizing emotional regulation for Capricorn. Do what you need to do to protect your peace, Seagoat. On the 7th, Mercury finds harmony with Neptune – a supportive transit for allowing yourself to dream big.

On the 8th there's a New Moon in Sagittarius. This lunation encourages you to scrutinize your coping mechanisms for stress and ensure they're not self-destructive in nature. This lunation is the ideal time to carve out a sanctuary space at home you can retreat to if you need some peace and quiet. This could be a designated room or section of a room (even a bathtub) where you can be left undisturbed. Venus squares off with Pluto one more time on the 9th, further emphasizing the importance of rest and relaxation at this time. The 11th and 12th feature harmonious alignments which support tying up loose ends before the end of the year. On the 11th, Mercury and Saturn find harmony. On the 12th, Venus and Mars do the same.

On the 21st, the Sun exits Sagittarius and enters your sign. Happy birthday! Capricorn season is your annual spotlight on your relationship with yourself. This is the ideal time to set goals around what you seek to accomplish in 2027. Your sign is represented by the seagoat that looks to the top of the mountain and to the bottom of the ocean. Know that while it may take a while to get there, you'll accomplish those goals – take the mentality of the seagoat with you into 2027, sweet Capricorn. On the 25th, Mercury enters your sign. Mercury finds tension with Saturn which encourages you to approach your big goals in small, bite-sized chunks.

Aquarius

~~~

THE WATER-BEARER

Birthdays from
January 20
to February 18

Personality Profile

AQUARIUS AT A GLANCE

Element – Air

Ruling Planet – Saturn
  Career Planet – Mars
  Love Planet – Sun
  Money Planet – Jupiter
  Planet of Health and Work – Moon
  Planet of Home and Family Life – Venus
  Planet of Spirituality and Mental Health – Saturn

Totem – the Spokesperson

Colours – electric blue, grey, ultramarine blue

Colours that promote love, romance and social harmony – gold, orange

Colour that promotes earning power – aqua

Gems – black pearl, obsidian, opal, sapphire

Metal – lead

Scents – azalea, gardenia

Quality – fixed (= stability)

Qualities most needed for balance – warmth, feeling and emotion

Strongest virtues – great intellectual power, the ability to communicate and to form and understand abstract concepts, love for the new and avant-garde

Deepest needs – to know and to bring in the new

Characteristics to avoid – coldness, rebelliousness for its own sake, fixed ideas

Signs of greatest overall compatibility – Gemini, Libra

Signs of greatest overall incompatibility – Taurus, Leo, Scorpio

Sign most helpful to career – Scorpio

Sign most helpful for emotional support – Taurus

Sign most helpful financially – Pisces

Sign best for marriage and/or partnerships – Leo

Sign most helpful for creative projects – Gemini

Best Sign to have fun with – Gemini

Signs most helpful in spiritual matters – Libra, Capricorn

Best day of the week – Saturday

Understanding an Aquarius

In the Aquarius-born, intellectual faculties are perhaps the most highly developed of any sign in the zodiac. Aquarians are clear, scientific thinkers. They have the ability to think abstractly and to formulate laws, theories and clear concepts from masses of observed facts. Geminis might be very good at gathering information, but Aquarians take this a step further, excelling at interpreting the information gathered.

Practical people – men and women of the world – mistakenly consider abstract thinking as impractical. It is true that the realm of abstract thought takes us out of the physical world, but the discoveries made in this realm generally end up having tremendous practical consequences. All real scientific inventions and breakthroughs come from this abstract realm.

Aquarians, more so than most, are ideally suited to explore these abstract dimensions. Those who have explored these regions know that there is little feeling or emotion there. In fact, emotions are a hindrance to functioning in these dimensions; thus Aquarians seem – at times – cold and emotionless to others. It is not that Aquarians haven't got feelings and deep emotions, it is just that too much feeling clouds their ability to think and invent. The concept of 'too much feeling' cannot be tolerated or even understood by some of the other signs. Nevertheless, this Aquarian objectivity is ideal for science, communication and friendship.

Aquarians are very friendly people, but they do not make a big show about it. They do the right thing by their friends, even if sometimes they do it without passion or excitement.

Aquarians have a deep passion for clear thinking. Second in importance, but related, is their passion for breaking with the establishment and traditional authority. Aquarians delight in this, because for them rebellion is like a great game or challenge. Very often they will rebel strictly for the fun of rebelling, regardless of whether the authority they defy is right or wrong. Right or wrong has little to do with the rebellious actions of an Aquarian, because to a true Aquarian authority and power must be challenged as a matter of principle.

Where Capricorn or Taurus will err on the side of tradition and the status quo, an Aquarian will err on the side of the new. Without this virtue it is doubtful whether any progress would be made in the world. The conservative-minded would obstruct progress. Originality and invention imply an ability to break barriers; every new discovery represents the toppling of an impediment to thought. Aquarians are very interested in breaking barriers and making walls tumble – scientifically, socially and politically. Other zodiac signs, such as Capricorn, also have scientific talents. But Aquarians are particularly excellent in the social sciences and humanities.

Finance

In financial matters Aquarians tend to be idealistic and humanitarian – to the point of self-sacrifice. They are usually generous contributors to social and political causes. When they contribute it differs from when a Capricorn or Taurus contributes. A Capricorn or Taurus may expect some favour or return for a gift; an Aquarian contributes selflessly.

Aquarians tend to be as cool and rational about money as they are about most things in life. Money is something they need and they set about acquiring it scientifically. No need for fuss; they get on with it in the most rational and scientific ways available.

Money to the Aquarian is especially nice for what it can do, not for the status it may bring (as is the case for other signs). Aquarians are neither big spenders nor penny-pinchers and use their finances in practical ways, for example to facilitate progress for themselves, their families or even for strangers.

However, if Aquarians want to reach their fullest financial potential they will have to explore their intuitive nature. If they follow only their financial theories – or what they believe to be theoretically correct – they may suffer some losses and disappointments. Instead, Aquarians should call on their intuition, which knows without thinking. For Aquarians, intuition is the short cut to financial success.

Career and Public Image

Aquarians like to be perceived not only as the breakers of barriers but also as the transformers of society and the world. They long to be seen in this light and to play this role. They also look up to and respect other people in this position and even expect their superiors to act this way.

Aquarians prefer jobs that have a bit of idealism attached to them – careers with a philosophical basis. Aquarians need to be creative at work, to have access to new techniques and methods. They like to keep busy and enjoy getting down to business straightaway, without wasting any time. They are often the quickest workers and usually have suggestions for improvements that will benefit their employers. Aquarians are also very helpful with their co-workers and welcome responsibility, preferring this to having to take orders from others.

If Aquarians want to reach their highest career goals they have to develop more emotional sensitivity, depth of feeling and passion. They need to learn to narrow their focus on the essentials and concentrate more on the job in hand. Aquarians need 'a fire in the belly' – a consuming passion and desire – in order to rise to the very top. Once this passion exists they will succeed easily in whatever they attempt.

Love and Relationships

Aquarians are good at friendships, but a bit weak when it comes to love. Of course they fall in love, but their lovers always get the impression that they are more best friends than paramours.

Like Capricorns, they are cool customers. They are not prone to displays of passion or to outward demonstrations of their affections. In fact, they feel uncomfortable when their other half hugs and touches them too much. This does not mean that they do not love their partners. They do, only they show it in other ways. Curiously enough, in relationships they tend to attract the very things that they feel uncomfortable with. They seem to attract hot, passionate, romantic, demonstrative people. Perhaps they know instinctively that these people have qualities they lack and so seek them out. In any event, these relationships do seem to work, Aquarian coolness calming the more passionate partner while the fires of passion warm the cold-blooded Aquarius.

The qualities Aquarians need to develop in their love life are warmth, generosity, passion and fun. Aquarians love relationships of the mind. Here they excel. If the intellectual factor is missing in a relationship an Aquarian will soon become bored or feel unfulfilled.

Home and Domestic Life

In family and domestic matters Aquarians can have a tendency to be too non-conformist, changeable and unstable. They are as willing to break the barriers of family constraints as they are those of other areas of life.

Even so, Aquarians are very sociable people. They like to have a nice home where they can entertain family and friends. Their house is usually decorated in a modern style and full of state-of-the-art appliances and gadgets – an environment Aquarians find absolutely necessary.

If their home life is to be healthy and fulfilling Aquarians need to inject it with a quality of stability – yes, even some conservatism. They need at least one area of life to be enduring and steady; this area is usually their home and family life.

Venus, the generic planet of love, rules the Aquarian's 4th solar house of home and family, which means that when it comes to the family and child-rearing, theories, cool thinking and intellect are not always enough. Aquarians need to bring love into the equation in order to have a great domestic life.

Horoscope for 2026

Using your voice is the name of the game in 2026 for you, Aquarius. The cosmic weather of the year empowers you to not be afraid to speak up when advocating for your needs or for the needs of others. This year is a major turning point astrologically, as several planets that were oscillating between two signs finally settle into a new sign which they'll occupy for a significant frame of time. In other words, several signs that were oscillating between the past and future make a concerted step forward this year.

Most notably, Saturn, your traditional planetary ruler, leaves Pisces and enters Aries on February 13. In addition to simply entering a new sign, Saturn wraps up an almost 29-year cycle transiting the entire zodiac. For Aquarius, this shift significantly centres around communication and how you either use your voice or deny it from being heard. Saturn rules limiting patterns of thought and behaviour and its gaze is squarely set on patterns involving communication. In addition to Saturn, Neptune, the planet of dreams, compassion and the collective, also leaves Pisces and enters Aries early in 2026, on January 26. Neptune takes roughly 160 years to transit the zodiac, so there is a noteworthy collective shift around Neptunian themes being cemented this year. Overall, a whole new way of how people dissociate and unplug is likely to emerge over the next few years as Neptune stays in Aries until 2039. Moreover, dreams, compassion and the collective are major themes to be watched on the societal level this year. For you, Aquarius, Saturn and Neptune co-present in Aries work together to not only challenge existing patterns of communication, but to encourage you to make your dreams a reality through using your voice.

Your modern planetary ruler, Uranus, also switches signs this year. Uranus moves from Taurus to Gemini on April 25. Uranus rules individuality, instability and innovation, among many other significations. For the collective, the ways in which technology is interwoven with learning and communication are only going to exponentially evolve. For Aquarius, Uranus in Gemini encourages utilizing your unique individuality as a means to creatively self-express. Owning your story and using it as creative fuel is another way to interpret this astrological transit for Aquarius. All three of these outer planets aspect each other and other slow-moving bodies like Jupiter and Pluto throughout the year. The monthly forecasts below will always highlight when a noteworthy aspect between these planets is occurring, so make sure you read these sections.

Another notable astrological event this year for Aquarius is the north node entering your sign for the first time in about 18 years. The north node functions like a north star the collective journeys towards. When the north node is in your sun sign, it typically marks a period of increase or stepping into your power. However, it also means that eclipses are going to be present in your sign (and your polar sign, Leo, as well). Eclipses are evolutionary transits which catalyse growth through scrutiny and shake-ups.

For a quarterly view of the year ahead, the first quarter of 2026 features significant cosmic weather around communication and your relationship with yourself. The second quarter features a focus on creativity and romance. The third quarter once again highlights communication and also centres on partnership. The final quarter of the year features several career- and higher education-oriented transits.

Health (1st/6th/12th houses)

(Please note that this is an astrological perspective on health and not a medical one. Any health-related symptoms should be evaluated by a qualified healthcare professional.)

Aquarius's physical health planet is the Moon and, as a result, it's especially important for you to always be informed on when eclipse seasons, New Moons and Full Moons are. Moreover, just as the lunar calendar is cyclical and follows a routine, so should you when it comes to diet and exercise. This year's eclipses occur on February 17 (in your sign), March 3 (in Virgo), August 12 (in Leo) and August 28 (in Pisces). Given the effects of eclipses are typically felt within the lunar cycle they exist in, it's fair to state that essentially all of February, most of March and all of August count as 2026's eclipse seasons. It is important that during these eclipse seasons you aren't overexerting yourself, as eclipses can be felt in the body. Arguably, this is especially the case for the first eclipse of the year since it's in your sign. Furthermore, Jupiter, the great augmenter, is in your physical health sector until June 30, drawing more attention to how you either care for or neglect your body.

Aquarius's mental health planet, Saturn, undergoes a significant change this year as it formally moves into fiery Aries on February 13. Aries is the first sign of the zodiac, often signifying our relationships to ourselves. This is a year to address any forms of self-criticism which are unhealthy or deleterious to your emotional wellness. Aries, ruled by Mars, is inflammatory in nature, so monitor your inner narrator and when you notice an increase in self-demeaning narration, make concerted efforts to intervene. Moreover, it is recommended to work with a professional on resetting internal patterns of communication to more positive or growth-mindset oriented ones.

Here are the specific areas of the body to focus on this year:

- Ankles: these are a perennial area of focus for Aquarius as it rules this part of the body in medical astrology. Consistent bodywork or acupuncture to support the ankles is recommended this year.
- Lungs and breasts/chest: Jupiter will continue its transit of Aquarius's physical health sector in the sign of Cancer, which rules this part of the body, for the first half of the year. Avoiding smoking or other behaviours deleterious to these parts of the body is especially recommended this year.
- Digestive system: your physical health planet, the Moon, will undergo a lunar eclipse in Virgo on March 3. Virgo rules this part of the body in medical astrology. It's highly recommended to avoid inflammatory foods during this eclipse season. Consult a medical professional for more information around which foods may be uniquely triggering for you.

Love and Social Life (5th/7th/11th houses)

Romance and partnership are two chart sectors with significant activations for Aquarius in 2026. Uranus, the planet of individuality, instability and innovation, enters your romance sector on April 25, where it will stay until 2032/2033. Uranus brings a new way of approaching the themes of the chart sector it transits. With romance being one of these themes, this transit is noteworthy regardless of partnership status. A couple of months after this happens, Jupiter, the planet of expansion and convictions, enters Aquarius's partnership sector and then forms aspects with several influential planets shortly thereafter. Bookmark July as a super-noteworthy month for partnership, as Jupiter will find harmony with Neptune on July 20 and Uranus on the 21st, and will find tension with Pluto on the 21st as well. These are slow-moving transits and you could begin to feel them as early as the start of the month. For those Aquarians who are single, there's ample activity around securing partnership or planting seeds for relationships to blossom over the summer. For those Aquarians who are already partnered, anticipate the summer to be a time of notable growth or development in these existing relationships.

Aquarius's social life chart sector does not feature any outer planetary transits. However, your social life planet, Jupiter, makes a shift from home/family-oriented Cancer to radiant Leo on June 30. The latter half of 2026 is especially ripe with possibility when it comes to networking. Say yes to opportunities which can put you in the room with new and potentially supportive people. Joining professional organizations or new hobby-oriented groups is supported by your social planet's foray into popular Leo. As mentioned above, Jupiter is especially busy in the month of July, so also be mindful not to overload yourself with too many social commitments over the summer.

Career and Finances (10th/2nd/8th houses)

Venus, the modern planetary ruler of personal finances, turns retrograde in Aquarius's career sector on October 3. Venus's retrogrades are periods of time centred around values realignment and reviewing relationships. For Aquarius, the end of 2026 is a time you'll likely be prompted with reassessing your satisfaction with your current work situation and identifying what changes need to be made for you to feel more satisfied or fulfilled. The two metrics to analyse your satisfaction should revolve around whether your current career matches up with the values you seek to live your life by, and if you feel comfortable with whatever financial compensation you're currently receiving or will receive in the long-term investment of your career. Your career planet, Mars, does not turn retrograde this year, which supports advancement and even exploration in this area of life.

Last year was a big year for Aquarius in all realms of navigating finances. This year eases a little bit of the scrutiny of 2025 but asks the question 'Where are we going from here?' in relation to securing/maintaining financial freedom. Neptune moves out of Aquarius's finance sector on January 26, Saturn exits on February 13 and the north node leaves this sector on July 27. There is one final eclipse that is explicitly financially related for Aquarius on August 28. The autumn should be a season of intentional frugality, with Venus's retrograde occurring through almost all of October and half of November. Your finance planet, Jupiter, moves into Leo on June 30 and highlights how your finances are interwoven with partnership (regardless if you're partnered or single). Prior to this, Jupiter in Cancer highlights finances being wrapped up in the physical home or in matters related to health/wellness for Aquarius. Jupiter in Leo supports Aquarius in building new streams of income with a business partner.

Home and Domestic Life (4th house)

This area of life is relatively neutral as there are no outer planetary transits through this chart sector for Aquarius after April, and no eclipse activity in this chart sector either. For the first four months of the year, Uranus will be wrapping up its eight-year stint transiting Aquarius's home chart sector. Uranus leaving this sector brings a sense of stability to this area of life. That being said, your home planet, Venus, will turn retrograde from October 3 to November 13. Venus's retrograde influences this area of life by forcing you to take stock of how you may have neglected your physical home or how your home's set up inhibits personal/family connections. Work with Venus during this time to investigate if there are ways to spruce up or reorganize your home as a way to revitalize the energy of the space. In addition to revitalizing the energy, another theme of this retrograde period pertains to how your home supports career pursuits or gets in the way of them. This may be something as minor as changing the organization of your home office, or something more behavioural like preventing yourself from working in specific rooms as a means to allocate them for pleasure or relaxation.

Self-improvement (1st/3rd/5th/9th houses)

You're at the very beginning of a 20-year cycle of massive transformation with Pluto moving into Aquarius at the end of 2024. This is noteworthy as its own astrological event, but especially so this year given that the north node moves into your sign for the first time in 18 years. The north node is a destiny point and highlights that this year is about stepping into your power. Aquarius is going to accomplish this through using your voice. Using your voice not only for yourself but for the collective is highlighted by Saturn and Neptune moving into Aquarius's communication sector this year. As an exercise, take note of how often you censor yourself or forgo the opportunity to ask for what you want/need. Communication in all forms, written and verbal, are highlighted by Saturn and Neptune this year.

In addition to communication, utilizing technology as a means to progress yourself or to create is another self-improvement strategy. Uranus, the planet of innovation, moves into Aquarius's creativity sector in April. Be open to parting with outdated methods of creativity and adopting newfound, more efficient methods to express yourself or get your message across.

Month-by-month Forecasts

January

Best Days Overall: 19-23
Most Stressful Days Overall: 10-14
Best Days for Love: 13-16
Best Days for Money: 6-9
Best Days for Career: 12-15
Power Word: Steady

Happy New Year, Aquarius – it's almost your season! The cosmic weather for 2026 begins on the 1st with Mercury entering Capricorn. There's now a significant build-up of Capricorn energy with the Sun, Mercury, Venus and Mars all in the earth sign. A cluster of Capricorn energy indicates for you that it's important to make sure you're fully recharged from an eventful 2025 before you go ahead and chase your 2026 goals. Emotional regulation to start the year off is the name of the game for Aquarius. The Full Moon in Cancer also highlights the importance of making sure your physical body is healthy and prepared to start the year off right. This lunation encourages you to examine your existing routines and make changes which support physical wellness.

The Sun joins up with Venus on the 6th, which is a great day to nest, rest and plan out your 2026 next steps. Remember, the astrology of this month really wants you to be 'slow and steady' about how you approach the year. You may be feeling restless between the 9th and the 10th when the Sun, Venus and Mars all find tension with Jupiter. Being methodical about how you start the year off will pay dividends in the long run. On the 18th, the New

Moon in Capricorn encourages you to take what you've reflected on regarding physical and emotional wellness and integrate it into newfound routines.

On the 19th, the Sun exits Capricorn and enters Aquarius. Happy birthday! Aquarius season does start off a little rockily this year as the Sun, Venus and Mars all meet up with Pluto between the 20th and the 27th. Ever since Pluto entered your sign a couple of years ago, you've been tasked with a 20-year journey of not only personal transformation but being a change agent for others. These meet-ups with Pluto also encourage you to shed beliefs, aspects of your identity or attitudes from 2025 which won't serve you in 2026 or may even stifle you. The month ends with Neptune formally entering Aries after bouncing to and from the sign last year. This shift in energy affects your year as a whole and is described in detail in your annual Horoscope overview, above.

February

Best Days Overall: 9–14
Most Stressful Days Overall: 16–21
Best Days for Love: 1–4
Best Days for Money: 10–13
Best Days for Career: 19–22
Power Word: Transform

Aquarius's season rolls on into February. If you haven't already, it may support your yearly goal-setting to identify two or three adjectives you seek to embody this year now that you're embarking upon a new trip around the Sun. The astrology of February begins with a Full Moon in your polar sign, Leo. This lunation illuminates partnership for you. Regardless of partnership status, your attitudes towards partnership and the emotions surrounding this area of life are focused on in this Full Moon. Advocating for your needs in relationship to partnership is vital at this time. Mercury moves into watery Pisces on the 6th, bringing a little more of your attention to budgeting and finances. This is a major area of life for you over the next couple of months.

Venus follows suit and enters Pisces on the 10th. Once Pisces's season begins in a few short weeks' time, there will be a cosmic audit of your relationship to finances. You may want to get a head start and make sure you truly understand all the ways you spend and save. On the 13th, Saturn follows Neptune and enters Aries. This transit affects your year as a whole and is delineated in your annual Horoscope, above. On the 17th, the first eclipse of the year occurs in your sign! Eclipses are evolutionary transits and this is the first eclipse in a while to be in your sign. You're going to be entering into a roughly two-year period of rapid growth and transformation as the north node will be entering your sign in a few months' time for the first time in about 18 years.

Pisces season begins on the 18th. As mentioned when Mercury and Venus entered the sign, Pisces season as a whole functions as a spotlight on finances for you. This year it functions more like an audit because Mercury turns retrograde in Pisces on the 26th. Mercury's retrograde periods centre around reviewing, revisiting and revising specific areas of life. For you, the focus now is on doing these 're-' words with finances and budgeting. Gaining insight into your finances early in the year will set you up for success as the next couple of years should be a whirlwind of growth for you. The month ends with a turbulent alignment between Mars and Uranus on the 27th. Think before you speak around this date, Aquarius.

March

Best Days Overall: 25–30
Most Stressful Days Overall: 3–8
Best Days for Love: 10–13
Best Days for Money: 19–23
Best Days for Career: 28–30
Power Word: Exorcise

Mercury's retrograde and eclipse season continue into March. The month's cosmic weather kicks off with a lunar eclipse in Virgo. This eclipse illuminates personal demons you need to exorcise in order to really capitalize on the growth potential of this year's astrology. Prioritize emotional regulation at this time given this is very likely a stressful week for you, sweet Water-bearer. Thankfully, the Sun finds harmony with Jupiter which supports quality time with a special someone (either a partner or a best friend). Venus enters Aries on the 6th further reinforcing the impact of the words you use with everyone around you and yourself. Mercury finds harmony with Jupiter on the 9th, encouraging you to reconnect with friends you haven't spoken to in a while (a common theme during a Mercury retrograde).

The New Moon in Pisces occurs on the 18th and ushers in a new emotional cycle around finances and budgeting. This lunation encourages you to apply all the reflections you've made around finances and create a new budgeting framework to use for the remainder of the year. Given Mercury will turn direct in a few days, this lunation can also be utilized to identify new streams of income which you could pursue once Mercury is direct: Mercury turns direct on the 20th giving you the greenlight to press ahead. In general, please note that while Mercury is no longer retrograde come the 20th, it won't be moving at its fully functional speed for another couple of weeks so you may still experience communication, transport or technological glitches for a bit longer.

The 20th is also when the Sun exits Pisces and enters Aries. Happy (astrological) new year! Aries's season is your annual spotlight on both internal and external communication. This also includes expressive and receptive communication. One important prompt for this Aries season is for you to observe how efficiently and effectively you listen to others. The end of the month features two productive transits. Saturn finds harmony with Pluto, supporting career efforts, and Venus enters Taurus, encouraging you to cultivate abundance within your home.

April

Best Days Overall: 1-5
Most Stressful Days Overall: 15-19
Best Days for Love: 27-30
Best Days for Money: 11-14
Best Days for Career: 22-26
Power Word: Influence

April's astrology begins with a Full Moon, this time in Libra. The Full Moon in Libra highlights the importance spirituality and higher education play in your life, and how they correlate to the transformative period you're going to enter when the north node enters your sign in a few months. Do you have a routine spiritual practice which grounds you or helps you navigate life? Have you received all the training or certifications you need to achieve your year-end and long-term goals? These are questions to ponder under the light of this Full Moon. On the 9th, Mars enters Aries emboldening you in the realm of communication. Once again, this month features a spotlight on both expressive and receptive communication. Listen as much as you speak, Water-bearer.

The New Moon in Aries ushers in a new emotional cycle around your local community. This lunation is the ideal time to explore parts of your neighbourhood, town or city you've always been curious about but haven't ventured into. This lunation also encourages you to spend quality time with siblings or those you're as close to as siblings. On the 19th, the Sun exits Aries and enters Taurus, bringing your annual spotlight on home and family dynamics.

Taurus is the fixed earth sign of the zodiac associated with its principled nature. While it gets the reputation for being stubborn, it is actually just rooted in its values. This Taurus season is also the time for you to analyse how your home and/or upbringing has influenced the values which root you. Do you need to update, modernize or change any of these values? Ponder this over the next couple of weeks and then work with the next New Moon to implement these changes. On the 25th, Uranus formally moves into Gemini after spending last year oscillating to and from the air sign. Uranus will stay in Gemini until 2032/2033. More information on how this impacts the remainder of your year can be found earlier in your annual Horoscope overview. The month ends with a harmonious aspect between Venus and Pluto supporting romantic connections.

May

Best Days Overall: 8–12
Most Stressful Days Overall: 23–26
Best Days for Love: 20–22
Best Days for Money: 1–4
Best Days for Career: 29–31
Power Word: Shift

Happy May, Aquarius! The cosmic weather for this month features a Blue Moon, meaning there's double the number of Full Moons this month. On the 1st, the first Full Moon of the month occurs in Scorpio. This lunation illuminates career, public perception and moves you're making to cement your legacy. Contemplating what you want to be remembered for is a good way to tap into the energy of this lunation. On the 2nd, Mercury enters Taurus, which results in it finding tension with Pluto three days later. Also, on the 5th, Mars and Jupiter square up to each other as well. The first week of May features scrutinizing energy around each person's individual relationship to anger and confrontation. Thankfully, on the 13th, this energy will have dissipated by then and Mercury and Jupiter find harmony on this day. This transit supports getting organized both at home and in furthering progress on your year-end goals.

The New Moon in Taurus on the 16th is a juicy lunation supporting you in the realm of home and domestic life. If you've been considering a move, this lunation would support that search or decision. This is also a useful lunation to repair or modify your existing home, if that's something you've intended to get round to doing. Outside the physical home, this lunation supports spending quality time with those you consider family to deepen those relationships. Taurus is a Venus-ruled earth sign centred around connection affording you security. The next day, Mercury enters Gemini and begins to draw your cosmic focus towards creative self-expression, romance and relationships with children. Mars enters Taurus and Venus enters Cancer on the 18th as well, providing a shift in energy.

Speaking of shifts, the Sun moves into Gemini on the 20th, indicating the seasons are changing. In the northern hemisphere, summer is approaching. In the southern hemisphere, Gemini's season represents moving into winter. Gemini season provides your annual spotlight on creativity, romance and your relationship to the younger generation. This is an excellent time of year to lean into hobbies or preferred types of recreation which bring you joy as a means to balance out all the ways you work hard. Mars and Pluto plus Venus and Saturn each find tension with one another on the 26th and 28th respectively, further emphasizing the importance of self-care. The month ends with the second Full Moon of May, this time in Sagittarius. This lunation highlights the company you keep and encourages you to prioritize relationships with friends who also function as personal cheerleaders.

June

Best Days Overall: 10; 20-23
Most Stressful Days Overall: 25-29
Best Days for Love: 15-18
Best Days for Money: 13-16
Best Days for Career: 4-8
Power Word: Network

The first nine days of June start off neutrally with only one planet shifting signs - Mercury moves into Cancer. Aside from that, the overarching Gemini themes for Aquarius of placing value on creative self-expression and relationships with the younger generation prevail. On the 10th, Venus and Jupiter meet up, supporting you in efforts to regulate your physical health or to get back into your fitness routines. Your thoughts and behaviour around physical wellness will be scrutinized by this month's Mercury retrograde, so get an early start if you've been slacking in this department. Venus enters your polar sign, Leo, on the 13th, encouraging quality time with significant others, if you're partnered, or putting yourself out there if you're single and ready to mingle.

On the 14th, the New Moon in Gemini occurs, encouraging you to network, schmooze and get your name out there. Gemini is known as the marketeer and the storyteller of the zodiac. Use this energy either in your professional life or in your personal life to expand your networks. Venus in Leo finds harmony with Uranus and Neptune, but tension with Pluto between the 16th and the 18th. Be mindful about actively supporting and embracing your own individuality at this time. Venus and Pluto finding tension can spark some insecurity around self-esteem or worthiness.

On the 21st, the Sun exits Gemini and moves into Cancer, bringing your annual spotlight on physical wellness and routines. This Cancer season especially functions like this, given Mercury will be retrograde entirely in the sign as well. In addition to general physical wellness and your fitness routine, this retrograde also centres around your attitude or mindset related to body image. Learning to embrace every part of you that makes you unique is an important takeaway from this three-week period of review. The Full Moon in Capricorn on the 29th highlights the link between physical wellness and emotional regulation. On the 30th, Jupiter moves into Leo for the first time in 12 years. Jupiter will stay in Leo for close to a year and brings its expansive energy to the realm of partnership and collaboration for Aquarius.

July

Best Days Overall: 13–18
Most Stressful Days Overall: 26–31
Best Days for Love: 5–8
Best Days for Money: 20–23
Best Days for Career: 9–12
Power Word: Cycle

It's July, Water-bearer! If you were to circle one month of 2026 with the most noteworthy and jam-packed astrology, it's this one! July's astrology begins on the 4th with kinetic Mars meeting up with frenetic Uranus. These two planets create – figuratively and literally – explosive energy when they meet. Expect tempers to flare and if you're handling fireworks or anything flammable around this date, do so with an excess of caution. Mars then finds harmony with both Neptune and Pluto the next day, supporting efforts around networking and forming connections with others. Venus enters Virgo on the 9th, encouraging you to give back or support those in need.

Between the 15th and the 21st, some of the most exciting astrology of the year occurs. As mentioned in previous months' forecasts, Uranus and Neptune both shifted into new signs this year. It takes Uranus roughly 84 years to transit the zodiac and Neptune takes about 160 years, meaning they don't enter new signs that often. Moreover, they rarely enter new signs within just a couple of months from one another. Pluto entered Aquarius a couple of years ago, but given it is the slowest of the bunch, the three planets are hanging out at the same degree of their respective signs. This means that on the 15th, Uranus and Neptune harmoniously align.

Then on the 18th, Uranus and Pluto do the same. These two transits affect the collective more so than you on the personal level. What does influence you on the personal level is Jupiter, the planet of growth and expansion, newly in Leo, forming aspects to all three slow-moving influential planets between the 20th and the 21st. This astrology actually functions as a check-in moment for you to pause and track how much you've grown since 2020. Jupiter and Pluto met up three times that year and this aspect functions as the halfway point of that cycle.

Leo's season begins on the 22nd and is your annual spotlight on partnership. The next day, Mercury ends its retrograde period. The Full Moon in Aquarius lights up the night sky on the 29th. This lunation spotlights your relationship with yourself. Do you embrace all the facets of what makes you unique? This lunation encourages you to partner with yourself to the best of your ability.

August

Best Days Overall: 7–10
Most Stressful Days Overall: 21–25
Best Days for Love: 16–19
Best Days for Money: 10–13
Best Days for Career: 29–31
Power Word: Priority

How are you doing, Water-bearer? July's astrology was jam-packed and August also seems to be a busy month astrologically because it is officially eclipse season once again! The cosmic weather kicks off with Venus entering Libra on the 6th. Venus will begin to slow down in a few weeks' time as it will turn retrograde in a couple of months. The Sun in Leo harmoniously aligns with your traditional planetary ruler, Saturn, on the 7th. This is an ideal transit for relationship building or checking items off your to-do list. If you've been craving any sort of aesthetics change, Venus and Pluto find harmony on the 10th support this.

On the 12th, the solar eclipse in Leo occurs. Any lunation in Leo is partnership-oriented for Aquarius, but an eclipse is especially so.

Eclipses are evolutionary transits, so this influences this area of life regardless of your actual partnership status. If you're single, the methods you use to put yourself out there or your attitude towards partnership is influenced by the eclipse. If you're partnered, making sure your emotional needs are being met in the relationship is up for review. Mercury finds tension with Pluto on this date, so it is important you prioritize self-care. Mercury and Pluto at odds can heighten your inner critic, so be kind to yourself, Aquarius.

On the 22nd, the Sun exits Leo and enters Virgo. Virgo's season is your annual spotlight on joint ventures and your relationship with anxiety. Speaking of which, the second eclipse of the month (and final eclipse of the year) occurs in Pisces on the 28th. Prioritizing emotional regulation is paramount at this time. This eclipse scrutinizes patterns of spending and your general relationship with money. It is recommended to adopt a frugal mindset at this time. Moreover, this eclipse also encourages growth and evolution around how you integrate spirituality into your daily or weekly routines. To reiterate, emotional regulation is integral at this time, so finding ways to ensure your routines ground and centre you is a top priority. The month ends with Jupiter and Saturn harmoniously aligning, supporting interpersonal communication for Aquarius.

September

Best Days Overall: 2–6
Most Stressful Days Overall: 15–19
Best Days for Love: 22–26
Best Days for Money: 4–7
Best Days for Career: 26–29
Power Word: Advocate

Happy September! The cosmic weather for the first week of this month mostly surrounds the energy of the Lunar Eclipse in Pisces which occurred at the tail end of August. On the 10th, Venus enters Scorpio and really begins to slow down, as it will turn retrograde in a few weeks. As a heads-up, contemplating career trajectory is a major theme of the astrology of the next couple of months for Aquarius. The 10th also features the New Moon in Virgo. This lunation firstly centres around joint ventures or business collaborations for Aquarius. If you were planning on going into business with another person or party, now would be the time to do so as multiple planetary retrogrades define October and November. Moreover, this New Moon encourages new beginnings around changing coping mechanisms for stress you recognize may be more destructive than positive. You may seek the advice of a mental health expert on how to approach this.

The Sun in Virgo finds harmony with Mars in Cancer encouraging you to make sure you're moving your body this month. This is an excellent transit for playing sports or immersing yourself in nature. On the 16th, Venus and Pluto find tension in the first of multiple encounters over the next four months. Venus will be dancing around Pluto during its retrograde period. As a result, everyone will be grappling with their own insecurities more than they typically do. For Aquarius, insecurities around public perception, career and career aspirations are likely to arise for you to confront.

On the 22nd, the Sun exits Virgo and enters your fellow air sign Libra. Libra's season provides your annual spotlight on spirituality and higher education. The Full Moon in Aries shines brightly on the 26th, begging the question, 'Do you advocate for your needs in all of your closest relationships?' If not, which ones do you censor yourself and why? The Full Moon in Aries is an ideal time to take yourself on a date or just generally make your happiness a priority. Mars enters your polar sign, Leo, on the 27th bringing some much-needed kinetic energy to the realm of partnership over the next six or so weeks.

October

Best Days Overall: 10–14
Most Stressful Days Overall: 23–27
Best Days for Love: 12–16
Best Days for Money: 15–18
Best Days for Career: 6–9
Power Word: Aspirations

It's October, Aquarius! October's astrology begins with the long-anticipated Venus retrograde period, which officially begins on the 3rd although you have been feeling Venus slow down for a few weeks. Venus's retrograde periods function as reflections and audits on relationships and value systems for everyone. Within that, there are specific unique themes for each sign. For Aquarius, this Venus retrograde also functions as an audit on career aspirations, your existing career, public perception and how your guiding values inform these. Venus's retrograde periods encourage re-evaluation as well, so don't be surprised if you feel the urge to change direction in some respect related to career or career aspirations. Questioning the root causes for your career aspirations is another theme of this retrograde for Aquarius. This should of course be handled with care, especially given Mars and Pluto find tension on the 3rd as well.

The Sun and your traditional planetary ruler Saturn find tension on the 4th, which can make you feel like you're spreading yourself too thin or like you're working too hard with no payoff. This feeling will dissipate but be open to exploring possible tweaks to your routine to support yourself with this. The New Moon in Libra occurs on the 10th and centres around how your spiritual values inform how you approach interpersonal relationships. Moreover, this New Moon supports planning a trip which would provide you with some enlightenment or deepen your connection to the collective.

On the 23rd, the Sun exits Libra and enters Scorpio. Scorpio's season is your annual spotlight on career, although this year this theme is extended because of Venus's retrograde. The next day,

Mercury formally turns retrograde in Scorpio, too. General career reflection, career-goal reconsiderations and your interpersonal relationships in this space are all under review at this time. On the 25th, Venus re-enters Libra, shifting more focus to auditing inter-personal relationships. The Full Moon in Taurus also spotlights family relationship dynamics and relationships within your physical home. Pluto finds tension with this lunation, making it more likely issues which had been buried or left unaddressed rise to the surface at this time.

November

Best Days Overall: 27–30
Most Stressful Days Overall: 12–16
Best Days for Love: 24–26
Best Days for Money: 2–5
Best Days for Career: 8–11
Power Word: Build/Bolster

Happy November, Aquarius! The first two weeks of this month are primarily defined by the two existing retrograde periods occurring with Mercury and Venus. The New Moon in Scorpio on the 9th functions as a check-in on any reflections that have been made during the retrogrades around your existing career, future career aspirations or your attitudes about how the public perceive you. Thankfully, both Mercury and Venus end their retrograde periods on the same day – November 13. However, the planets will take a few weeks before being back to their fully functional speeds, so anticipate the vibes to still feel retrograde-y for a bit longer. If you're planning on launching any new business endeavours, you have the green light to do so now that these retrograde periods are over.

Mars in Leo meeting up with Jupiter in Leo provides a lot of kinetic energy in the realm of partnership for you. It would be an opportune time to take your significant other out on a romantic date or, if you're single, to put yourself into environments where you could meet prospective partners. On the 22nd, the Sun exits

Scorpio and enters fiery Sagittarius, bringing your annual spotlight on your circles of friends and professional networks. The Full Moon in Gemini shines brightly two days later and centres around creative self-expression and romance for you. This is the opportune time to partake in hobbies or types of recreation which can help you build new communities or bolster existing communities.

Sagittarius is represented by the centaur and is often associated with spontaneity. This solar season is the ideal time to shake off the retrograde periods by going on some spontaneous adventures with close friends. Though it may surprise you, Sagittarius is also commonly associated with wisdom. Be open to what these friends or community members can teach you this solar season. Mars enters Virgo on the 25th also encouraging you to support community members in need. The month ends with the Sun in Sagittarius finding harmony with Saturn in Aries. This transit concludes the month on a productive and motivational note going into December.

December

Best Days Overall: 14–19
Most Stressful Days Overall: 8–9; 28–31
Best Days for Love: 1–4
Best Days for Money: 15–18
Best Days for Career: 21–24
Power Word: Envision

It's December, Water-bearer! Sagittarius season continues with Venus entering Scorpio on the 4th. Venus re-entering Scorpio now shifts you from reflecting on career/career aspirations to actually making a plan around the goals you seek to achieve in 2027. Mars and Uranus square off the next day, making the first week of December one where most people will be a little more quick to anger. Mercury enters Sagittarius on the 6th and then the New Moon in Sagittarius on the 8th builds the Sagittarian energy to its peak for the year. The New Moon in Sagittarius strongly encourages you to investigate new communities or networks you can tap into that would support you achieving your 2027 goals. December's astrology primarily centres around envisioning and planning for next year.

Venus finds tension with Pluto one more time on the 9th, which can rile up insecurities. Thankfully, Mercury finds harmony with Sagittarius on the 11th and Venus finds harmony with Mars on the 12th. It is vital not to isolate yourself during this week and to use your interpersonal relationships as a means to support emotional regulation. Sagittarius's season rounds out with the prompt to identify different areas of study or matters to educate yourself on which will support you in achieving your 2027 goals. Sagittarius is often associated with higher education, so consider identifying if there is any type of certification or training which would greatly benefit you in the new year. Moreover, be open to opportunities to both mentor others and receive mentorship.

On the 21st, the Sun exits Sagittarius and enters Capricorn. For Aquarius, a build-up of Capricorn energy would support shying away from the limelight. Hopefully you capitalized on your social-izing during Sagittarius's season, because the cosmic weather strongly encourages you to strike a balance between social and solo time. Self-effacing patterns of thought and behaviour are up for review during the last week of the year as Mercury and Saturn find tension, which is exact on the 31st. With Mercury and Saturn find-ing tension during this last week, it is vital you prioritize emotional regulation at this time.

Pisces

THE FISH

Birthdays from
February 19
to March 20

Personality Profile

PISCES AT A GLANCE

Element – Water

Ruling Planet – Jupiter
   Career Planet – Jupiter
   Love Planet – Mercury
   Money Planet – Mars
   Planet of Health and Work – Sun
   Planet of Home and Family Life – Mercury
   Planet of Fun, Entertainment, Creativity and Pleasure – Moon

Totem – the Regulator

Colours – aqua, violet

Colours that promote love, romance and social harmony – earth tones, yellow, yellow-orange

Colours that promote earning power – red, scarlet

Gem – selenite

Metal – tin

Scent – lotus, petrichor

Quality – mutable (= flexibility)

Qualities most needed for balance – structure and the ability to handle form

Strongest virtues – psychic power, sensitivity, self-sacrifice, altruism

Deepest needs – spiritual illumination, liberation

Characteristics to avoid – escapism, keeping bad company, negative moods

Signs of greatest overall compatibility – Cancer, Scorpio

Signs of greatest overall incompatibility – Gemini, Virgo, Sagittarius

Sign most helpful to career – Sagittarius

Sign most helpful for emotional support – Gemini

Sign most helpful financially – Aries

Sign best for marriage and/or partnerships – Virgo

Sign most helpful for creative projects – Cancer

Best Sign to have fun with – Cancer

Signs most helpful in spiritual matters – Scorpio, Aquarius

Best day of the week – Thursday

Understanding a Pisces

If Pisces have one outstanding quality it is their belief in the invisible, spiritual and psychic side of things. This side of things is as real to them as the hard earth beneath their feet – so real, in fact, that they will often ignore the visible, tangible aspects of reality in order to focus on the invisible and so-called intangible ones.

Of all the signs of the zodiac, the intuitive and emotional faculties of the Pisces are the most highly developed. They are committed to living by their intuition and this can at times be infuriating to other people – especially those who are materially, scientifically or technically orientated. If you think that money, status and worldly success are the only goals in life, then you will never understand a Pisces.

Pisces have intellect, but to them intellect is only a means by which they can rationalize what they know intuitively. To an Aquarius or a Gemini the intellect is a tool with which to gain knowledge. To a well-developed Pisces it is a tool by which to express knowledge.

Pisces feel like fish in an infinite ocean of thought and feeling. This ocean has many depths, currents and undercurrents. They long for purer waters where the denizens are good, true and beautiful, but they are sometimes pulled to the lower, murkier depths. Pisces know that they do not generate thoughts but only tune in to thoughts that already exist; this is why they seek the purer waters. This ability to tune in to higher thoughts inspires them artistically and musically.

Since Pisces is so spiritually orientated – though many Pisces in the corporate world may hide this fact – we will deal with this aspect in greater detail, for otherwise it is difficult to understand the true Pisces personality.

There are four basic attitudes of the spirit. One is outright scepticism – the attitude of secular humanists. The second is an intellectual or emotional belief, where one worships a far-distant God-figure – the attitude of most modern church-going people.

The third is not only belief but direct personal spiritual experience – this is the attitude of some 'born-again' religious people. The fourth is actual unity with the divinity, an intermingling with the spiritual world – this is the attitude of yoga. This fourth attitude is the deepest urge of a Pisces, and a Pisces is uniquely qualified to pursue and perform this work.

Consciously or unconsciously, Pisces seek this union with the spiritual world. The belief in a greater reality makes Pisces very tolerant and understanding of others – perhaps even too tolerant. There are instances in their lives when they should say 'enough is enough' and be ready to defend their position and put up a fight. However, because of their qualities it takes a good deal to get them into that frame of mind.

Pisces basically want and aspire to be 'saints'. They do so in their own way and according to their own rules. Others should not try to impose their concept of saintliness on a Pisces, because he or she always tries to find it for him- or herself.

Finance

Money is generally not that important to Pisces. Of course they need it as much as anyone else, and many of them attain great wealth. But money is not generally a primary objective. Doing good, feeling good about oneself, peace of mind, the relief of pain and suffering – these are the things that matter most to a Pisces.

Pisces earn money intuitively and instinctively. They follow their hunches rather than their logic. They tend to be generous and perhaps overly charitable. Almost any kind of misfortune is enough to move a Pisces to give. Although this is one of their greatest virtues, Pisces should be more careful with their finances. They should try to be more choosy about the people to whom they lend money, so that they are not being taken advantage of. If they give money to charities they should follow it up to see that their contributions are put to good use. Even when Pisces are not rich, they still like to spend money on helping others. In this case they should really be careful, however: they must learn to say no sometimes and help themselves first.

Perhaps the biggest financial stumbling block for the Pisces is general passivity – a *laissez faire* attitude. In general Pisces like to go with the flow of events. When it comes to financial matters, especially, they need to be more aggressive. They need to make things happen, to create their own wealth. A passive attitude will only cause loss and missed opportunity. Worrying about financial security will not provide that security. Pisces need to go after what they want tenaciously.

Career and Public Image

Pisces like to be perceived by the public as people of spiritual or material wealth, of generosity and philanthropy. They look up to big-hearted, philanthropic types. They admire people engaged in large-scale undertakings and eventually would like to head up these big enterprises themselves. In short, they like to be connected with big organizations that are doing things in a big way.

If Pisces are to realize their full career and professional potential they need to travel more, educate themselves more and learn more about the actual world. In other words, they need some of the unflagging optimism of Sagittarius in order to reach the top.

Because of all their caring and generous characteristics, Pisces often choose professions through which they can help and touch the lives of other people. That is why many Pisces become doctors, nurses, social workers or teachers. Sometimes it takes a while before Pisces realize what they really want to do in their professional lives, but once they find a career that lets them manifest their interests and virtues they will excel at it.

Love and Relationships

It is not surprising that someone as 'otherworldly' as the Pisces would like a partner who is practical and down to earth. Pisces prefer a partner who is on top of all the details of life, because they dislike details. Pisces seek this quality in both their romantic and professional partners. More than anything else this gives Pisces a feeling of being grounded, of being in touch with reality.

As expected, these kinds of relationships – though necessary – are sure to have many ups and downs. Misunderstandings will take place because the two attitudes are poles apart. If you are in love with a Pisces you will experience these fluctuations and will need a lot of patience to see things stabilize. Pisces are moody, intuitive, affectionate and difficult to get to know. Only time and the right attitude will yield Pisces' deepest secrets. However, when in love with a Pisces you will find that riding the waves is worth it because they are good, sensitive people who need and like to give love and affection.

When in love, Pisces like to fantasize. For them fantasy is 90 per cent of the fun of a relationship. They tend to idealize their partner, which can be good and bad at the same time. It is bad in that it is difficult for anyone to live up to the high ideals their Pisces lover sets.

Home and Domestic Life

In their family and domestic life Pisces have to resist the tendency to relate only by feelings and moods. It is unrealistic to expect that your partner and other family members will be as intuitive as you are. There is a need for more verbal communication between a Pisces and his or her family. A cool, unemotional exchange of ideas and opinions will benefit everyone.

Some Pisces tend to like mobility and moving around. For them too much stability feels like a restriction on their freedom. They hate to be locked in one location for ever.

The sign of Gemini sits on the cusp of Pisces' 4th solar house of home and family. This shows that Pisces likes and needs a home environment that promotes intellectual and mental interests. They tend to treat their neighbours as family – or extended family. Some Pisceans can have a dual attitude towards the home and family – on the one hand they like the emotional support of the family, but on the other they dislike the obligations, restrictions and duties involved with it. For Pisces, finding a balance is the key to a happy family life.

Horoscope for 2026

In the wake of a heavily Piscean 2025, 2026 appears to be a year you will be focused on regulating various areas of your life to sustain the growth made last year, Pisces. This is a notable year because all three influential placements that were in your sign for at least part of last year – Saturn, Neptune and the north node – will all shift out of Pisces and not return for a sizable amount of time. As a result, 2026 functions as an important checkpoint for Pisces to audit how each area of life has been influenced by such a concentration of energy in your sign for an entire year. Moreover, the planets shifting signs greatly influence the areas of life especially under review for you.

One major area of life under review for Pisces this year is finances. Saturn, the planet of responsibility and reality, leaves Pisces and enters Aries early in the year, on February 13. Saturn moves into Pisces' finance sector just after Neptune, the planet of dreams and illusion, undergoes the same shift on January 26. A deep dive into how these planets influence finances will be provided in that section of this Horoscope, below. On the collective level, Saturn and Neptune entering Aries will shift people's focus and prioritization to building and creating. Aries is the cardinal fire sign known for campaigning and pioneering. Not biting off more than you can chew and maintaining balance this year will strongly support sustaining the growth you underwent in 2025.

Along these lines, another area of life brought into focus in 2026 is health for Pisces. The north and south nodes will shift into Pisces' mental and physical health chart sectors respectively. More specifics will be provided below. For society at large, the north node moving into Aquarius from Pisces draws a collective focus to communities and equity as opposed to monarchy and class divisions. Anticipate how class influences society will become a hot topic in 2026 and one which catalyses major changes politically and socially. The eclipses this year will be split between the Leo/Aquarius and Virgo/Pisces axis, drawing the focus to this theme.

Jupiter, the planet of growth and conviction, equally divides itself this year between Cancer and Leo (making the switch on June 30). For Pisces, this move is actually a bit sobering as Jupiter moves its focus for you from romance and creativity to physical health and routines. In 2026, being of service to others, non-profit work and/ or any sort of philanthropy is the key to unlocking growth and expansion. As clichéd as it sounds, with Jupiter's shift mid-year, small acts of kindness will cumulatively have a major impact this year. Embodying the Regulator this year means being responsible for what energy you both put out and invite into your life in 2026.

For a quarterly view of the year ahead, the first quarter has a financial and mental health focus to it. The second quarter of the year also centres on home and family dynamics. The third quarter of 2026 emphasizes physical health and routines, while the final quarter reinforces finances and health but also the importance of tackling fears and anxieties.

Health (1st/6th/12th houses)

(Please note that this is an astrological perspective on health and not a medical one. Any health-related symptoms should be evaluated by a qualified healthcare professional.)

For the first time in nine years, Pisces will be experiencing eclipses centred around mental and physical health. This is because the north node shifts into Pisces' mental health sector and the south node shifts into Pisces' physical health sector on July 27. Where the north node is transiting in a person's chart signifies where they're being called to grow or come into their own. For you, Pisces, after all the activity and expansion last year you're being called to prioritize your peace this year. Developing a balance between social and solo time is one strategy for Pisces strongly supported by the north node moving into Aquarius. Moreover, where the south node is transiting is an area of life you're called on to audit and shed any outdated behaviours. Pisces is being informed of the urgency to address long-standing behaviours around physical health which are either deleterious or just not beneficial. The adage 'your body is a temple' should be taken seriously this year given how the eclipses are affecting your sign.

As a reminder, eclipses are evolutionary transits which stimulate growth through scrutiny and shake-ups. The first health-oriented eclipse is actually the first eclipse of 2026, which occurs on February 17. Astrologers debate how long eclipses impact us because their effects don't dissipate in the same way a typical transit does. It's safe to bookmark February as a major month for regulating and improving mental health. Taking social media breaks or limiting who has access to your energy would likely benefit you when things feel especially heavy. The second health-oriented eclipse occurs on August 12 and centres around habits which promote or detract from your physical wellness. Furthermore, your general daily routines are up for review over how they impact your physical health. It is recommended to approach August like a detox month and try to integrate healthful routines that you could sustainably maintain for the remainder of the year.

Here are the specific areas of the body to focus on this year:

- Feet: this part of the body is a perennial area of focus for Pisces as Pisces rules this part of the body in medical astrology. Foot reflexology or other forms of reparative therapy is strongly recommended to support your feet this year. Being aware of your gait and having proper-fitting shoes are also ways to improve quality of life this year.
- Ankles: your physical health planet, the Sun, meets up with Pluto when it's in Aquarius, the sign which rules this part of the body. Proper stretching prior to routine exercise should not be overlooked and strengthening the legs is an important physical health priority this year.
- Skin: the Sun, your physical health planet, faces off with Saturn when in Libra, the sign which rules this part of the body. Prioritizing how you regulate sun exposure and overarching skin health is strongly recommended this year.

Love and Social Life (5th/7th/11th houses)

Last year was a noteworthy year for partnership with multiple eclipses occurring in Pisces' partnership sector and Jupiter shifting into your romance sector, and 2026 continues this trend. Jupiter will be occupying Pisces' romance sector for the first half of 2026 and one eclipse will occur in your partnership sector on March 3. Your partnership planet, Mercury, turns retrograde three times this year to boot: from February 25 to March 20 in your sign, from June 29 to July 23 in Cancer, and from October 24 to November 13 in Scorpio. Mercury's retrograde periods are not meant to be feared, but rather looked to as times to slow down and check in with yourself on whether you need to course correct within the areas of life Mercury rules for you. In relation to love, these three Mercury retrogrades are times to intentionally regulate your schedule so you can identify whether partnership is a priority and, if so, readjust your schedule to accommodate this. This also means that Mercury will be retrograde in all three water signs and, as a result, will spend over 50 per cent of the year in that element. Water is the element associated with emotions and intuition. This is a noteworthy year for getting comfortable with vulnerability in partnership.

Social life is an area you're being called on to regulate in 2026. Your social life planet, Saturn, shifts in Aries on February 13. One mantra for Aries is 'I am'. This is a year where you should check in with yourself and finish that sentence when you are with, and after spending time with, the various circles and groups you are currently immersed in. I am ... welcomed? I am ... disrespected? I am ... cherished? I am ... you fill in the blank. Given the importance of striking a balance between social and solo time this year, only affirmative groups should be given your time and energy in 2026.

Career and Finances (10th/2nd/8th houses)

While there are no outer planetary transits in Pisces' career sector in 2026, your career planet, Jupiter, does shift into fiery Leo on June 30. As a result, career is an area of life which can be viewed in two distinct halves this year. The first part of the year, when your career planet is in Cancer, is more centred on the importance of creative self-expression and emotional fulfilment in your career. Jupiter in Leo catalyses activity in this area of life as Jupiter forms aspects with the other slow-moving influential planets. July is a noteworthy month for career as Jupiter in Leo finds harmony with Uranus and Neptune and finds tension with Pluto. Jupiter will also find harmony with Saturn in August.

Finances is a major area of focus for Pisces as both Saturn and Neptune formally shift into this chart sector. Saturn and Neptune are essentially antithetical in nature, as Saturn rules restriction and reality and Neptune rules dreams and fantasy. That being said, the combination of these two planetary energies centring on this area of life highlights the importance of embodying your 2026 totem, the Regulator. Saturn is the ruler of consequences, and this year it's especially prudent to be informed about budget and spending. That being said, positive consequences are rewards (which are also under Saturn's domain by extension), and there's substantial energy supporting concerted moves to making your money multiply itself. This can be achieved through investing and working with a financial planner.

Home and Domestic Life (4th house)

Pisces is embarking upon an eight-year cycle centred around shifts and changes in this area of life this year. Just like Saturn and Neptune, Uranus oscillated between two signs last year and is now officially making the shift into a new sign. Uranus moving into Gemini on April 25 means it begins its transit of Pisces' home sector. Uranus is the planet of innovation, instability and individuality. While this transit is slow to unfold its full effects, one common outcome is a move. Given Uranus's modern rulership over technology, integrating new, cutting-edge technology to better support your quality of life at home is a clever way to honour this new cycle. This transit especially influences those Pisceans who have multiple placements in the sign or in fellow mutable signs: Gemini, Virgo and Sagittarius. July is a noteworthy month for this area of life as Mars meets up with Uranus early in the month and Jupiter harmonizes with Uranus later on in the month.

Self-improvement (1st/3rd/5th/9th houses)

Your totem this year is the Regulator because a major form of self-improvement this year is making a concerted effort to set boundaries with others. Venus, the planet of values and worthiness, will be retrograde in the area of your chart related to co-dependency or blurred lines in relationships. Venus's retrogrades function like a values audit, with this one absolutely zeroing in on your ability to maintain healthy and balanced interpersonal relationships. Venus will be retrograde for most of the autumn, from October 3 to November 13. Venus will spend the first part of its retrograde period in the sector of your chart related to philosophy, so it is strongly advised to educate yourself on the topic of boundaries by reading or watching experts who have studied it. Coupled with enforcing boundaries is the need for meaningful self-esteem or self-confidence work. This is a year which cements the societal shifts observed last year. Amid a changing world with so many planetary shifts, being able to centre yourself assuredly, without the need for validation from others, is highly recommended. Your planetary ruler, Jupiter, enters Leo mid-year. Leo rules the heart in medical astrology, and Jupiter in this sign emphasizes the importance of regulating who or what you give full access to your own heart. Being able to navigate 2026 with the compassion and wholeheartedness Pisces is known for, while maintaining healthy boundaries with others, is the ultimate goal for you this year.

Month-by-month Forecasts

January

Best Days Overall: 14-18
Most Stressful Days Overall: 27-31
Best Days for Love: 8-11
Best Days for Money: 10-13
Best Days for Career: 3-6
Power Word: Sustainable

Happy New Year, Pisces! January's astrology kicks off with Mercury entering Capricorn on the 1st. The energy at the start of the year supports using your networks and the groups you immerse yourself in to assist in helping you achieve your 2026 goals. The first Full Moon of the year in Cancer occurs on the 3rd. This lunation centres around your relationship to play and pleasure. With the start of the year, you may be reluctant to hit the gas pedal when it comes to work. This lunation encourages you to also find time this month for recreation and creative self-expression. An ideal day to do this would be on the 6th when the Sun and Venus meet up in Capricorn. Ideally, you'll find friends you can have fun with or even go on an adventure.

The kinetic energy builds up around the 9th and 10th when the Sun, Venus and Mars all find tension with Jupiter, the planet of growth and expansion. January is all about identifying a balance between work and play that you can sustainably keep all year long. The New Moon in Capricorn on the 18th also encourages you to seek out new communities you can immerse yourself in this year. If there are any professional organizations which could assist you in achieving your year-end goals, this is the time to join them or get more involved.

On the 19th, the Sun exits Capricorn and enters Aquarius. Aquarius's season is your annual spotlight on emotional regulation. Speaking of balancing work and play, this first week of Aquarius's season calls on you to not spread yourself too thin and to prioritize your peace. Multiple planets meet up with Pluto, the edgy planet of transformation, between the 20th and 27th. The month concludes with Neptune entering Aries after spending all last year bouncing between your sign and the fire sign. This influences your year as a whole and is discussed in detail in your annual Horoscope, above.

February

Best Days Overall: 9–13
Most Stressful Days Overall: 18–22
Best Days for Love: 1–4
Best Days for Money: 22–25
Best Days for Career: 8–10
Power Word: Energy

Happy February, Pisces! This month's astrology begins with a roaring Full Moon in Leo. This lunation illuminates physical health and wellness for you. Specifically, if there are deleterious habits in your daily or weekly routine you need to scale back on or root out completely. Moreover, this lunation reminds you that there's a link between physical wellbeing and emotional wellness. On the 5th, Mercury squares off with Uranus right before entering your sign on the 6th. Many people are going to be speaking without a filter around the 5th, so think before you talk, Pisces.

Venus joins Mercury and enters your sign on the 10th. The build-up of Pisces energy brings a cosmic focus to your relationship with yourself. This is a major theme for the next six weeks based on certain transits occurring later this month. On the 13th, Saturn joins Neptune by entering Aries after exhibiting the same back and forth behaviour between your sign and the fire sign last year. Just like Neptune, this shapes your year as a whole and is delineated in your annual Horoscope.

The first eclipse of 2026 occurs in Aquarius season and centres around emotional health and wellness. More specifically, this eclipse scrutinizes if you've found a balance between social and solo time. Pisces is a sign strongly affected by the energy of its environment. It is important you carve out time to recharge in a sanctuary space. A sanctuary space could be a room in your home, the bathtub or a nature path – anywhere that can bring you peace and solitude.

Your solar season begins on the 18th. Happy birthday! Pisces season starts off with Mercury turning retrograde in your sign on the 26th. This retrograde period has you reflecting on and revising the ways you communicate with yourself. Pay particular attention to hypercritical, self-deprecating or limiting communication. Mercury's retrograde periods always centre around patterns of communication, but this one will feel especially potent as it is in your sign. The month ends with Mars and Uranus finding tension and making the energy feel fairly frenetic. Lean into spiritual practices or other routines you have which help you ground and centre yourself.

March

Best Days Overall: 21–25
Most Stressful Days Overall: 2–6
Best Days for Love: 7–8; 29–30
Best Days for Money: 20–23
Best Days for Career: 18–20
Power Word: Support

Pisces season rolls on into March with more dynamic astrology. On the 2nd, Mars joins the Sun, Mercury and Venus in Pisces and the next few days feature strong Piscean energy until Venus leaves the sign at the end of the week. The next day, on the 3rd, the second eclipse of 2026 occurs – a lunar eclipse in Virgo. This eclipse centres around partnership for Pisces. If you're single, this eclipse scrutinizes your attitude towards partnership and may very well motivate you to put yourself out there in new or different ways. If you're partnered, this eclipse functions as an audit of the interpersonal dynamic between you and your significant other. Is there reciprocity in how you support one another? Are all of your emotional needs being met (assuming you're advocating for them)? The Sun finds harmony with Cancer on the 5th, which is the ideal day for a romantic date. On the 6th, Venus leaves your sign and enters Aries, where it meets up with Neptune on the 7th and Saturn on the 8th. Be mindful of seeing things through rose-tinted glasses around this date.

The New Moon in Pisces occurs on the 18th and provides fertile energy to elevate the support you provide yourself. This could be through doing a better job at enforcing boundaries or it could be through how you provide yourself with love and motivation. This New Moon invites you to begin a new cycle centred around self-compassion and self-love. On the 20th, the Sun exits your sign and enters Aries, bringing your annual spotlight on personal finances.

The 20th also features Mercury ending its retrograde period in your sign. Mercury will take a couple of weeks to be back to functioning at full speed, so anticipate that some communication, technology or transport glitches are still likely to occur until then. The Sun meets up with Neptune on the 22nd and then with Saturn on the 25th. This is an opportune time to check in on personal finances and your budgeting activity. Are you aware of how all your money enters and exits your bank accounts? The beginning of Aries's season marks a new astrological year. Start the year off on an informed note by educating yourself around your finances.

April

Best Days Overall: 2–6
Most Stressful Days Overall: 23–27
Best Days for Love: 28–30
Best Days for Money: 14–17
Best Days for Career: 7–9
Power Word: Trailblaze

Happy April, Pisces! April's astrology kicks off with the Full Moon in Libra. This lunation centres around two different themes for Pisces. Firstly, for those Pisceans who currently are involved in any sort of joint venture, business collaboration or who have shared finances, this lunation brings an emotional focus to how equitable and fair this relationship is. Moreover, this lunation also spotlights fears, insecurities or anxieties that you need to confront in order to bring yourself more long-lasting emotional balance. On the 9th, Mars enters Aries. Mars entering Aries may feel like a hole is being burned into your wallet, so it's best to adopt a more frugal mindset for the next six weeks.

The New Moon in Aries occurs on the 17th. This day there are *six* planets in Aries: the Sun, the Moon, Mercury, Mars, Saturn and Neptune. Aries is a Mars-ruled sign associated with drive, ambition and trailblazing. Aries is also not known for sensitivity in the same way Pisces is. Be mindful that people this week may be hyper-fixated on their goals and a little less sensitive in how they act. This lunation encourages you to adopt new strategies towards conserving and raising funds. This could be through identifying new streams of income or working with a financial expert.

On the 19th the Sun exits Aries and enters Taurus. Taurus is the fixed earth sign of the zodiac associated with security and sensuality. Taurus attains security through its principled nature, even at the expense of being called 'stubborn'. This Taurus season it is paramount you identify and utilize your values system as a way to root yourself and better inform your boundaries to preserve and bolster your closest interpersonal relationships. On the 24th, Venus enters chatty Gemini, and on the next day, Uranus finally formally enters Gemini after spending the last year oscillating between Taurus and the air sign. This transit influences your year as a whole and is discussed in detail in the overview of your annual Horoscope, above. The build-up of Gemini energy brings a cosmic focus to home and family dynamics. The month ends with a supportive alignment between Venus and Pluto on the 28th. This is a softer supportive transit for interpersonal relationships and also would support any sort of aesthetic change if you were considering some sort of home makeover.

May

Best Days Overall: 2–3; 12–15
Most Stressful Days Overall: 24–28
Best Days for Love: 18–20
Best Days for Money: 15–17
Best Days for Career: 21–24
Power Word: Wholehearted

Taurus's season continues into May with the Full Moon in Scorpio on the 1st. It is important to note that this isn't the only Full Moon occurring this month. The Full Moon in Scorpio is a spiritual lunation which encourages you to immerse yourself in nature as a means to ground yourself. The Full Moon in Scorpio is also an interpersonal lunation which could rile up feelings of co-dependency, if that is something you've been struggling with. Be gentle with yourself, sweet Pisces. On the 2nd, Mercury enters Taurus, where it finds tension with Pluto three days later. This transit is known to heighten your inner critic in order for you to confront this self-deprecating behaviour. The astrology of this first week in May requires you to be your biggest ally. Mars finds tension with Jupiter on this day too, meaning emotions are generally running higher and there's a general feeling of restlessness.

There's a harmonious and beautiful connection between Mercury and Jupiter on the 13th. This transit facilitates an opportune time for you to open up to your special someone on how you've been feeling, or to wholeheartedly connect with someone you care about. These are also good vibes for any sort of writing or composing. On the 16th, the New Moon in Taurus ushers in a new emotional cycle around how you communicate with yourself or others.

On the 20th, the Sun exits Taurus and enters Gemini. Gemini season is your annual spotlight on home, domestic life and family dynamics. Gemini is the mutable air sign associated with networking and storytelling. Gemini is *not* two-faced, as many claim it to be. It is in fact just the sign which embodies duality. This Gemini season you're tasked with holding space for multiple truths to exist at once. Moreover, you're asked to redefine how the stories of your childhood influence your present. Mars finds tension with Pluto on the 26th bringing emotions to a boil. Do your best to stay cool, calm and collected around this date. May ends with a Blue Moon in Sagittarius: a second Full Moon. This lunation centres around career and public perception for you. The summer's astrology is chock-full of opportunities to change course when it comes to the goals you're chasing this year. Be open to what presents itself, Pisces.

June

Best Days Overall: 13-17
Most Stressful Days Overall: 26-30
Best Days for Love: 7-10
Best Days for Money: 21-24
Best Days for Career: 5-8
Power Word: Play

It's June, Pisces! June's astrology begins on the 1st with Mercury entering Cancer. Anticipate being influenced a bit more by your emotions than normal. The first week of June is strongly coloured by the Full Moon in Sagittarius that lit up the night sky on the last day of May. As mentioned before, this lunation brings an emotional focus to your existing career, future career aspirations and your relationship with public perception. Sagittarius is a visionary Jupiter-ruled sign, so allow yourself to do what you do best and daydream about the career you've always wanted to have, and the legacy you want to be remembered for. Venus in Cancer finds harmony with Jupiter on the 10th making it an excellent week for romance or prioritizing play. Venus enters Leo three days later, encouraging you to find joy in physical wellness routines.

The New Moon in Gemini ushers in a new emotional cycle around family dynamics on the 14th. This lunation creates fertile energy to engage in any conversations with family (or those you live with) which need to be had. This New Moon also encourages you to analyse how the layout of your home influences the energy you feel in this space. Venus finds tension with Pluto on the 18th. This transit can have you grappling with lingering self-esteem issues or insecurities. Self-esteem is a major theme of the astrology of the last quarter of the year for you, Pisces, so take time now to make a note of what themes arise around this date.

On the 21st, the Sun exits Gemini and enters Cancer. Cancer's season is your annual spotlight on creative self-expression, romance and children/the younger generation. This Cancer season, the astrology really has you reflecting on your relationship with these themes as Mercury turns retrograde in the sign on the 29th. The 29th also features a bright Full Moon in Capricorn, which illuminates friendship, professional networks and the communities you immerse yourself in. Pay attention to how you feel before, during and after spending time with these different groups of people. On the 30th, Jupiter enters Leo for the first time in 12 years. Jupiter in Leo centres around growing and expanding the ways you integrate physical health and wellness into your daily regime.

July

Best Days Overall: 14–18
Most Stressful Days Overall: 23–27
Best Days for Love: 13–16
Best Days for Money: 6–10
Best Days for Career: 28–31
Power Word: Cycle

Happy July, Pisces! July marks an astrological turning point in the year as it contains some of the most anticipated astrology of 2026. The cosmic weather begins on the 4th with Mars and Uranus meeting up and creating very combustible energy. Mars and Uranus together are notorious for rapid bouts of anger or erratic shifts in mood. Mars and Uranus conjoined is also literally associated with combustion, so if you're handling anything flammable or fireworks around this date, please be careful. Thankfully Mars finds harmony with Neptune and Pluto the next day, supporting drive and ambition. Venus enters your polar sign, Virgo, bringing some much-needed kinetic energy to the realm of partnership. If you're single, tap into this energy and put yourself out there.

Uranus takes about 84 years to go around the zodiac, so it really only enters a new sign every six to eight years, based on its orbit. Neptune takes about 160 years to circumnavigate the zodiac, so it's usually in a sign for 12–13 years. This year has been special as both Uranus and Neptune entered new signs. The middle of the month features highly anticipated harmonious alignments between Uranus and Neptune, on the 15th, and Uranus and Pluto on the 18th. These transits influence society at large and centre around cementing the changes in the collective observed last year. That being said, they also set the scene for Jupiter, the planet of growth and expansion, to form aspects with all three slow-moving bodies between the 20th and 21st. This is super-important for you on the personal level, Pisces, because it functions as a major point in the cycle of transformation you embarked upon in 2020 when Jupiter and Pluto met up that year. Take time to pause and reflect on the ways you've grown and changed since 2020.

On the 22nd, the Sun exits Cancer and enters Leo. Leo's season kicks off with Mercury turning retrograde in Cancer. This Mercury retrograde has you reflecting on and revisiting the role recreation, play and pleasure take in your life. This transit also pertains to your relationship with your inner child. What hobbies did you partake in as a child which would heal you or bring you bliss if you revisited? This Mercury retrograde has you reflecting on the way you nurture or communicate with your inner child as well. The Full Moon in Aquarius on the 29th centres around prioritizing emotional regulation going into eclipse season next month.

August

Best Days Overall: 15-20
Most Stressful Days Overall: 8-12; 28-29
Best Days for Love: 1-4
Best Days for Money: 29-31
Best Days for Career: 9-12
Power Word: Audit

Whether it's summer or winter where you live, there's no denying that there's been some seriously powerful astrology so far this season. The trend continues into August, Pisces, because it is officially eclipse season once again! Remember, eclipses only create tension in order to stimulate growth or evolution. Part of growing is shedding what no longer serves you. Remember that this month. August's astrology begins though not with an eclipse, but with Venus entering Libra. Pay attention to this because Venus will turn retrograde in a couple of months' time and spends part of its retrograde in this sign. On the 7th, the Sun in Leo finds harmony with Saturn in Aries, encouraging fiscal responsibility for Pisces. Venus finds harmony with Pluto in air signs, supporting efforts around interpersonal communication.

The first eclipse of August occurs on the 12th and is a solar eclipse in roaring Leo. This eclipse can be felt in the body as its primary focus for Pisces is on physical health and wellness. It is vital you do not overexert yourself this month. Moreover, if you haven't done an audit of your routine behaviours which are deleterious to your health, now is the time to take this seriously. Tied to this, if you're overdue for a check-up or have been delaying seeing any sort of health expert, now is the time to do this. You only have one body, sweet Pisces. While this eclipse does bring an emotional focus to physical health, it is important you are not hypervigilant or over-anxious about this. Mercury and Pluto find tension on this day, which can spike obsessive or compulsive behaviour. Just be mindful that you're being advised to treat your body like the temple it is.

On the 22nd, the Sun exits Leo and enters your polar sign, Virgo. Virgo's season is your annual spotlight on partnership and collaboration. Mercury joins the Sun three days later, supporting communication within your most intimate one-to-one relationships. The lunar eclipse in your sign occurs on the 28th. Once again, this is an eclipse that can be felt in the body so don't assume unnecessary or excessive burdens at this time. A major theme of this year for you has been your relationship to yourself and empowering you to be your biggest ally. This eclipse encourages you to really embody your 2026 totem, the Regulator.

September

Best Days Overall: 22–27
Most Stressful Days Overall: 11–16
Best Days for Love: 10–13
Best Days for Money: 2–5
Best Days for Career: 5–8
Power Word: Self-compassion

Happy September, Pisces! The cosmic weather is shifting from energy pushing you to go-go-go to energy encouraging you to take your time and reflect. The first week of September is primarily influenced by the lunar eclipse in your sign last month. Make sure your needs are being met. If you want to spend additional time out of the public eye or nesting and resting, prioritize doing so. On the 10th, Venus enters Scorpio and it is already slowing down as it will turn retrograde in a few weeks. This day also features the New Moon in Virgo. This New Moon encourages you to spend quality time with your significant other or to treat yourself to a self-date. This lunation is especially potent for those Pisceans in the early phases of dating. This is a fertile New Moon for planting seeds around growing a new partnership. This lunation is further supported a few days later by the Sun and Mars finding harmony.

However, the vibes shift come the 16th as Venus and Pluto square off for the first of several times over the next few months. Venus and Pluto finding tension with one another is commonly associated with insecurities or self-esteem issues coming to the surface for you to address. Lean into self-compassion at this time,

Pisces. On the 22nd, the Sun exits Virgo and enters Libra. This is apt timing for Pisces as Libra season is your annual spotlight on how your fears or anxieties influence your goals, dreams and over-arching outlook on life. Libra is represented by the scales, so the goal isn't necessarily to rid yourself of anxiety, but rather to find a balance with it.

The Full Moon in Aries illuminates finances and budgeting for Pisces. Next month's Venus retrograde will be financial in nature, so it is advised to get a head start on identifying themes and trends you have around spending and saving. With this retrograde now imminent, it is best to work with this lunation to get all your infor-mation in order around this area of life, but not to launch any new endeavours or try to start a new stream of income. Wait until after Venus's retrograde to do so if you can. Mars enters Leo on the 27th, encouraging you to move your body and be more disciplined around physical fitness. The month concludes on the 30th with Mercury entering Scorpio. Mercury will begin to slow down now as it will also turn retrograde next month.

October

> Best Days Overall: 10–15
> Most Stressful Days Overall: 1–4; 23–25
> Best Days for Love: 26–28
> Best Days for Money: 11–14
> Best Days for Career: 13–16
> Power Word: Values

Ready for the retrogrades, Pisces?! October begins with Venus turning retrograde in your fellow water sign Scorpio. Venus in Scorpio cares about certainty almost above all else, so this retro-grade period will have you evaluating your relationship to ambigu-ity and certainty. Moreover, this retrograde period will have you evaluating how fear or anxiety holds you back in the realm of part-nership or general interpersonal connection. Venus's retrograde periods also function as an audit of our one-to-one relationships and value systems. Be receptive to what is shown to you over the next six weeks. October 3 also features a tense alignment between Mercury, Mars and Pluto. Both Mercury and Mars have so much to do with expression, as Mercury rules communication and Mars rules anger and conflict. Your relationship to anger and how you approach conflict is up for review with this retrograde, given how it coincides with these transits.

On the 10th, the New Moon in Libra encourages you to approach fear and anxiety in new or innovative ways. If you've never worked with a mental health expert, this would be an opportune time to do so. If you've never meditated or done somatic work to get out of your head and into your body, this would also be the ideal time to experiment with this kind of supportive behaviour. If you're involved in any joint ventures or business collaborations, this lunation encourages you to ensure the dynamic is still equitable and balanced. Venus in Scorpio squares off with Pluto in Aquarius once again on the 20th. As mentioned before when Venus and Pluto squared off, it is fundamental to prioritize emotional regulation. This could mean spending less time on social media or in environments which are associated with spiking anxiety, insecurity or stress around comparisons with others.

The Sun and Venus switch places on the 23rd and 25th as the Sun leaves Libra and enters Scorpio on the former date and Venus retrogrades out of Scorpio and re-enters Libra on the latter date. In between this switch, Mercury turns retrograde in Scorpio on the 24th. Mercury being retrograde concurrently with Venus only further reinforces the importance of reflection and re-evaluation of the progress you've made this year. This is not the ideal time to endeavour to start something new. Moreover, these retrograde periods could be bringing 'ghosts' from your past back to remind you of values or patterns of thinking you exhibited when you knew them. This is done to show you how much you've grown, or to remind you what self-effacing patterns of thought or behaviour to avoid.

November

Best Days Overall: 26–30
Most Stressful Days Overall: 3–7
Best Days for Love: 25–28
Best Days for Money: 16–19
Best Days for Career: 24–27
Power Word: Accomplish

Happy November, Pisces! The first two weeks of this month are primarily defined by the existing retrogrades. Remember, Scorpio is the sign most desiring certainty as a form of security. In life, very few things are certain. Work with these retrogrades to sift through how your relationship with or desire for certainty influences the fears and anxieties which are being brought up by these planetary retrogrades. On the 9th, the New Moon in Scorpio is a fertile lunation for cultivating community around your spirituality or spiritual practices. On the 13th, Mercury *and* Venus both end their retrograde periods. While this gives you the green light to start any new initiatives or endeavours, remember that the planets won't be back at their fully functional speeds for a couple of weeks.

Mars, the planet of drive and ambition, finds harmony with Jupiter, the planet of growth and expansion. This puts some fuel back in your tank to tackle the rest of the year. If you feel like you have a massive amount to still accomplish, work with the energy of this alignment and tackle what's most in your control first. A bunch of little wins will add up to a big victory, Pisces. On the 22nd, the Sun exits Scorpio and enters Sagittarius, bringing your annual spotlight on career, public perception and legacy. After those concurrent retrogrades, have your career goals changed at all? This is the ideal solar season to set goals around what you seek to accomplish next year.

On the 24th, the Full Moon in Gemini illuminates home and family dynamics for you. If there are any conversations that need to be had with family based on what you experienced during the retrogrades, this is the opportune time to have them. Moreover, this lunation encourages you to strike a balance between social and solo time going into the end of the year. On the 26th, the Sun and Uranus find tension, encouraging you to lean in and embrace what makes you unique. How do your individual strengths and quirks influence your career goals? The month concludes with the Sun in Sagittarius finding harmony with Saturn in Aries. For Pisces, this is a helpful transit for building financial abundance with investing, identifying new streams of income or working with a finance expert.

December

Best Days Overall: 17–22
Most Stressful Days Overall: 28–31
Best Days for Love: 6–9
Best Days for Money: 12–15
Best Days for Career: 8–11
Power Word: Validation

It is the last month of the year, sweet Pisces! December's cosmic weather kicks off with Venus re-entering Scorpio on the 4th, placing a value on quality time with your closest connections. Mars finds tension with Uranus, which likely will be making you feel extra spontaneous considering it's Sagittarius season. December is a very community-oriented month for Pisces, so take this opportunity to plan some fun adventures with friends. The New Moon in Sagittarius is on the 8th and centres around new beginnings in regards to career and public perception. Whether it's changing what you're seeking to become or making an effort to market your existing services more, this lunation is a fertile time to grow in this area of life.

For the last time this year, Venus and Pluto find tension on the 9th. This transit reinforces the importance for Pisces not to seek external validation as a means to help yourself when battling with self-esteem, but rather to unlock an intrinsic means of combating self-deprecating narratives. Mercury and Saturn find harmony on the 11th, which is another transit which supports financial investments. On the 12th, Venus and Mars find harmony as well. This transit reinforces the importance of reciprocity in your friendships and prioritizing spending time with those people.

On the 21st, the Sun exits Sagittarius and enters Capricorn once again. Capricorn season is Pisces' annual spotlight on friendships, professional networks and communities you immerse yourself in. This Capricorn season begins with the Full Moon in Cancer on the 23rd. This lunation illuminates creative self-expression, romance and recreation for Pisces. Carve out time in your schedule to play or prioritize pleasure. This lunation also highlights your relationship with children or the younger generation. December winds down with Mercury entering Capricorn on the 25th and encouraging you to check in on friends and express gratitude for your connection. The month ends with Mercury and Saturn finding tension. Don't put too much pressure on yourself regarding conceptualizing all the details of your goals for next year. Instead, it may be helpful to identify feelings or adjectives you seek to embody in 2027.

Acknowledgements

This edition of *Your Personal Horoscope* is dedicated to the memory of Joseph Polansky. I am so grateful for your contributions to the astrology community and how your words brought comfort and guidance to so many. You are sincerely missed. Your memory lives on in the hearts of all you uplifted with your profound wisdom.

I would like to express my profound gratitude to the people of STAR ★ DATA, who truly fathered this book and without whom it could not have been written.

Thank you to Rachel Lang, my dear friend and incredible colleague, for believing in me.

Thank you to my parents, brother and family for their unconditional support.

And thank you to Megan, the person who introduced me to astrology. I'm so grateful.